ROUTLEDGE LIBRARY EDITIONS: THE ADOLESCENT

Volume 11

ADOLESCENT DRINKING AND FAMILY LIFE

ADOLESCENT DRINKING AND FAMILY LIFE

GEOFF LOWE, DAVID R. FOXCROFT
and
DAVID SIBLEY

LONDON AND NEW YORK

First published in 1993 by Harwood Academic Publishers

This edition first published in 2023
by Routledge
4 Park Square, Milton Park, Abingdon, Oxon OX14 4RN

and by Routledge
605 Third Avenue, New York, NY 10158

Routledge is an imprint of the Taylor & Francis Group, an informa business

© 1993 by Harwood Academic Publishers GmbH, Poststrasse 22, 7000 Chur, Switzerland.

All rights reserved. No part of this book may be reprinted or reproduced or utilised in any form or by any electronic, mechanical, or other means, now known or hereafter invented, including photocopying and recording, or in any information storage or retrieval system, without permission in writing from the publishers.

Trademark notice: Product or corporate names may be trademarks or registered trademarks, and are used only for identification and explanation without intent to infringe.

ISBN: 978-1-032-37655-4 (Set)
ISBN: 978-1-032-38142-8 (Volume 11) (hbk)
ISBN: 978-1-032-38158-9 (Volume 11) (pbk)
ISBN: 978-1-003-34373-8 (Volume 11) (ebk)

DOI: 10.4324/9781003343738

Publisher's Note
The publisher has gone to great lengths to ensure the quality of this reprint but points out that some imperfections in the original copies may be apparent.

Disclaimer
The publisher has made every effort to trace copyright holders and would welcome correspondence from those they have been unable to trace.

ADOLESCENT DRINKING AND FAMILY LIFE

Geoff Lowe, David R. Foxcroft and David Sibley
University of Hull, UK

harwood academic publishers
Switzerland • Australia • Belgium • France • Germany • Great Britain • India • Japan • Malaysia • Netherlands • Russia • Singapore • USA

Copyright © 1993 by Harwood Academic Publishers GmbH, Poststrasse 22, 7000 Chur, Switzerland. All rights reserved.

Harwood Academic Publishers

Private Bag 8
Camberwell, Victoria 3124
Australia

3-14-9, Okubo
Shinjuku-ku, Tokyo 169
Japan

58, rue Lhomond
75005 Paris
France

Emmaplein 5
1075 AW Amsterdam
Netherlands

Glinkastrasse 13-15
O-1086 Berlin
Germany

820 Town Center Drive
Langhorne, Pennsylvania 19047
United States of America

Post Office Box 90
Reading, Berkshire RG1 8JL
Great Britain

Library of Congress Cataloging-in-Publication Data

Lowe, Geoff, 1940–
    Adolescent drinking and family life / by Geoff Lowe, David R. Foxcroft & David Sibley.
        p.   cm.
    Includes bibliographical references and indexes.
    ISBN 3-7186-5413-X (hard). -- ISBN 3-7186-5414-8 (soft)
    1. Teenagers--Great Britain--Alcohol use. 2. Teenagers--Great Britain--Family relationships. I. Foxcroft, David R., 1963–
II. Sibley, David.z. III. Title.
HV5135.L69 1993
362.29′23′0835--dc20

93-19119
CIP

No part of this book may be reproduced or utilized in any form or by any means, electronic or mechanical, including photocopying and recording, or by any information storage or retrieval system, without permission in writing from the publisher. Printed in Singapore.

Contents

List of illustrations and tables	vii
Preface	ix
Acknowledgements	xi
Chapter 1: Introduction and outline	1
SECTION 1: ALCOHOL AND TEENAGERS	13
Chapter 2: Alcohol, use and abuse	14
Chapter 3: Alcohol expectancies and reasons for drinking	28
Chapter 4: Psychosocial aspects of teenage drinking	40
SECTION 2: FAMILY DYNAMICS	48
Chapter 5: Family process	49
Chapter 6: The family socialization of teenage alcohol use	74
Chapter 7: Family profiles of teenage drinkers	104
SECTION 3: DOMESTIC SPACE AND FAMILY DYNAMICS	128
Chapter 8: Home environments	129
Chapter 9: Domestic space, modes of control, and problem drinking	149
SECTION 4: CONCLUSIONS AND IMPLICATIONS	164
Chapter 10: Teenage drinking: home and family influences	165
Bibliography	182
Author Index	197
Subject Index	200

List of illustrations and tables

FIGURES

Figure 5.1:	The circumplex model	59
Figure 5.2:	A two-dimensional classification of parenting patterns	62
Figure 6.1:	The reciprocal relationship between behaviour, person and the environment	76
Figure 6.2:	Odds of being a heavy drinker according to parental attitude and parental drinking	87
Figure 6.3:	Family socialization factors which influence the development of teenage drinking	88
Figure 6.4:	Family socialization: a model for teenage drinking	90
Figure 7.1:	Mean drinker score: school year and sex	120
Figure 7.2:	Mean drinker score: family support and control	121
Figure 7.3:	Mean drinker score: parental attitude and family drinking	122
Figure 7.4:	Mean drinker score: selected family profiles	125
Figure 8.1:	Mixed and homogenous spatial arrangements	138
Figure 8.2:	Private and public spaces in the home environment	140
Figure 9.1:	Alternative partitions of domestic space	154

TABLES

Table 3.1:	Drinking behaviour – youth trainees	31
Table 3.2:	Reasons for drinking: sex and alcohol use	32
Table 3.3:	Mean number of reasons: sex and alcohol use	33
Table 5.1:	Drinking behaviour variables identified in the meta-analysis	67
Table 5.2:	Family variables identified in the meta-analysis	68
Table 5.3:	Total significant and non-significant results for the relationship between drinking behaviour and family environment	68
Table 6.1:	Total significant and non-significant results for the relationship between adolescent drinking behaviour and family social learning factors	81
Table 7.1:	Drinking behaviour according to weekly consumption for adult drinkers and teenage drinkers	113
Table 7.2:	Drinking behaviour—secondary school students	114
Table 7.3:	ANOVA of drinker score and family socialization variables	119
Table 7.4:	Seven distinct family profiles	124

Preface

In this book we are concerned with adolescent drinking, primarily from the perspective of family socialization and the influence of the home environment. We identify family life behaviours which seem to be significantly linked to the development of teenage drinking characteristics.

Of course, many other factors may influence alcohol use/misuse amongst young people. Such factors might include, for instance, culture, socioeconomic status, social network, personality characteristics, locality and school/work. Nevertheless, we feel that much important research in recent years has focused on family socialization and home environment factors, and that the time is ripe for a review and assessment of theoretical developments and empirical studies in this particular area.

During the last decade, serious concerns (fanned by the media) were raised about the "rising levels" of teenage and underage drinking. Having looked in detail at the extent and nature of teenage drinking, we feel that there is still cause for concern but that alcohol misuse amongst teenagers is not the escalating problem which many media pundits predicted in the late 1980s.

Although young problem drinkers are a major source of concern, we have tried to portray teenage drinking as a normal development in the context of an adolescent's psychosocial environment. Drinking is predominantly a social behaviour and the family is a major agent of adolescent socialization. Our research, together with that of others in the field, has revealed a range of family interaction styles operating within a variety of domestic regimes. Although most young people drink within the normal range, those with alcohol-deviant behaviours (non-drinkers and heavy drinkers) seem more likely to emerge from families where the home environment and dynamics are more extreme.

For many years one of us (G. L.) has been especially interested in alcohol-behaviour interactions, the study of which increases our understanding not only of alcohol itself but also—and more importantly—of human behaviour. In collaboration with Hull & District Alcohol Advisory Service and related agencies we were able to develop projects concerned with the drinking behaviour of adolescents. These studies confirmed the notion of teenage drinking as a normative, developmental transition, and highlighted the role of alcohol in relation to adolescent social identity. Furthermore, parental attitudes were observed to be particularly influential.

It was becoming increasingly clear that family influences would be worth studying in more detail. D. R. F. joined the Alcohol Research Unit to investigate family socialization factors in adolescent drinking, and many of the main theoretical developments and empirical observations from that project are presented in this book (see section 2).

In the meantime, D.S. (a geographer) was busy researching "deviant" groups and the use of space. It just so happens that the Departments of Geography and Psychology at the University of Hull share a close "domestic environment" in that we occupy the same building. Initial "corridor conversations" between G. L. and D. S. led to ideas about boundary enforcement and transgression (see section 3), which were linked to adolescent alcohol use and abuse in a pilot study initially funded by the ESRC.

The three of us met regularly to further develop our ideas about family dynamics and the use of space in the home. The "problem" of adolescent alcohol use/abuse offered considerable scope for testing these ideas. Or, to put it the other way round, the "phenomenon" of teenage drinking might be best understood in terms of family socialization processes and the use of domestic space. A special feature of this book lies in the interaction of ideas from family life psychology and the geography of the home.

In the book we explore psychosocial family dynamics in detail and develop a theoretical model of family socialization and teenage drinking. What we have tried to do is put forward a particular perspective regarding the development and maintenance of adolescent drinking behaviour—namely, the influence of family life and of the home environment. This approach has implications for intervention strategies aimed at adolescent alcohol misuse, and, in terms of prevention, for alcohol education and guidance. We suggest and outline the potential directions in which this family perspective could benefit counsellors and therapists working with teenage problem drinkers. Moreover, we hope the book might contribute to therapeutic practice because of the problems it uncovers regarding family dynamics and relationships between families and domestic space. If we want our teenagers to use alcohol sensibly and appropriately we need to raise awareness of the role of parents in achieving this.

We have aimed to present theoretical issues in relation to drinking patterns, family socialization and modes of control in the home which should be of general interest to researchers in the field of adolescent behaviour, and to students in psychology, geography and other social sciences concerned with relationships between behaviour and the domestic environment.

Geoff Lowe
David R. Foxcroft
David Sibley

Acknowledgements

Firstly, we would like to thank the Departments of Psychology and Geography at the University of Hull for supporting our research and writing about adolescent drinking, the family and home environments. Special thanks are also due to the thousands of young people, parents and teachers who have contributed to our research. We are especially grateful to Steve Baber and Mike Woodward of Humberside Education Authority; Ian Warner, Wendy Leedham, James Greer, Deborah Sharp and Tamsin Black for their involvement in this project over the last few years; Anne Quigg for her help with the production and indexing of the manuscript; Paul McSherry for producing the figures; and Dorothy Sheridan of the Mass-Observation Archive at the University of Sussex for her cooperation. We also appreciate the help of the Economic and Social Research Council and the Alcohol Education and Research Council for funding this research. Finally, we would like to express our thanks to our own families for their warm support and interest in our work, and for their patience with us as we laboured to complete this book.

Chapter 1

Introduction and outline

> *"Today's level of under-age drinking has triggered fears of an alcohol abuse 'time-bomb'. Welfare counsellors in Hull are warning that the rising volume of drinking by under-18s will result in rocketing numbers of alcohol-related problems."*
> (Hull Daily Mail, 3 May 1989)

In a period of approximately ten years, young people go from individuals who have never had an alcoholic drink to individuals who, as an age group, comprise the heaviest drinking section of the population. Many youngsters report having their first drink between the ages of 9 and 11. A substantial proportion of teenagers drink excessively. What happens in this relatively short phase to bring about what is widely perceived as a dramatic and potentially costly change? This question reflects the largely media-generated public concern or even panic about teenage drinking.

Yet, despite all the emotive headlines and images of yobbism in action, objective data stubbornly continue to show that alcohol is not an increasing problem among the young. Although society purports to be shocked to discover that over 90 per cent of all 13-year-olds have tasted an alcoholic drink (Bagnall 1988), such observations are hardly surprising when about the same proportion of adults are drinkers of one sort or another. By the age of 17 many teenagers are drinking adult amounts of alcohol regularly and, over the next few years, before domestic and job responsibilities set in some may be indulging wildly. Fortunately, we are physically most capable of recovering from drinking binges when our body tissue is young, and it is comparatively rare to find alcohol dependence in anyone under 25 (Plant *et al* 1982).

Definitions

Before embarking on a discussion about adolescent drinking it is useful to define the terms used. Coleman (1980, p.viii) defined **adolescence** as:

> "that stage in the life cycle that begins at puberty and ends when the individual reaches maturity."

Although it is difficult to delimit the adolescent period in terms of lower and upper ages, most young people experience their adolescence between the ages of ten and eighteen. This is a period when young people are in their secondary school years (in the U.K.), or have just left school. The terms adolescent, young person, youth, teenager, etc, will be used interchangeably to describe this age group. The transitional stage from late childhood to adolescence is a critical period in which significant involvement with alcohol begins (May 1992; Plant & Plant 1992). Although girls and boys mature at different rates, and individual variation is considerable, most complete puberty within this age range.

Some social scientists believe that adolescence is universally a time of stress and strife. However, as Furnham and Gunter (1989) point out, this stress seems not to be a necessary result of physical and emotional maturation. Instead, any strain probably derives from the long interval during which the adolescent feels personally ready to accept independence and social responsibility, but actually remains financially dependent on his/her parents.

Traditional conceptualizations of adolescents' functioning in the family context have been based on the premise that adolescence is a time of separating from families (Gecas & Seff 1990). These days, such separation may be more psychological than physical. Despite earlier and possibly more rapid development in adolescence these days, there is in Western societies a longer period of dependence on parents, economically and socially. Hence, parental/family dynamics at this stage are important both in terms of contributing to, and influencing concern-generating behaviours (including alcohol and substance use).

Drinking refers to consumption of alcohol, and in many studies alcohol content is estimated using standard units of alcohol (SAU). One SAU is one millilitre of alcohol. Half a pint of beer, cider or lager contains one unit of alcohol as does a standard glass of wine or a measure of spirits. Clearly, this only approximates to the true alcohol content of drinks; extra strong beers and lager may contain twice as much alcohol as conventional beers. Also, glasses and measures vary, especially if not sold by a publican/bartender. However, absolute measures of alcohol are not usually appropriate for the types of study in our review. For the interested reader, Miller *et al* (1991) have compared alcohol measures and standard drink units across different countries.

What do we mean by the **family**? One of the difficulties in defining the family is that different individuals have different perceptions of who the members of their family are. Are intimacy or blood (genetic) ties the predominant influence in the perception of what constitutes a family? Is it the people you live with? On another level, the legal notion of what constitutes a family differs from the sociological notion, which differs from the anthropological, which differs from the psychological, and so on.

Defining the family unit is a fairly idiosyncratic thing to do. Nevertheless, the family constitutes the most important social grouping of human beings, and indeed of other animals. For the purpose of this book, and generally speaking within a psychological framework, the family can be considered to be an intimate group of people. What then constitutes intimacy? We can discriminate between intimate relationships and casual ones in that intimate relationships involve more intense liking and loving; more exchange of information; longer time periods; and exchange of resources of greater value and variety. For the adolescents in our studies, this sort of intimacy is typically manifested between themselves and their parents and siblings. However, for some individuals, other adults may take on a child-rearing (parental) role, fostering intimate relationships, for example grand-parents, foster parents, or legal guardians. We can therefore refer to adolescent **family life** as the behaviours, relationships and experiences - the characteristics of the intimacy - of the family unit.

The 'problem' of adolescent drinking

To many, any study of youthful drinking is synonymous with an investigation of the 'problem' of adolescent drinking. But why is adolescent drinking a problem? Disregarding media sensationalism, the main problem for young drinkers is the law. English law states that

> *"A child under the age of five years must not be given intoxicating liquor except under the orders of a doctor....."*
> (Children and Young Persons Act 1933)

and that

> *"No intoxicating liquor may be sold to a person under eighteen years of age"*

or

> *"delivered to such a person whether he is the purchaser or not"*
> (Licensing Act 1964)

Most youthful alcohol use involves breaking the law - it is 'under-age drinking'. The laxity with which the licensing laws are enforced is an indication of how lightly they are taken by both the police and licensees. Most young people have no trouble in obtaining alcohol.

There are, however, young people who have genuine drinking problems. Many young offenders blame alcohol for their crimes (McMurran 1990) but the links between alcohol and crime are not obvious (Standing Conference on Crime Prevention 1987). Other teenagers may damage their health or develop serious drink problems later in life. Because much of the evidence is equivocal, the relationship between youthful drinking and later alcohol use is unclear (Plant *et al* 1985; Andersson & Magnusson 1988).

Rather than investigating the 'problem' of teenage drinking, most U.K. research concentrates on youthful alcohol use as an example of adolescent social behaviour. In addressing the scope of the phenomenon several types of questions can be addressed. How do young people drink? How often and how much? When do they start using alcohol and when do they first get drunk? What are the roles of parents and friends? Do parents approve? Why do young people drink? Indeed, why do young people say they drink? What do they expect to get out of it?

If we consider the problem of adolescent alcohol abuse, further questions arise. What are the predictors and antecedents of problem drinking among youth? What are the links between problem drinking and other forms of social deviance? What are the characteristics of teenage alcohol abusers who seek treatment for alcohol problems?

Adolescents and alcohol

To put the issues in a broader context, we briefly review alcohol use and abuse in general before going on to outline the scope of teenage drinking.

Early work on the topic of adolescent alcohol use has already established that 'it goes on', and has addressed the who, when and where questions. Our aims are initially to confirm and comment on those scenarios in somewhat more detail, but more importantly to explore the reasons *why* adolescents do or do not drink, together with their attitudes and expectancies.

Teenage drinking is described as a normal developmental behaviour marking the progression from child to adult, and we consider this behaviour from a social, psychological and cultural perspective, and not from a 'legal' one. This perspective confirms and emphasizes the 'normality' of underage drinking, especially in the U.K., a prime example of an alcohol use culture.

Next we refer to example surveys which document epidemiological aspects, and discuss these observations in relation to psychosocial characteristics and implications. Such discussions need to be tempered with regard to various methodological issues involved in survey studies. So these are addressed before introducing notions of predicting alcohol abuse.

More recent studies are concerned with alcohol expectancies (i.e. what do teenagers expect from alcohol?). Here we will discuss research into the reasons underlying the drinking (and non-drinking) habits of teenagers. Our own work here has shown that such expectancies differ between the sexes and change over the age groups - but in rather complex ways. Moreover, these expectancies are modulated - both directly and indirectly - by parental/family influences.

We conclude this first section by stressing that the influences of the family and home are of primary importance in the development of an individual's behaviour and attitudes.

Family dynamics

Familial influences in the aetiology of 'alcoholism' have been well documented. However, much of this research considers possible genetic influences. It is only quite recently that the importance of family environmental factors has been established. It seems sensible therefore to broaden this outlook, and examine not only the familial aetiology of problem drinking, but the familial aetiology of drinking behaviour in general.

The family can be considered to be a major agent of adolescent socialization, as Minuchin (1974, p.48) states:

> "...the family is the matrix of its members' psycho-social development."

Since drinking behaviour is predominantly a social behaviour, and since the onset of drinking usually occurs in early adolescence, then it is important to look at family influences on early (adolescent) drinking behaviour.

What aspects of family life are important? Family systems theories have brought family dynamics to the forefront of current thinking. Family dynamics can be assessed and measured within the framework of family systems models. Two influential models - Minuchin's and the Circumplex Model of Olson and his colleagues - describe properties of the family system along two dimensions, cohesion and adaptability. Extreme levels of cohesion (enmeshed, disengaged) and of adaptability (rigid, chaotic) are seen as dysfunctional. Socialization theories also outline the importance of two family dimensions - support and control, as well as social learning factors, such as modelling of parental behaviour. We acknowledge that there is considerable overlap in concept and measurement between cohesion and support and between adaptability and control. The support dimension comprises behaviours which foster in an individual feelings of comfort and belonging, and the development of emotional bonds with each other. Control comprises family interactions which are concerned with rules, strictness, and power negotiation.

Within family systems there is a subset of family behaviours which are directly linked to drinking behaviour. We draw from Bandura's (1977) social learning theory to describe two important alcohol-specific family influences. These are imitation/modelling - parental and family models of alcohol use; and social reinforcement, characterized by the attitude of parents towards their teenager's actual or potential alcohol use.

Family process

Family process refers to those social and psychological interactions between family members which contribute to the climate and functioning of the family. Family systems can be observed both at the micro level (clock time interactions) and the macro level (calendar time interactions). The focus in this chapter is the calendar time process of parent-offspring socialization, in which two main dimensions of family environment - support and control - are important.

Knowledge of the aetiology of alcohol *misuse* is probably at a more advanced level than knowledge of the aetiology of alcohol use. Previous research and theory into the aetiology of problem drinking, carried out with the offspring of problem drinkers (a high-risk group for the development of alcohol-related problems), provides a useful guide and rationale for the investigation of family life and the aetiology of drinking behaviour. Although this might seem a backward way of going about trying to understand the development of normative drinking behaviour - using the family aetiology of misuse as a basis for investigating the family aetiology of use - the former relationship has received much more scientific attention, due mainly to the considerable social, economic and health impact of alcohol misuse.

People generally begin drinking in their early teenage years, and most young people learn to drink sensibly and moreover continue to do so. In this chapter we focus specifically on those elements of family process which are important for the socialization of drinking alcohol. Drawing from a range of diverse academic disciplines and theoretical perspectives of family life, we point out commonalities and integrate these similar perspectives into a useful framework for the investigation of family process and teenage drinking. Two main family process factors - support and control - are identified and included in this framework. This approach enabled us to carry out a comprehensive meta-analysis of numerous research studies, many of which employed different constructs.

The results of the meta-analysis were clear. Levels of family support and control, and also family structure (parental intactness), were directly related to teenage drinking. On the whole, low support, low control and a non-nuclear family were all linked with heavier teenage drinking. We go on to describe optimal levels of support and control for the socialization of sensible drinking. We also clarify the family systems perspective, where extremes of support and control are viewed as dysfunctional, by pointing out that non-drinking in an environment in which most young people drink sensibly and teenage drinking is accepted and condoned, is also a 'deviant' behaviour. We use the term 'deviant' in a statistical sense, meaning different from the norm, rather than the more moralistic and emotive sense in which deviant means socially problematical behaviour. Whereas low support and low control may socialize an individual towards heavier drinking, high support and high control may socialize an individual towards non-drinking.

Family socialization

Family process, through support and control, is only part of the picture. Family process refers to non-alcohol-specific general family behaviours. But what about alcohol-specific family behaviours?

In this chapter we turn to social learning theory to see how family models of alcohol use and parental reinforcement of teenage drinking relate to adolescent alcohol use. We describe the elements of social learning theory as put forward by Bandura (1977), and using a sorting meta-analytic technique we examine the results of numerous published studies. Most of these studies reported that heavier drinking by teenagers was related to heavier parental alcohol use. Similarly, parental social reinforcement was also an important factor. Parental indifference to their teenager's drinking was linked with heavier teenage alcohol use. Conversely, teenage non-drinking was linked with parents who do not drink and also parents who disapprove of their offspring drinking. We also discuss peer influences and point to how they may have been over-emphasized or misunderstood in relation to the socialization of teenage alcohol use.

In the second part of this chapter we bring together non-alcohol-specific and alcohol-specific family factors and describe a model for the investigation and understanding of family influences on the development of adolescent drinking behaviour. Given that teenage drinking is a common and socially and culturally accepted behaviour, our conceptualization of family socialization theory contained within this model gives a global view of family influences and teenage drinking, going beyond the more usual non-problem drinker/problem drinker distinction to include non-drinkers as a statistically and socially distinct group.

We also draw attention to the combined effect of these family socialization behaviours, and what the consequences might be for teenage alcohol use when these behaviours are consistent with each other, and also what the consequences might be when the family socialization factors do not complement each other.

Moving on from the theoretical development and discussion, we end this chapter with some qualitative data. Contrasting case studies are presented of two teenage drinkers - Tony who reported that he went through a period of drinking a large bottle of vodka every day, and Darren, who drinks sensibly.

Family profiles of teenage drinkers

The qualitative data we present at the end of chapter 6 is supplemented in chapter 7 by the results of a large questionnaire study.

Over 4000 school students (mostly aged 11-16) participated in this survey by completing an adolescent drinking and family life questionnaire. We look first at age and sex differences in drinking behaviour. As expected, there were considerable differences according to the school year of the respondent, but sex differences were relatively small, although statistically significant.

We next focus on how the family socialization variables related to teenage drinking. We present the results of the family process factors - support and control - and then go on to look at the family social learning variables - family models of alcohol use and parental social reinforcement of alcohol use. As we expected, low support, low control, heavier drinking parents and an indifferent parental attitude were all independently and additively linked with self-reported teenage drinking.

To illustrate the impact of the combination of both alcohol-specific and non-alcohol-specific family behaviours for the socialization of adolescent drinking, in the final part of this chapter we present a comparison of drinking behaviour across seven groups of teenagers who reported a different pattern of family life. This family profiling technique demonstrates that although some family socialization factors may be more influential than others, the combination of all the behaviours is also important. This holistic point has implications for how alcohol education programmes are designed and set up.

Home environments

Unlike many studies of family dynamics, we will not isolate the family from the immediate environment or fail to consider the wider environmental influences on behaviour. So we focus on the home as a space which can be manipulated but which can also constrain relationships between family members. If the oppression of children or adolescents in family settings has possible connections with the onset of problem drinking, then space is also implicated because children can be controlled through the control of domestic space. First, the availability and configuration of space in the home influences interactions between individuals. Space may be highly compartmentalized and controlled. Thus, psychological boundaries between family members can be reinforced by the maintenance of boundaries in the home between 'adult space' and 'children's space', for example. However, the opportunities for controlling domestic space will be affected by the design of the home. The internal division of space in the home tends to be fixed and stable so the arrangement of rooms may reinforce or modify family control systems. In our analysis, we refer to a range of arguments about boundary control, drawn from social anthropology, environmental psychology and human geography, in order to demonstrate how families and space interrelate. This next section will demonstrate how anxiety and tension derive from conflict over the use of space in the home. Whilst some conflict is inevitable in 'normal' families, we aim to identify particularly problematic associations between families and the home which could well contribute to the onset and maintenance of adolescent problem drinking.

The home is not a closed system. It is important to recognize that domestic regimes can be influenced by external factors or, rather, that there is a reciprocal conditioning of individuals in families, the home, the neighbourhood, and larger collectivities and spaces. We stress the importance of values implicit in the ordered suburb, a concern with boundary maintenance and the rejection of social difference. Images of disorder and threat may heighten a concern for boundaries within the home which may, in turn, encourage transgressive behaviour in adolescents. Thus, views of the social geography of the city, such as 'the house as haven' or the suburb as a defence against threatening minorities, are relevant considerations.

Surprisingly, conflict and power relations rarely feature in studies of the home by environmental psychologists. The literature in this field concentrates on individual satisfaction provided by the home environment - the house as a 'haven in a troubled world' and as a store of cherished memories. The focus on the individual renders the family invisible so there is no place for conflicting views of the use of space or time. We reject this 'happy phenomenology' of the home and draw instead on theoretical schemata which clarify the way in which power is exercised over domestic space. From Goffman's front stage/back stage dichotomy, which translates into masculine/feminine domestic spheres, we move to Bernstein's scheme for analysing the transmission of educational knowledge. Bernstein is concerned with the question of boundary maintenance as a means of securing 'pure' academic disciplines within hierarchical educational institutions (strong classification) and, conversely, the dissolution of boundaries between subjects where, in non-hierarchical systems, a mixing of ideas is valued (weak classification) and his argument provides an appropriate analogue for the problem of boundary maintenance in the home, ranging from strong boundaries and 'pure' spaces to weak boundaries and heterogeneous spaces. Mass-Observation surveys on home environments provide some evidence for individuals' preferences for strongly or weakly classified spaces. Similarly, we can recognize contrasting rigid and relaxed temporal regimes in the home which relate to the use of space. In relation to both space and time, we note how the use of the home environment may be associated with anxieties and tensions in families.

In an attempt to explain conflict in the home, we examine the fundamental dichotomies, clean/dirty and ordered/disordered. The concept of dirt has been discussed in detail by the anthropologist, Douglas, and the psychoanalyst, Kristeva. Kristeva traces the source of the pure and defiled self, defilement generalizing into a concern with a range of abject things, sensations and people. In the home, abjection is reinforced by advertising which promotes purified environments and encourages the identification of defilement in goods and people, thus strengthening boundaries. The ideas reviewed in this chapter emphasize boundaries in the home. The presence or absence of boundaries (spatial, social, individual) is a central feature of family dynamics. We should not generalize from mainstream western studies because different cultures have different concepts of social and spatial division. We can argue, however, that the boundaries which partition domestic space are an important component of family dynamics and may be crucial in understanding problem behaviour.

A discussion of the wider environment will also include an account of media images which define boundaries between 'purified' domestic space and 'defiled' exterior spaces. Television commercials and films, for example, enter the home and sustain domestic regimes which emphasize the regulation of space. This issue will be discussed in order to present a more complete profile of problem cases - the domestic situations of teenagers exhibiting deviant drinking behaviour.

Domestic space, modes of control and problem drinking

In this next chapter we go on to examine possible connections between the manipulation and appropriation of space in the home and teenage problem drinking. We first characterize families in terms of the methods of social control, using Bernstein's positional/personalizing dichotomy. This dichotomy can be linked to typical domestic regimes and attitudes to space, positional families being identified by strong classification and personalizing families by weak classification. Families within the 'normal' range would have a mix of positional and personalizing traits but the dichotomy usefully identifies polar types.

Strong classification and positional forms of control are oppressive and, in particular, may have a confining effect on children. However, a more complex picture of problem-creating behaviour emerges from Minuchin's model of family dynamics. According to Minuchin, problems can be associated both with disengagement, where boundaries are rigid, and enmeshment, where boundaries are vague or absent. Combining Minuchin and Bernstein, we identify three problematic domestic regimes where family relationships and attitudes to space are combined, characterized, respectively, by strong classification/disengagement, strong classification/enmeshment, and weak classification/enmeshment. Family interactions are mediated by the home, however. Thus, we have to take account of the constraining or enabling effects of the physical space of the home, that is, the design and density of occupation, on family interactions. Taken together, a characterization of spaces and a characterization of families provide a basis for locating cases where problems of conflict, oppression and transgression can be anticipated.

We introduce some of our recent research based on surveys of teenagers' home life and drinking behaviour. These studies also included structured interviews with problem drinkers who recounted experiences of their family and home life as adolescents. Additional commentary relates to the potentially therapeutic aspects of the research process, and we draw out implications for intervention and treatment strategies.

Conclusions

There is a clear link between teenage drinking and family life. Most individuals are given their first drink of alcohol by parents and family, and much of an individual's knowledge (or lack of it) about alcohol is developed throughout childhood and adolescence by family-oriented interactions with alcohol (Davies & Stacey 1972; Jahoda & Crammond 1972). By far the majority of adolescents use alcohol - an estimated 90 per cent have started drinking by the age of 16. Given that drinking is predominantly a social behaviour, and that the family is especially influential in adolescent socialization, individuals should be encouraged to develop sensible drinking behaviour via optimal family socialization. Sub-optimal family socialization may lead to adolescent drinking behaviour which is socially and/or culturally deviant - abstention or excessive drinking. Thus, the distinction between non-drinker, sensible drinker and heavy drinker differs from the perspective normally taken, which is the classification of an individual as a 'problem drinker' or 'non-problem drinker'.

Extremes of cohesion/support and adaptability/control can be viewed as dysfunctional for the development of sensible drinking behaviour in teenagers. Low support and lax control are linked with heavier drinking in adolescents. Alcohol-specific family behaviours are also related to adolescent drinking. More frequent parental drinking and indifferent parental attitudes towards teenage drinking are linked with heavier adolescent drinking. But if an individual remains abstinent in a social and cultural environment which condones and encourages drinking, then this too is deviant drinking behaviour, and it could be that high support and strict control, non-drinking parents and parental disapproval, are associated with abstention. Moderate support and control, and sensible parental drinking and a moderating attitude towards their offspring's drinking, appear to be optimal for the development of sensible adolescent drinking. Interactions between these family dimensions at the extremes may also contribute to whether an individual abstains, drinks sensibly, or drinks excessively. Family life is also constrained by more physical parameters. Structural influences, such as parental intactness and family size are important, and can directly affect an individual's approach to alcohol.

We conclude by showing that an increased understanding of family dynamics, partly within the context of the geography of the home, should offer important insights into teenage drinking (and possibly other substance use) during the course of adolescent development.

We offer suggestions for future research directions which should include follow-up and longitudinal studies, participant observation and the use of Mass-Observation approaches. The theoretical issues developed in the book might be further pursued in terms of socioeconomic status and cross-cultural aspects (for example, in addressing the problem of alcohol and substance abuse in different cultures, or in comparative studies of family life and teenage drinking in European countries).

Finally, implications and applications are considered - for instance, in relation to the role of the family in alcohol education, and home technologies which influence boundaries and boundary control.

SECTION 1:

Alcohol and Teenagers

Alcohol is arguably the most complex psychoactive substance and certainly the most widely consumed. Research into alcohol use and abuse is also complex and extensive.

Adolescence is arguably the most complex psychosocial stage of human development - a period of considerable concern for all involved. Research into adolescence is probably equally complex and wide-ranging.

So when adolescents and alcohol interact the resulting phenomenon of teenage drinking is likely to be viewed as even more complex. In this first section we offer a brief overview of alcohol use and abuse, outline the scope of teenage drinking - including a review of research and theories (some of which refer to other types of adolescent substance use) and generally consider the question of why teenagers drink.

Chapter 2

Alcohol, use and abuse

Alcohol

Alcohol is both the oldest and most widely used intoxicant. Yet, in its raw form, its taste is unpleasant, and our taste for it in various forms, such as beer and spirits, has to be acquired. Technically, it is a poison and leaves bad after-effects.

Alcoholic beverages, however, are drunk and enjoyed by most people in society. They taste and look good. They are sold and consumed in 'fun' places (restaurants, clubs, pubs and parties). Alcohol promotes 'sharing' - implied in mutual buying of drinks. It provides the 'excuse' to attend social gatherings. It makes people feel good. Its mood-altering properties are greatly sought after and enjoyed by most drinkers. So its capacity to encourage relaxation, reduce inhibition, promote sociability, relieve tension and stress, and, for some, produce inebriation and loss of control/consciousness, is greatly valued in society. It is a most welcome substance. Alcohol is

> *"the chosen intoxicant of European peoples as it has been in many other parts of the world. It has been part of our lives from the very beginnings of our civilization and it is woven inextricably into our culture"* (Special Committee of Royal College of Psychiatrists, 1986, p.18)

Alcoholism/alcohol abuse

Various attempts have been made to provide a single and comprehensive definition. In 1951 the W.H.O. suggested that:

> *"alcoholism is any form of drinking which in its extent goes beyond the traditional and customary dietary use, or the ordinary compliance with the social drinking customs of the whole community concerned, irrespective of the aetiological factors leading to such behaviour, and irrespective also of the extent to which such aetiological factors are dependent upon heredity, constitution or acquired physiopathological and metabolic influences."*

They later used this to refer to 'excessive drinking' and redefined 'alcoholics' as:

> *"those excessive drinkers whose dependence on alcohol has attained such a degree that it shows a noticeable mental disturbance or an interference with their bodily and mental health, their interpersonal relations, and their smooth social and economic functioning; or who show the prodromal signs of such development. They therefore require treatment."* (W.H.O. 1952)

Most psychologists prefer the terms 'alcohol dependence' or 'problem drinking' to refer to the excessive and compulsive use of alcohol, since the label 'alcoholism' is too closely associated with a simple disease model. A distinction is made between dependence upon alcohol and the harm caused by excessive consumption. Alcohol dependence refers to the strength of the habit, the subjective experience of compulsion and the difficulty in resisting alcohol across a wide variety of situations (Hodgson *et al* 1979).

Adolescent alcohol abuse

The relationship between teenagers and alcohol is not a recent development in adolescent behaviour: teenagers have always been into drinking. Teenagers consume alcohol for a myriad of reasons and such drinking sometimes leads to alcohol abuse and dependence which, of course, can link with other problem behaviours. It may be helpful, therefore, to try to differentiate such alcohol abuse (or problem drinking) from 'normal' (or sensible) drinking.

Most studies report around 90 per cent of young people have at least tried a 'proper drink' by age 16 (Bagnall 1988; Ghodsian & Power 1987; Hawker 1978; Plant *et al* 1982). Boys typically report drinking more than girls and more often, but girls usually prefer a wider variety of drinks. Most adolescents do not claim to drink excessively (Hawker 1978; Marsh *et al* 1986).

However, not all reported adolescent drinking is sensible drinking. In *Adolescent Drinking* (Marsh *et al* 1986), half the 13-year-old girls surveyed claimed they had been a little drunk at least once and 17 per cent had been very drunk. These proportions rose to 80 and 50 per cent respectively for 17-year-old boys. Moreover, 4 per cent of boys and 3 per cent of girls reported drinking *purely* to get drunk. Indeed, younger adolescents in London occasionally saved up to go out and "get paralytic" (Dorn 1983). Other consequences of excessive drinking have been reported, such as hangovers, vomiting, memory lapses, and violence. Prevalence rates for such consequences in adolescents range from 10-25 per cent.

Much has been written on the problem of defining adolescent alcohol misuse (Hawkins 1982). For instance, White (1987) highlights the need for two distinct dimensions - intensity of use and use-related problems - rather than a unitary construct. Abuse typically involves both a determination by the drinker and a criticism by one or more observers of the drinker's alcohol habits.

Teenage drunkenness

Given the extreme complexity of this issue and the lack of comprehensive information about teenage drunkenness, any discussion of youthful intoxication represents only a contribution to the continuing analysis of this phenomenon and cannot provide any definitive conclusions. However, several relevant viewpoints are worth considering.

Many hold the concerned view that youthful drunkenness is a warning that problem drinking or alcoholism may develop in the future. Drunken behaviour is seen as a sign that a youngster may have an emotional or genetic predisposition toward problem drinking (Brown *et al* 1989; Goodwin 1989; MacKay 1961; White 1987). This perspective has much force. There are millions of adult problem drinkers, and studies show that many males amongst them reported drunken behaviour as youngsters and at a generally earlier age than adults who do not have drinking problems.

However, we have no way of knowing whether there is a *causal* link between youthful intoxication and problems with alcohol later in time. It is possible that adult problem drinkers and 'alcoholics' would still abuse alcohol even if they had been prevented or discouraged from getting drunk as youngsters. Moreover, most teenagers who get drunk do not become problem drinkers as adults (Smart 1980). For some teenagers, problem drinking is part of the process of growing up and will decrease with age and maturity (Donovan et al 1983). Of special concern to parents and counsellors who see youthful drunkenness from an 'ominous' perspective is the evidence that the very act of 'labelling' a youngster as a problem drinker may become a self-fulfilling prophecy (O'Gorman et al 1976). Nevertheless, we should all be concerned about the repeated drunken behaviour of any teenager and explore what appears to be responsible for it and, importantly, the context in which it occurs.

Another relevant perspective on teenage drunkenness is that it must be seen in the context of a culture's overall drinking norms. In this view, youthful intoxication, given its prevalence and enjoyment by many youngsters, can be seen as the natural and harmless expression of socially shared values, including the notion of 'time out' or natural break which adults also seek from the (heavy) responsibilities and harsh realities of everyday life. As such, it may represent a normal process of socialization towards adulthood (Sharp 1992).

However, it is not clear that drunkenness by teenagers is normative behaviour, nor do we really know if it is condoned by a majority of youngsters, let alone adults. Yet two things are clear: (i) for many teenagers getting drunk is a routine feature of their social lives and that of their friends, whether it occurs once a month, every weekend, or two or three times a week; and (ii) not getting drunk is certainly a competing social norm for a lot of other youngsters. In many cultures there simply has been no widespread consensus regarding the appropriateness of youngsters or adults becoming intoxicated. With the increasing force of 'health promotion' recently, however, the range of normative contexts for drunkenness is probably much narrower.

Adolescent problem drinking

It must be kept in mind that adolescents often encounter problems with alcohol because of a single acute episode rather than as the result of a chronic condition. However, problems which occur because of drunkenness, such as drunk driving or having a fight with a friend or aggression towards an authority figure, even though not indicative of a repetitive pattern of problems, are often precursors to referral. Many of these problems simply result from inexperience and carelessness. Young people drink less often than adults, but when they drink, they tend to drink in larger amounts (Harford & Grant 1987). Thus, they are at risk for suffering acute effects (eg. blackouts and hangovers) as well as for behaving adversely (eg. belligerence). Moreover, some social and interpersonal consequences are more likely because adolescents are legally under age and their drinking may violate parental norms as well as legal regulations.

Identifying problem drinking in adolescents requires certain departures from the widely used model of adult alcoholism. The usual measures of frequency, quantity and variability of alcohol use are not sufficient to accurately diagnose the problem status of adolescent drinking. The effects of alcohol can vary widely from one youth to another. So, information about negative consequences attributable to drinking, in addition to information on drinking patterns, would seem most appropriate for diagnosing problem drinking (White & Labouvie 1989).

Young problem drinkers

There are, of course, many factors which may lead a teenager to abuse alcohol. The age period of adolescence may foster a spirit of boundary transgression - challenging society and adult authority, possibly by illegal behaviour. Disregarding or even flouting alcohol regulations may be one example. Another factor is the need for independence from the parent. Teenagers like to appear 'grown-up' by assuming adult habits such as consuming alcohol. For many, there is also increased availability of money and leisure time, both of which can encourage unwise drinking habits. Add these and other factors (such as insecurity or inferiority complexes, low educational attainment, stress, and isolation or poor family relationships), and a problem drinker can emerge at an early age.

In problem drinking, several reasons may exist which propel the adolescent in attempts to solve problems through consumption of increasing amounts of alcohol - just as with many insecure, more experienced adults. Teenagers drink to experience the effects produced by alcohol: the more they consume, the greater the effects. One study distinguished young problem drinkers from the normal adolescent drinkers by their early use of alcohol for its effect (Addeo & Addeo 1975).

The troubled youth, caught in the upheaval of their adolescence, may well use alcohol, not for relaxation, but for coping with stress. Mitic *et al* (1987) compared perceived stress levels between problem and non-problem drinkers. In adolescent males, the differences were greatest in areas of money, parents and school work; while amongst adolescent females, parents, money and appearance were the main distinguishing concerns. The more stress encountered, the more alcohol is consumed until it becomes a 'crutch', even though it only compounds individual problems and indeed clouds good judgment.

Problem drinking may be linked with problem or deviant behaviour generally. The incidence of heavy drinking is higher among juvenile delinquents and young offenders (McMurran 1990). Many believe that adolescent problem drinking is one of a class of behaviours, commonly referred to as anti-social, which involves the potential for getting into trouble. It is the amount of alcohol consumed, the frequency, and the adverse effects that determine if individual teenagers are misusing alcohol. It becomes a problem when drinking interferes with normal relationships at school/college/work, with parents and family, among peers, or involves difficulties with the police or other authorities.

To summarize, alcohol misuse/abuse occurs whenever too much alcohol is consumed, whether it be alone, at a party, or on special occasions. There are signs that the number of identified teenage problem drinkers has given cause for concern - particularly during the 1980s. It has also been noted that alcohol abuse occurs in all ethnic and income groups and in all regions. However, certain ethnic groups may be more prone to problem drinking, and some localities regions contain more problem drinkers than others. Not all problem drinkers remain problem drinkers; nor, indeed, do all abstainers remain as such. These behavioural patterns are influenced by many diverse factors.

Alcohol and substance-related problems in adolescents

Some leading researchers view alcohol and other drug use as part of essentially similar behaviour (eg. Adger 1991; Jessor *et al* 1980; Kandel *et al* 1978). Much American research on adolescent substance use is based on this conceptualization and, as Hansen *et al* (1987) suggest: "*the use of tobacco, alcohol and marijuana by young adolescents may be considered a unitary phenomenon.*" However, few researchers in the U.K. and other parts of Europe would share this view, and use patterns of alcohol and other substances are often clearly differentiated - particularly so in adolescents. In trying to understand why people use substances and in developing prevention/treatment strategies for problem users it may be helpful to deal with drinking, smoking, and the use of heroin, solvents and other substances as separate and distinct behaviours (Davies 1992).

Nevertheless, there are inevitably some commonalities (Levison *et al* 1982), and individuals who use one drug are more likely to use others (for instance, there are very few smokers who do not also drink). American researchers in the forefront of theory development have tended to focus on the commonalities of alcohol and substance use in adolescents, and explanations of use/misuse cover a range of substances. So it seems appropriate to consider these approaches in order to sample the broader picture of adolescent substance use/abuse in which teenage drinking has a prominent role.

For British secondary school children, 10-20 per cent are regular smokers (Eiser *et al* 1991) and 60-90 per cent regularly drink alcohol (about 10 per cent drinking "more than moderately" (Sharp 1992)). Age of induction into alcohol use is generally about 11-13. This is made more significant by the evidence that the earlier initiation into alcohol and drug use, the higher the risk of progressing to more dangerous patterns of use and subsequent behavioural and social problems (Robins et al 1986).

One interesting observation is that although there has been a decrease in the reported prevalence of smoking and the use of most illicit drugs, there has been little change in the reported use of alcohol - which many claim to be the major drug of abuse. Moreover, there has been a trend toward earlier initiation of drug use, with the average age of starting alcohol or drug use being the early teens.

Health risks

A major factor in the deterioration of the health status of young people is use of alcohol and other drugs. It is a major contributor to disability and death in the 15-25-year-old group. Of equal concern is the impact of alcohol and other drugs on the cognitive and psychosocial development of young people.

'Epidemic' smoking and drinking

Prevalences of smoking and drinking increase markedly during adolescence. Most theories assume that peer influences have a prominent role in the initiation of these behaviours. If the source of influence is actually face-to-face peer interactions, then the spread of drinking (and smoking) behaviours may follow a predictable course. According to Rowe and Rodgers (1991), it may resemble the epidemic process associated with a contagious disease. They found model fits to be generally better for drinking than for smoking. Peer 'influence' is conceptualized not so much as pressure, but rather as opportunity. The epidemic model also emphasizes the inherent reward (eg. functional) value of these substances.

Causal theories of adolescent alcohol and other drug use

A number of theories on causation and initiation of use of alcohol and other drugs can be identified from the research literature.

Problem behaviour theory suggests that drug use is part of a range of problem behaviours with which it has common antecedents. Jessor and Jessor (1977) originally proposed that many problems, including substance abuse, could be explained by variations in individual personality characteristics, perceived environmental structures, socialization patterns, and demographic status. In a study by Hays *et al* (1987), these characteristics were about equally predictive of alcohol use. However, according to Jessor (1987), a better measure of psychosocial risk or proneness to problem behaviour can be obtained from the interaction of these factors.

Social learning theory suggests that behavioural patterns are more or less problematic depending on the opportunities and social influences to which one is exposed, the skilfulness with which one performs, and the balance of rewards obtained from participation in certain activities.

According to Bandura (1977), learning is shaped by the observation of other people's behaviour and its consequences for them. Bandura recognized the potential use for **modelling** as a way of directing and modifying behaviour through the transmission of messages depicting behaviour and attitudes that young people would like to initiate. Bandura also noted that the ability to anticipate both the consequences of one's behaviour and the attitudes of others toward such behaviour develops as an individual matures.

Kandel and co-workers (1978) proposed that drug involvement progresses through a series a stages which begins with experimentation, progresses to regular use, and then results in abuse/dependence. **Stage theory** proposes that within normal adolescent populations, substance use tends to follow several stages, each of which is necessary but not sufficient for progressing to the next stage. For those who progress beyond initial experimentation with tobacco and alcohol, regular use of alcohol is next, followed by use of marijuana in conjunction with tobacco and alcohol, and then the use of prescription drugs, inhalants and illicit substances.

Opponents of the stage theory argue that no one path leads to drug use or abuse: they suggest instead that drug abuse is a function of a number of problems experienced by adolescents. **Multiple-risk-factor theory** proposes that drug use is caused by a combination of factors, none of which alone is causative (Newcomb *et al* 1986).

The **biopsychosocial model** emerges from the field of behavioural medicine and from recent interest in competence and coping. It features strongly in health psychology, and is based on two central premises: (i) that substances may be used as a coping strategy to enhance desirable or reduce undesirable feelings or emotions; (ii) that skills used to cope with daily stresses are different from those used for coping with temptation to experiment with or experience the effects of a mood-altering substance. The model suggests that substance abuse is a product of a deficiency in coping skills that are relevant to a variety of stressors. Hence, when faced with personal or social pressure to use substances, adolescents with deficits in social skills are more likely to engage in drug use.

Rhodes and Jason (1988) integrated the traditional emphasis on individual and family variables with recent research on competence and coping. They viewed drug use as a long-term outcome of multiple experiences with significant others and social systems from birth to adolescence. Accordingly, adolescents who: (i) form positive attachments with family, teachers and peers; (ii) develop good coping skills; and (iii) have school and community role models in addition to resources in the community which provide opportunities for success are more likely to deal with stress effectively and less likely to engage in problem behaviours, including use of alcohol and other drugs. This **social stress model** suggests that it is important to examine the broader social context in an attempt to minimize the social and institutional obstacles to adjustment for youth, such as enhancing their educational opportunities and improving the quality of school systems. Additionally, it emphasizes the importance of examining broader variables, such as socioeconomic status, race, school environment, and community resources, in determining risk.

'At risk' groups

Early identification of youth at high-risk might permit the modification of behaviours or amelioration of circumstances that would otherwise lead to alcohol and other drug use and/or other dysfunctional behaviours. But this should be done without inappropriate negative labelling. In the earliest school years, youngsters at risk may be distinguishable from others by aggressive antisocial behaviour, combined with shyness and problems with truancy and school adjustments (Kaplan et al 1984). By the late elementary grades, youngsters at highest risk are those who have experienced school failure. By adolescence, a low commitment to school and associated academic failure may be evident, as may be delinquent, drug using friends (Kandel 1985), alienation from society (Kandel 1982) and associated rebelliousness.

Risk for alcohol misuse and other drug use can be seen as falling into five broad categories: biological factors, environmental factors, psychological factors, peer factors, and genetic and family factors. In addition to these broad categories, several demographic variables have been used to characterize youth at risk.

Demographic factors

Age, sex, ethnicity, race, socioeconomic status and other demographic variables have been examined with regard to their impact on adolescent alcohol and substance use (Martin & Pritchard 1991).

Age is most consistently associated with problem drug use. Kandel and others have shown that initiation of alcohol use at a young age influences the risk of using other drugs, which in turn increases the risk of further escalation. The earlier a person begins to drink or use other drugs, the greater the likelihood of later drug problems (Battjes 1985). In particular, using drugs before age 15 years greatly increases the risk of later drug use (Barnes & Welte 1986; Newcomb et al 1986). Recent research suggests that delaying the age of onset of experimentation with alcohol and other drugs may help to prevent later and more serious drug involvement.

Gender is not usually a good predictor of adolescent drug use. Differences between male and female drug use have declined over the past two decades. Such differences are relatively small and vary by type of substance, level of drug involvement, and age. In general, males are more likely to report higher levels of drinking and illicit drug use (Kandel 1982), whilst teenage girls report more involvement with smoking than do boys (Foxcroft & Lowe 1992d; Lader & Matheson 1991; Smyth & Browne 1992).

Ethnic and racial differences in substance abuse are difficult to determine because these variables are often confounded by socioeconomic status and living conditions (Wright & Watts 1988). Although white teenagers compared to non-white teenagers have reported consistently higher levels of use of alcohol (Morgan *et al* 1984), marijuana, cocaine and other illicit drugs, differences between these groups are now very small. However, there is a need to consider this within the overall culture.

Socioeconomic status alone is not strongly associated with substance abuse (Battjes 1985). Substance use, abuse, and dependency cut across all income and socioeconomic levels. Education, a factor closely associated with socioeconomic status, does correlate with substance use. Pupils who are doing well in school report lower rates of use than those who are doing poorly (Levine & Singer 1988). In addition, those who have plans for further education (after school) are less likely than those without such expectations to use illicit drugs (Johnston *et al* 1989).

Biological factors

In the past two decades there has been much exploration of the biological aspects of alcohol and other drug dependence. Some research suggests that once a person has been dependent on alcohol or other drugs, that individual remains biologically different from others who have never used drugs. This may be one factor which makes relapse common (Schuckit 1983). According to Goodwin (1989), the only known biological risk factor for alcohol abuse is a family history of alcoholism - although hyperactive children may also be at risk. However, much remains unclear, and the evidence for a predominantly biological basis of alcohol and drug dependence is limited.

Environmental factors

Environmental factors have long been known to play an important role in the causes of delinquency and, by extension, in the development of substance use. For instance, persistent drug use and delinquent activity (Kandel 1980), as opposed to infrequent or occasional alcohol/drug use, is associated with deprivation, population density and community disorganization.

Psychological factors

A wide variety of psychological factors are believed to be associated with substance use. These include school failure (Bloch *et al* 1991), low interest in school and achievement, rebelliousness and alienation (Kandel 1982; Norem-Hebeisen *et al* 1984), low self-esteem, early anti-social behaviour (Kaplan *et al* 1984; Wilcox 1985) and greater adjustment problems (Weintraub 1990-91). Although psychological factors are not well understood, a constellation of character traits has been linked with high risk of substance use problems. These characteristics include lack of empathy for the feelings of others, easy and frequent lying, favouring of immediate over delayed gratification, and insensitivity to punishment.

Peer-related factors

One of the most widely proposed predictors of substance use by an adolescent is the drug use of the youth's best friend (Kandel 1985; Norem-Hebeisen *et al* 1984). Adolescents whose friends use drugs are much more likely to use them than those whose peers do not. Additionally, youngsters having older siblings using alcohol or other drugs are also more likely to become involved themselves (Kandel 1985).

Genetic and family factors

There is some evidence for genetic factors, especially for sons of fathers who had early onset of drinking problems (Schuckit 1983). Individuals with a family history of alcoholism have a four- to six-fold increased risk for the same disorder when compared to the general population (Goodwin 1989). A family history of antisocial behaviour is another risk factor, as is family disorganization (Weintraub 1990-91). Additionally, poor parenting skills increase the risk of having children who use alcohol and other substances. Parental alcohol and drug use, as well as attitudes favourable to such use, are the other familial risk factors for teenage substance use (Kandel 1982; McLaughlin *et al* 1985).

A family systems perspective

Many studies point to the family system as a very salient factor in the aetiology of alcohol misuse in adolescents. There appears to be a high level of anxiety in these families, and the adolescent is rather withdrawn from the family. For example, Stacey and Davies (1970) report that parental models are influential in shaping early attitudes and behaviour with regard to teenage drinking. Conversely, MacKay (1961) found that, amongst adolescent problem drinkers, the family was the least influential. Jessor and Jessor (1974) studied the child-rearing practices of the mothers of high-school students, along with the responses of these students to a questionnaire on alcohol use. According to this study, the more traditional the mother's values, the less the adolescent's involvement in alcohol misuse. Others have found strong links between adolescent drunkenness and lax maternal control, parental rejection, and psychological tension in the relationship with either the father or mother.

Family links

In his review of research on alcohol and the family, Orford (1990) points to increasing concern over youthful excessive drinking. Its origins, he says, are frequently attributed to unsatisfactory aspects of family life. Causation is usually assumed to operate directly from a family deficiency to youthful problem drinking - and reports from Western Europe, Nigeria and especially from countries within Eastern Europe attest to this. However, the results are generally complex, involving multiple interactions with a number of variables, including sex and race.

Nevertheless, the results are consistent in showing positive links between parents' drinking and their children's drinking, although the size of these correlations is sometimes overshadowed by the degree of relationship between a young person's drinking and that of his or her peer group. Interesting work in this area includes an American study by Teusch (1980), who found that increased alcohol consumption in 13-15-year-olds was related to lack of parental emotional tension and/or a high degree of parental control. From Australia comes a study which seems to reflect the changing roles of women. Wilks and Callan (1984) investigated attitudes towards heavy drinking. They found a greater discrepancy between the views of daughters and their parents than between those of sons and their parents, and greater discrepancies between the views of mothers and their children than between the views of fathers and their children, mothers having less favourable attitudes.

Parental drinking

One theme that runs through the literature is that certain subgroups of adolescents (eg. those from lower social classes) are particularly 'at risk' as a consequence of parental influence. This is particularly so in the case of smoking in young males.

The literature about the association between parents and their children's drinking addresses slightly different issues as it tends to focus upon the development of problem drinking rather than drinking *per se* (Cotton 1978). Many argue that parental drinking is the most accurate predictor for adolescent drinking, and various studies cite examples of parents playing an active role in introducing alcohol to their children. However, there is some debate in the literature about the relative importance of parental drinking as compared with other factors including age, income, social class, religion, race, school achievement, independence, and friends' drinking behaviours and attitudes (Bank *et al* 1985; Davies & Stacey 1972; Jessor & Jessor 1975; Kandel & Andrews 1987).

The majority of children are offered their first drink at home, usually on a special occasion, and often at a very early age (Aitken 1978; Plant *et al* 1982). Drinking at home with parents is typical for adolescents and is generally deemed to be a safe and secure environment in which to learn to drink in moderation (Davies & Stacey 1972; Ghodsian & Power 1987). McKechnie *et al* (1977) indicate that parents who disapprove of drinking are more likely to 'force' their children to drink away from home which may lead to problems.

Green *et al* (1991) observed that adolescent drinking behaviour was linked with parental drinking in non-manual families. A possible explanation for this social class difference is provided by evidence in this cohort that the young people in non-manual families were more likely to drink with their parents, whether at home or in restaurants, than were young people in manual families. This fits in with role-modelling, and receives some support from the National Child Development Study (Ghodsian & Power 1987). Young people who only mentioned drinking in public houses at age 16 were more likely to be in the heavy drinking category at 23, whereas those only drinking at home at 16 were less likely to be heavy drinkers. Although young people from non-manual families are just as likely - if not more so (Green *et al* 1991) - to drink than those from manual families, it may be that introducing young people to alcohol within the family home is less likely to lead to problem drinking (Sharp & Lowe 1989a).

The risk factor approach

Research which examines the association between risk factors and adolescent alcohol/substance use has implications for prevention and intervention.

Unfortunately, as we have already seen, there is no general agreement about predictor variables. A wide variety have been proposed and many of these are likely to interact in complex ways. Bloch *et al* (1991), for instance, found family relations, family structure, marks in school, participation in academic activities, frequency of church attendance, and deviant behaviour to be significantly associated with adolescent alcohol use two years later. The age at which first intoxication occurred has been found to be strongly related to alcohol consumption among older adolescents (Barnes & Welte 1989) and is a strong predictor of substance use (Newcomb *et al* 1986). In middle-class adolescents, Levine and Singer (1988) found risk-taking attitudes to be strong predictors of delinquency and substance abuse. On the other hand, family attachment and involvement in school and church were negatively related. Burkett (1977) also noted a deterrent effect of religiosity on adolescent drug use. Whilst it may be difficult to identify particular factors as strongly reliable predictors, the *number* of risk factors at time 1 may well be more predictive of alcohol/substance use at time 2 (Bloch *et al* 1991).

It is important to recognize, of course, that risk factors are simply characteristics which refer to increased likelihood of a problem occurring. Many children who grow up under highly adverse conditions still manage to become healthy, well-functioning adults (Wolin *et al* 1980). Although the presence of risk factors may help to identify those who are most vulnerable, it does not mean that any individual who has these distinguishing features will inevitably develop problems.

Chapter 3

Alcohol expectancies and reasons for drinking

As we have seen, research on youthful alcohol and substance use has tended to focus on socio-demographic characteristics, familial and social influences, and various other behavioural antecedents of 'deviancy'. Many findings enable investigators to propose explanations or reasons for drinking, smoking and other drug use in general terms of, for instance, favourable attitudes (Moore *et al* 1982) or identity status and psychosocial maturity (Christopherson *et al* 1988). Sharp and Lowe (1989a), in their review of research into adolescent alcohol use in Britain, stated that:

> *"The way forward seems to lie in understanding what drinking means to a young person and how these meanings are propagated. To achieve this the interpretations of behaviour given by the young people themselves must be considered."* (pp. 305-306)

Reasons for drinking

So what reasons do young teenagers give for drinking alcohol? If we ask young people to indicate why they drink then their replies should offer further insights into the aetiology of teenage alcohol use and misuse.

Researchers who have explored such questions have found that heavier drinkers are more likely than others to say they drink to relax, to socialize, for curiosity, to relieve boredom, and because their friends all drink (Plant *et al* 1990, 14-16-year-olds). Sharp and Lowe (1989b) report that, in their sample of 11-16-year-olds, heavier drinkers were more likely than others to drink because they liked the taste, to feel relaxed, because everyone does, to get drunk, and because it makes a party fun. Bagnall (1988), in her three-country investigation of the drinking behaviour of 13-year-olds, found that males were more likely than females to give as reasons for drinking: 'so as not to be the odd one out in a group', 'to help me mix more easily with other people', 'to help me talk to members of the opposite sex more easily', and 'to look good in front of other people'. It seems that the heavier drinkers among teenagers are more likely than others to drink for reasons of recreation, and that males are more likely to drink for reasons of social confidence and enhancement than females. In all the studies mentioned above, however, the upper age limit was sixteen. In a recent study, (Foxcroft & Lowe 1993), we were interested in the reasons for drinking given by an older and (consequently) heavier-drinking age group - i.e. those individuals between the ages of sixteen and nineteen. Furthermore, in the above-mentioned studies, all of the individuals were school attenders, but Marsh *et al* (1986) have shown that individuals who have left school have higher levels of alcohol consumption than those still at school. These individuals are more likely to be seen as adults and, in turn, are more likely to view themselves as adults, than same age individuals still at school. Our sample of youth trainees therefore offered more scope for exploring reasons for drinking - since many more of the sample would be doing so.

Number of reasons

The reasons that a person gives for an action can be seen as an attempt to explain that action. A person's reasons for drinking make up multiple sufficient causes. Thus an individual is likely to use alcohol more often and perhaps more heavily if he or she has more reasons for using alcohol.
  Reasons for action are explanations at an individual level. Inter-group attribution research has generally focussed on differences between in-group attributions and out-group attributions about the behaviour of a particular group (Hewstone 1989). However, in this study we addressed a slightly different question - namely, do self-attributions for a particular behaviour, such as reasons for drinking, vary as a function of group membership? To this end we explored sex differences in reasons offered for alcohol use in the present sample of youth trainees.
  In sum, we were interested in the reasons for drinking in a slightly older and perhaps more 'adult' sample of teenagers than has previously been investigated - primarily because these older teenagers are heavier drinkers. We aimed to determine how these reasons varied as a function of (i) reported

level of alcohol use; and (ii) sex differences. We also hypothesized that level of alcohol use would be directly related to the number of reasons an individual gave for drinking.

The study

We recruited 430 teenagers between the ages of 16 and 19 to take part in the study (237 females). All the teenagers were either engaged in youth training or were on a vocational course.

Participants completed an anonymous and confidential questionnaire, which included a retrospective seven-day drinking diary, and questions about frequency of alcohol use, amount of alcohol usually consumed, and reasons for drinking alcohol. The total number of units of alcohol consumed over the week was classified according to the guidelines for weekly consumption put forward by the Department of Health, namely *'low risk'* through to *'dangerous levels'* of use (Royal College of Physicians 1987). These guidelines are different for males and females. Quantity of use was indicated by one of five responses, ranging from *'never had a drink'* to *'enough to get drunk'*. This is a novel method of assessing amount of alcohol usually consumed, in that it goes beyond the actual volume usually consumed, to measure the effects of alcohol use each individual usually likes to achieve. We chose this method because of the dose related variability amongst people in the physical and psychological effects of alcohol.

As a snapshot of drinking behaviour, the seven-day retrospective diary technique is a useful measure. However, longer term alcohol use may not be reflected in this seven-day report. By combining the frequency, quantity, and seven-day diary responses, we derived a composite measure of alcohol use. Three levels of alcohol use were created - *low, moderate* and *high*. Individuals whose composite score was in the lower third of the distribution were classified as 'low users', the mid-third as 'moderate users', and the upper third as 'high users'. A typical 'low user' would, for instance, drink only on special occasions, would usually only have a few sips, and would have consumed no alcohol in the previous seven days, whereas a typical 'high user' would perhaps drink more than once a week, usually enough to get merry or drunk, and in the past seven days would have consumed more than the recommended sensible limits. This composite measure gives a better picture of longer term alcohol use, and was the one used in our study to examine the relationships between alcohol use and reasons for drinking. In a closed-response format, 11 possible reasons were presented, and respondents indicated for each reason, on a true/false dichotomy, why they drank alcohol.

The vast majority of the sample reported drinking on a regular basis. Of these, over 44 per cent drank more than once a week (Table 3.1a). Most people said that they like to get merry or drunk when they drink (25 per cent usually drink enough alcohol to get drunk - Table 3.1b). In the previous seven days the majority of respondents reported drinking sensibly. A sizeable proportion (almost a third) reported drinking more than the recommended sensible limits, and six per cent admitted to dangerous levels of alcohol use (Table 3.1c).

Drinking behaviour	n	%
(a) last 7 days		
0 no alcohol	90	21
1 light/sensible use	216	50
2 moderate/increased risk	64	15
3 heavy/risky use	35	8
4 very heavy/dangerous use	25	6
(b) frequency of drinking		
0 do not drink	11	3
1 only on special occasions	54	13
2 every few months	37	9
3 a few times a month	137	32
4 more than once a week	188	44
(c) usual consumption		
0 never had a drink	7	2
1 do not usually drink	36	8
2 few sips/one or two drinks	39	9
3 enough to get merry	238	55
4 enough to get drunk	109	25

Table 3.1: Drinking behaviour - Youth Trainees

Table 3.2 lists 11 reasons for drinking alcohol, and for each reason shows the percentage of male and female respondents in each of the alcohol use categories (low, moderate or high) who indicated that they drank for that reason.

Reason for drinking	Overall %	Alcohol use		
		Low %	Moderate %	High %
like the taste	86			
males		82	90	83
females		78	93	90*
to escape problems	13			
males		3	18	16
females		7	13	21
to be confident	20			
males		9	24	27
females		11	13	35***
to feel relaxed	64			
males		64	79	78
females		55	53++	56++
to get drunk	33			
males		24	27	63***
females		9	25	54***
because my friends do	13			
males		0	18	23*
females		10	10	8
to be sociable	62			
males		55	68	74
females		53	55	65
to celebrate	90			
males		85	85	88
females		91	94	90
because I'm under pressure	8			
males		0	5	7
females		10	11	13
I like the effects	41			
males		27	47	65***
females		23	28+	57***
It cheers me up	62			
males		48	69	72*
females		47	61	79***

Level of use differences (χ^2): *$p<0.05$; ***$p<0.001$
Sex differences (χ^2): +$p<0.05$; ++$p<0.01$

Table 3.2: Reasons for drinking: sex and alcohol use

Results

Most respondents said they drank alcohol for the following reasons - 'like the taste', 'to feel relaxed', 'to be sociable', to 'celebrate', 'it cheers me up'. Few significant sex differences emerged from these analyses. In the moderate and high alcohol use groups, three quarters of the males said they drank to relax, compared to just half of the females. In the moderate alcohol use group only, males were significantly more likely than females to say they drank because they liked the effects. Interestingly, high alcohol using females were over two and a half times as likely to say they drank to boost confidence than moderate or low alcohol using females. Looking at the reasons for drinking between the different alcohol use groups, three reasons seem important. High alcohol users, both males and females, were over twice as likely as others to say they drink to get drunk. Similarly, heavier drinkers were significantly more likely to say they drink because they like the effects and to cheer themselves up. Moreover, for these three reasons the proportion in the high alcohol use group saying they drink for that reason is considerable - ranging from 54 per cent to 79 per cent.

Now consider the total number of reasons for drinking each individual reported. As predicted, the number of reasons varied between alcohol use groups (Table 3.3). For males and females, alcohol use was highly significantly related to the number of reasons for drinking, with more reasons related to higher use. So, our study showed that those teenagers who exceeded recommended limits for alcohol intake gave reasons more connected with the effects of alcohol, and overall offered a greater number of different reasons. A study of early adolescent substance use by Shilts (1991) also showed that users differed from abusers in their reported reasons for substance use.

	Alcohol Use		
	Low	Moderate	High
Males	4.00	5.33	5.95 ***
Females	3.95	4.49	5.72 ***

Level of use differences (ANOVA):   *** $p<0.001$

Table 3.3: Mean number of reasons: sex and alcohol use

Clearly, the reasons for drinking that most respondents gave were positive reasons for alcohol use. The taste of alcohol, relaxation, celebration, and socializing are all reasons in which alcohol use is appropriate, if not favourable. The young people in our present study were no exception to this, because even if for some their alcohol use is illegal, it is a socially and culturally condoned activity. As we mentioned earlier, similar previous research with younger age groups tended to show that heavier drinkers were more likely than others to drink for reasons of recreation, and that males were more likely than females to drink for reasons of social confidence and enhancement. Although comparing studies is problematical because of methodological differences, generally, in our sample of older teenagers, these findings were not replicated. The majority of individuals drank recreationally, regardless of level of use. The reasons which were important in differentiating level of use were generally physiologically focussed ('to get drunk'; 'like the effects'). One similarity between this study and earlier research (Sharp & Lowe 1989b) was the finding that heavier drinkers were more likely than others to give as a reason for drinking 'to get drunk'. Amongst older teenagers, heavier drinking females, but not males, were significantly more likely to drink to boost their confidence, whereas in earlier research (Bagnall 1988), males were more likely to drink for reasons of social confidence than females.

Other sex differences have been reported elsewhere. Carman *et al* (1983) found that problem drinking in females was positively associated with reasons deriving from alienation and negatively linked with social/convivial reasons. These correlations were not observed in males. Common reasons reported by teenagers in other studies include: experimentation, social and recreational reasons, and relaxation (Johnston & O'Malley 1986); excitement-seeking, pleasurable (Windle & Barnes 1988); and family reasons for initial drinking (Milgram 1982). Over a range of studies the most frequently reported reason for drinking was 'because I like the taste' (eg. Alvarez *et al* 1991).

A different set of reasons come into play when teenagers are asked why they do not or should not drink. Reeves and Draper (1984) found that reasons rated important by the majority of their adolescent drinking groups, including heavy drinkers, were related to health, self-esteem, self-control, and parental disapproval/disappointment. Amongst younger teenagers, (Christopherson *et al* 1988) fear of parents finding out and fear of arrest were frequently cited as reasons for not trying alcohol.

Socialized processing

Although we have presented reasons for alcohol use as offering insights into the aetiology of teenage drinking, we are well aware that reported reasons may be post-hoc rationalizations for drinking behaviour. Yet such rationalizations may become genuine reasons for further use, in the form of a self-fulfilling prophecy. If this is so, then it serves to complicate research into the aetiology of alcohol use in young people. Furthermore, can young people report accurately on their mental processes? If so, can they know that the causes of their behaviour are what they say they are? We need to learn more about the psychological and social processes through which people learn about causes and adopt cultural explanations for behaviour.

Socialized processing refers to the fact that much of our knowledge about causes is learned through language based communications (Wells 1981). Hewstone (1989) calls for such socialized processing to be more thoroughly investigated in the future. One such explanation for alcohol use in young people, as put forward by academics and educationalists, is the 'peer-pressure hypothesis'. This theory has enjoyed considerable popularity, but has recently been called into question by Eiser *et al* (1991) and May (1991a). The use of the peer-pressure hypothesis may be an example of socialized processing, not necessarily by young people who tend not to invoke peer influences as reasons for drinking, but by academics and educationalists who do describe peer pressure as a powerful aetiological factor in young people's drinking behaviour.

Alcohol expectancies

On a related note, expectancy effects of alcohol use are linked to reasons for drinking. If one drinks to get drunk, then this sets up a certain expectancy about the outcome of drinking. McMurran (1991) suggests that the identification of alcohol-related expectancies may help in the development of cognition-modification components of alcohol interventions, and enable better matching of clients with programmes. Although alcohol expectancies are learned early in life (Christiansen *et al* 1982) and seem resistant to corrective information (Gustafson 1986), they vary with many factors like consumption level and sex (Brown *et al* 1980), level of intoxication (Southwick *et al* 1981), and drinking environment (Brown 1985). It is also clear that most people expect predominantly positive effects for themselves and at the same time more negative effects for others (Rohsenow 1983; Gustafson 1987).

Given that heavy drinkers spend more time drinking larger quantities than their lighter drinking counterparts, it is perhaps not surprising that they should also be more likely to experience a large number of effects from drinking, both pleasant and unpleasant. At the same time, they perceive the 'good' effects of drinking as more pleasurable, and the 'bad' effects as not so bad. Both of these judgments may then contribute to continued heavier drinking (Critchlow 1986).

Individual differences

In addition, the meanings of these effects may be very different for different people; certain consequences of drinking may be viewed very negatively by some (and indeed maybe all of the 'dry' movement) and not as negatively by others. A utility analysis of drinking behaviour (Bauman *et al* 1985) proposes that drinking is a function of expectations about the probability of experiencing effects and evaluations of the desirability of those effects. Thus, influences on drinking behaviour come not only from expectancies about positive consequences but from the belief that negative effects are not particularly bad, or are less bad for oneself than for others.

Rohsenow (1983) found that college social drinkers expect other people to be more strongly affected by alcohol than they expect to be affected themselves, for both positive and negative consequences. However, moderate and heavy drinkers expected themselves to experience the same enhancement of social and physical pleasure as others: only light drinkers expected less pleasure for themselves than others experience. This is understandable for light drinkers. Anticipating little pleasure may be a primary reason why they drink little.

Williams and Wortley (1991) observed some sex differences in young adults. Light drinking females revealed lower levels of expectancy than did light drinking males, whereas heavier drinking females reported higher levels of expectancy than did males at a comparable level of consumption.

Similarly, in a laboratory study of psychomotor performance (Lowe & Buikhuisen 1989), we observed sex differences in alcohol-expectancy effects. When male students expected and indeed received alcohol, they performed slightly better, seemingly compensating for the alleged pharmacological effect; whereas female performance deteriorated in this condition and was even worse than when they expected placebo but received alcohol. Strong expectations of alcohol-induced performance disruption are apparently still common in women, whereas men are characteristically encouraged to compensate against any such effects (i.e. 'hold their drink').

Adolescent alcohol expectancies

A number of studies have highlighted the role of expectancies in adolescent drinking behaviour. Bauman and Bryan (1980) observed a positive relationship between children's drinking and their expectations of positive consequences of drinking. In a study of predictor variables and adolescent drinking, Christiansen and Goldman (1983) found that expectancies can improve on the predictive power of background and demographic variables. More specifically, different kinds of expectancies lead to particular drinking behaviours. Expectancies of alcohol altering social behaviour are frequently reported by low-risk drinkers, whereas high-risk drinkers expect more in the way of cognitive and motor function effects, tension reduction, personal and power motive effects (McLaughlin et al 1987).

Adolescents undergoing treatment for alcohol abuse generally have higher alcohol expectancies than non-abusers (Brown et al 1987). Also, those with alcohol abusing parents have higher expectancies of cognitive and motor enhancement from alcohol. Christiansen et al (1989) used alcohol expectancies to predict adolescent drinking after one year. They showed that some expectancies discriminated between non-problem drinkers and those subsequently beginning problem drinking. In their study, negative expectancies were less likely to influence behaviour.

The development of alcohol expectancies

Christiansen et al (1982) noted that preconditions for reinforcement from drinking are present on an individual's first drinking occasion. To the extent that positive effects can occur due to placebo factors, drinking then becomes an instrumental behaviour performed to achieve reinforcing consequences. Thus, expectations of positive consequences may lead to initiation of drinking behaviour, subsequent drinking experience then modifies (strengthening or attenuating) expectations, and these modified expectancies then affect future consumption (Bauman & Bryan 1980). Bauman et al (1985) have reported data supporting this reciprocal model. In a longitudinal study with adolescents, Time 1 utility scores were related to Time 2 drinking habits, and Time 1 drinking habits were related to Time 2 utility scores, although the magnitude of both relationships was small. On the level of the individual drinker, then, beliefs about alcohol's effects may be important as reinforcers for drinking behaviour. Although negative effects are expected as well as positive effects, drinkers are less likely to believe that negative effects will occur and also perceive them less negatively; thus, expectations of reinforcement may 'swamp' expectations of unpleasant consequences. Moreover, the negative effects of drinking are typically less well remembered than positive effects (Cowan 1983; Tamerin et al 1970).

In their earlier study of adolescents, Christiansen et al (1982) addressed the question of whether expectancies develop from pharmacological experience with alcohol or from social learning factors. They looked at groups aged 12-14, 15-16, and 17-19, categorized according to low and high experience of alcohol. Amongst non-drinkers or very low drinkers, expectancies in the youngest age group were not markedly different from those of the older groups. Thus it appears that expectancies develop in the absence of personal drinking experience. Many expectancies seem to be present before personal drinking begins.

When comparing low drinkers with heavy drinkers (overall), five factors derived for low drinkers replicated those in the 12-14 age group, whilst four of the high drinkers' factors replicated those found in the 17-19-year-old group. The most striking observation was that all factors found for the 'low' drinkers included items that reflected enhancement of pleasure and interpersonal functioning. In contrast, the 'high' drinking factors emphasized items tapping increased expectations of power, sexuality, and tension reduction. Expectancy factor content did, however, alter with increasing drinking experience and age to become more homogeneous. Hence, relatively well-developed expectancies do exist prior to alcohol usage, but pharmacological experience with alcohol may 'crystallize' existing expectancies.

Dose-related expectancies

Obviously, dose-related effects of alcohol will influence expectations which, in turn, will vary with drinking experience. Connors *et al* (1987) have examined such interactions. They found that drinker group membership and rated dose level interacted in predicting subjects' estimates of the usefulness of alcohol for them. On the 'useful for feeling better' factor, the greatest benefit was expected from a moderate dose, particularly among alcoholics. On the 'useful for relieving emotional distress' factor, usefulness ratings increased with dose, with alcoholics expecting the greatest rate of increase. A similar pattern was found for the 'useful for feeling in charge' factor, except that the ratings for problem drinkers and alcoholics paralleled each other. These findings have implications for our understanding of drinkers' motivations to initiate and continue drinking.

In a recent study of adolescent alcohol expectancies (Sharp & Lowe 1990), we investigated ways in which expectancies (derived from imagined effects of various alcohol doses at a party) varied as a function of age, drinking experience and sex. There were distinct age changes. Older pupils did not expect much effect from two units of alcohol, whilst younger respondents generally expected this amount to produce quite marked psychological changes. Similar shifts occurred in relation to drinking experience, but this had less overall influence. Although heavier drinkers expected the same negative effects as did lighter drinkers, they also expected greater positive effects from larger amounts of alcohol. In this study of 11-16-year-olds, we found clear support for the notion that expectancies about alcohol are evident before first experience of drinking and that they do change with age and drinking experience (see also Christiansen *et al* 1982).

Implications

Taken together, accumulating data on alcohol expectancies indicate that the strengths and types of several specific alcohol expectancies correlate strongly with the extent and range of both current and future drinking behaviours. In relation to possible alcohol misuse amongst teenagers, strategies aimed at altering expectancies may provide useful interventions. For example, cognitive restructuring would seem appropriate. Overly positive expectations about the short-term benefits of alcohol should be counterbalanced by a greater appreciation for alcohol's long-term negative consequences. Investigating reasons and assessing expectancies may also prove to be useful diagnostic tools for identifying teenagers who may be at risk for developing alcohol-related problems.

Chapter 4

Psychosocial aspects of teenage drinking

Reviews of epidemiological evidence show that alcohol is the most widely used drug among teenagers and that its use in this age group is markedly patterned by age. There are also some notable differences in distribution and extent of drinking by sex (particularly at the heavier drinking levels), ethnicity, region, urbanicity, and between those teenagers who aim for further education and those who do not. The main psychosocial aspects of teenage drinking relate to personality, social functions and influences, and to parental and family factors.

Personality correlates

Early research on the personality correlates of adolescent problem drinkers prominently featured the characteristics of aggressiveness, impulsiveness, low self-esteem, high anxiety, depression, and a general lack of success in the attainment of life goals (Braucht 1980). Some subsequent research seemed to corroborate the presence of psychopathology-like characteristics among teenage drinkers. Hartcollis (1982) tested young problem drinkers on the Minnesota Multiphasic Personality Inventory (MMPI) and found that they had very similar personality profiles to 'alcoholics'. Rydelius (1983) suggested that alcohol-abusing teenage boys have more psychopathic personality traits compared with abstainers.

In their four-year longitudinal study of the development of problem behaviour in youth, Jessor and Jessor (1975) examined personality, perceived environmental and behavioural variables as they related to the development of drinking behaviour. Several of their personality measures obtained at year 1 were significantly predictive of the timing of onset of drinking. Those who made the earlier transitions to drinker status generally placed lower value on achievement, placed higher value on independence relative to achievement, had lower expectations of achievement, were more tolerant of deviance, had lower religiosity scores, and endorsed fewer negative functions (reasons) for not drinking. In addition, values on independence and alienation were generally higher for those making the earlier transitions.

In later analyses of these data, Jessor and Jessor (1977) showed that several of the personality variables were correlated with the number of times the adolescents reported being drunk during the past year. For both sexes, being drunk more often was significantly related to lower value on academic achievement, higher tolerance for deviance, more positive relative to negative functions (reasons) for drinking and drug use.

The Jessors's programme of research has shown that teenage abstainers differ from drinkers on a number of personality variables. The pattern of these variables seems to be strongly suggestive of a syndrome reflecting personal unconventionality or nonconformity. They have also shown that the drinkers' pattern of personality characteristics represents a later developmental level than the abstainers' pattern - more so for those who became drinkers earlier than later. They cautiously interpreted these findings as being in line with the conclusion of Stacey and Davies in their earlier review (1970, p.210):

"Consumption of alcohol at an earlier age...may...indicate more precocity in development."

Whilst several personality needs have fairly consistently been identified as placing adolescents at heightened risk for the relatively intensive use of alcohol and other drugs, less is known about the natural history of personality change during adolescence as it relates to substance use behaviours. Recently, Bates and Pandina (1991) collected prospective longitudinal data to find that those adolescents who maintained a stable, low-risk personality profile showed quite conservative substance use patterns over three years compared with all others. Generalized personality changes were linked to more intensive substance use behaviours in males. In contrast, personality change, per se, did not appear as relevant to females' alcohol and other drug use behaviours until combined with information regarding their level of high-risk personality needs.

In another longitudinal study (Kellam et al 1980), a similar male-oriented personality link with substance use was observed. Boys rated as 'shy' in first grade (age 6) used drugs least 10 years later; those rated as 'aggressive' used them most; and those rated as 'adapting' used alcohol and drugs moderately. This association was less clear cut for girls.

Overall, there is credible evidence that a number of relatively enduring individual difference (personality) variables are linked at a rather low level with problem drinking, and this seems to be particularly the case among the junior/senior high school population of the U.S.A. And these are somehow differentially salient in various sex-ethnic subpopulations.

Social functions of alcohol use

Alcohol use may serve several functions for adolescents: it relieves stress, it regulates moods and it reinforces gender identity - to list but a few. However, these processes obscure the fact that drinking takes place primarily in groups and must therefore serve some kind of social function for adolescents as well as help ease psychological distress. Adolescent orientations toward alcohol use are clearly associated with group interaction (Jessor & Jessor 1975; Johnson 1984).

Thompson (1989) investigated the role of early alcohol use in enhancing youths' relations with peers (and also self-esteem) over time. Early alcohol use has been linked with a high need for social approval (Scherer *et al* 1972). This void is generally created by an unsupportive home environment (Jessor & Jessor 1975; Pulkkinen 1983) and may be exacerbated by rejection by conventional age-mates. Thus, drinking may help to re-establish feelings of acceptance in several ways; for instance, by facilitating the sharing of confidences. The disinhibiting effects of alcohol may encourage this process. Drinking may also crystallize friendship through the efforts required to obtain and share alcohol. Such activities (eg. sneaking out of the house, buying alcohol) leading to a common goal may be highly rewarding, especially if the activity undermines the normative expectations of conventional groups.

Thompson's (1989) study showed that drinking may be functional only for youths who seek to use alcohol for explicit purposes. For example, alcohol used in early adolescence (grades 7-8) as a vehicle for group membership appears to improve relations in later adolescence. It was also found that drinking boosts self-esteem when youths hold a sophisticated image of drinking in early adolescence. However, alcohol consumption had no demonstrable effect on these status indicators in the absence of such conditions. This suggests that alcohol use will produce desired time-ordered effects only when consumption is tailored to a matched set of cognitive expectancies (see Crawford 1984).

Social influence

Middle adolescence is a period involving a great deal of maturation and changes in status and norms. Nevertheless, it might be expected that early alcohol use under the influence of the drinking group will have some kind of sustained effect on adolescents' identities and relations, since the continued use of alcohol implies that the deviant group still serves as a frame of reference. It may be that the social functions of adolescent drinking are rather limited, so that the drinking group's chief accomplishment is simply to shield adolescents from further conventional bases of rejection.

Graham *et al* (1991) proposed a framework which identified three types of social influence: active social pressure in the form of explicit offers to try a substance, and two types of passive social pressure; namely, social modelling of behaviour and misperception of peer use of a substance. It is likely that the effect of each is linked to conformity pressure and the need to be accepted by peers.

Social modelling operates through the adolescent's perceptions of others. Perceptions reflect modelling to the extent that they are accurate representatives of peer behaviours. We would not, however, expect all or even most adolescents to be completely accurate in their perceptions of peer drug use. Other factors may contribute to misperception. For instance, a young person's own current substance use may increase his or her perceptions of friends' use. This effect, referred to as 'assumed similarity', is likely to be related to the adolescent's future substance use.

Interestingly, Graham *et al* (1991) found that over-estimation of friends' use of alcohol was the only predictor of onset of alcohol use. Thus, the more passive forms of social pressure, especially misperceptions, may be the key predictor of future use among former non-users. It should be noted, however, that in this study the subjects were non-users by the age of 12 (seventh grade). When initial substance use onset is earlier, then a different set of influences may be involved.

Adolescent social identity

Sharp (1992) has linked youthful drinking to adolescent social identity. She viewed the youthful drinking culture as an example of social creativity - an attempt to enhance adolescent social status in comparison with adults. In her questionnaire survey of Humberside secondary school pupils, the youngest respondents reported drinking mainly with their families. However, the amount of drinking with peers, outside of parental control, rapidly increased with age, supporting the idea of a distinct adolescent drinking culture. Moreover, many parents were perceived to be unaware of their offspring's drinking.

Age of first drink without parents and age of first drunkenness (as reported by respondents) were shown, in Sharp's study, to be important factors in the development of drinking.

Parental and family influences

The adolescent's circle of friends can have a significant effect on weekly alcohol consumption. Perhaps even more pervasive - and certainly more complex - is parental influence. The double standard whereby parents and other authorities endeavour to prohibit drinking amongst young people, while conveying by their actions that it is acceptable and distinctive 'adult' behaviour, only serves to make alcohol seem more attractive to young people as a means of marking their own transition to adulthood (Manson & Ritson 1984).

Parents transmit their beliefs and attitudes to their children. This includes their drinking habits and views about drink. Adolescents who grow up in a home where alcohol is given disproportionate significance are more likely to drink abnormally themselves (Davies & Stacey 1972). Paradoxically, this outcome is as likely when the parents are strongly anti-drink as when a parent has a drinking problem. It seems that to drink or not to drink becomes an emotionally charged decision, if drinking has become part of the emotional currency of a particular home.

Levels of influence

Most investigators regard the acquisition of drinking behaviour as a developmental phenomenon which starts in the home for the majority of youths and then moves towards a more peer-controlled context. A few researchers have attempted to conceptualize the pathways by which parental influences systematically produce differences in children's drinking patterns. Zucker's heuristic model (1976) delineates a six-level process of indirect and direct parental and family influences. The first level includes traditional socioeconomic and sociocultural influences which are considered to be transmitted via the behaviour, ideology and values of the parents. The second and third levels focus on the parents as an interacting dyad and as separate individuals, respectively. The fourth level considers peer effects whilst the fifth level is concerned with the child's personality. Finally, the youngster's actual drinking behaviour comprises the sixth level of Zucker's model.

Mothers and fathers

Zucker's research has shown that both mothers and fathers of heavier-drinking and problem-drinking boys were heavier drinkers themselves, were more antisocial - compared to other parents - and used social isolation and deprivation as disciplinary techniques. Father's worries about his own drinking were negatively related to his son's problem drinking whereas mother's worries were positively related. These results, however, were based on data collected from the parents and stand in contrast to the adolescents' reports.

Heavier-drinking boys saw their mothers as less often present but neutral figures. They saw their fathers in a highly negative perspective, as being emotionally distant and unrewarding and uncaring about their son's achievements. Mothers of heavier-drinking girls were heavier drinkers themselves, were characterized as having an aggressive sociability style, and used social isolation and little praise or affection to shape behaviour. Father's physical absence and drinking problems were related to daughters' heavier drinking. Problem-drinking girls saw their fathers as using more effective punishment. Thus, these studies found the family environments of problem drinkers to be marked by harsher and more negative, tension-filled interactions and lacking parental involvement.

In an early clinical investigation of 20 adolescent alcohol abusers MacKay (1961) found that all had alcoholic fathers and some had alcoholic mothers. Nineteen fathers had left the family. There were violent parental arguments and other forms of family hostility. These families were characterized by poor relationships and poor control. Adolescents reported a strong need to belong.

Zucker (1979) went on to suggest that all these observations and those of Jessor's group point to major disturbances in three areas of families of adolescent problem drinkers: (a) parental deviance in personal behaviour and heavier drinking; (b) parental disinterest and lack of involvement; and (c) lack of positive parent-child interaction, affection and nurturance. All three aspects may be interpreted in terms of family socialization behaviours, which we shall be examining more closely in subsequent chapters.

Prendergast and Schaefer (1974) investigated the importance and interrelations of three mechanisms through which parental influence might operate on adolescent drinking: (a) parents as models; (b) parents as educators; and (c) parents as sources of general support for adolescent problems. They found parent-child relationship variables to be the best predictors of frequency of drinking or drunkenness. After controlling for parents' drinking behaviour, lax maternal control and perceived rejection and psychological tension in the relationship with the father accounted for 46 per cent of the variance in frequency of adolescent drinking. Lax maternal control and perceived paternal rejection also accounted for 34 per cent of the variance of frequency of drunkenness.

More recent evidence has shown that parent-youth relationships influence a developing youngster's use of alcohol and other drugs. Coombs and Paulson (1988) reported that non-users felt closer to their parents, considered it important to get along with them, and wanted to be like them. Parents of non-users set more limits, provided more praise and encouragement, and were less likely to use substances themselves. In a study of family cohesion, Protinsky and Shilts (1990) found that teenagers who reported not using drugs/alcohol were more enmeshed with their families, whilst those who reported using or abusing drugs/alcohol viewed their families as more disengaged. We shall be looking at the enmeshed-disengaged dimension later on in the context of the home environment (Chapters 8-9). DeJong et al (1991) investigated memories of parental rearing styles in alcohol and drug addicts. Reports by 'alcoholics' featured more rejection and overprotection, and less emotional warmth.

Conclusions

During the last two decades there has been an increasing quantity of research on teenage drinking and drug use. We now know a good deal about teenage drinking and its correlates. In broad brush outline, we know that drinking is widespread among teenagers and poses an immediate problem for 10 to 20 per cent of them. During the teenage years, there are differential probabilities of problem drinking within different age, sex, ethnic, and regional groups.

We also know that drinking and problem drinking are associated with a number of parental, peer group, and other perceived environmental influences. The important influence of family environment has been increasingly emphasized. Several personality characteristics which lean towards non-conformity are also related at somewhat lower levels. Finally, there have been converging lines of evidence which suggest that problem drinking is a significant part of a syndrome of progressive involvement in unconventional, deviant social problem behaviours among particular subgroups of teenagers.

More recent research has tried to establish if there are different pathways from non-drinking to drinking to problem-drinking status (and so on). Braucht (1980) raises another interesting question: Are different kinds of adolescents in situ (who may have arrived at a given level of drinking via different pathways) differentially receptive to various kinds of influences (either naturally occurring ones or planned interventions) toward or away from greater involvement with alcohol and other substances?

In the next sections we put forward a particular perspective regarding the development and maintenance of adolescent drinking behaviour - namely, the influence of family life and of the home environment.

SECTION 2:

Family Dynamics

In this section we focus in on psychosocial aspects of family life. In relation to adolescent alcohol use, family dynamics can be grouped into non-alcohol-specific family influences and alcohol-specific family influences. Non-alcohol-specific family behaviours can be described as those general family behaviours which characterize family interactions and family relationships. We look at this aspect of family dynamics - family process - in chapter 5. We take a family systems perspective, but one which also integrates other family theories and models. From this systems perspective extremes of family behaviours are seen as dysfunctional, and we incorporate this point into our own theoretical model. Importantly, this has enabled us to clarify the family systems model for dysfunctional extremes of behaviour.

In chapter 6 we discuss alcohol-specific influences, taking a lead from social learning theory. We also look at social learning constructs from a systemic perspective, in which extremes of behaviour are dysfunctional. We go on to combine family process and family social learning influences into a theoretical model of family socialization and teenage drinking, and conclude this chapter with contrasting case studies from teenage drinkers.

Chapter 7 reports on a large survey we carried out in Humberside, U.K. In this study we predicted, and found, that perceived family process and family social learning influences were both linked with adolescents' reported drinking. In line with the systems model, extremes of these family behaviours were linked to extremes of adolescent alcohol use. In addition, alcohol-specific family influences were found to be more directly related to reported drinking than non-alcohol-specific family behaviours.

This section then, (chapters 5 to 7) focusses in on psychosocial family dynamics. In section 3 we extend this to look at psychosocial dynamics and spatial relationships in the family and home.

Chapter 5

Family process

Family environment is an important, arguably the most important, influence in the socialization of children and adolescents. Although other environments, for example school, neighbourhood or peer, do make a substantial contribution to the socialization process, family life is the arena of most intense psychosocial interaction. Family life can be described by those interactions between family members which contribute to the social and psychological functioning of the family. There are different levels of functioning in different families, varying from severely dysfunctional to optimal patterns of behaviour. In this context, families have the greatest capacity for inflicting emotional harm on their members: physical and sexual abuse of children by parents in some families is a horrific example of dysfunctional family behaviour.

The intensity of family relationships also makes family life a likely area of interpersonal conflict. If we argue or fall out with a family member it is much more difficult to avoid the resulting tension than with friends or acquaintances. If we grow apart from other family members we cannot join a new family as we would make new friends. At the same time the potential for love, support and guidance is strongest within a family. Affective ties tend to be strongest with other family members, throughout the family life cycle, and a successful family environment contributes positively to the socialization process.

We have begun this chapter by drawing attention to the functionality of family environmental relationships. Given that adolescent drinking is a social behaviour, we take family process to mean those aspects of family life which are influential in the acquisition and development of adolescent social behaviours. These general family interactions and behaviours are distinct from family behaviours which are specific to a particular adolescent social behaviour. In this chapter we focus on the former (non-alcohol-specific family behaviours), and discuss the latter (alcohol-specific family behaviours) in the next chapter.

There are different ways of commenting on functionality of behaviour. Whilst it is more usual, although possibly not more useful, to point to (family) influences on dysfunctional behaviour, we think it is also important to contrast this focus with (family) influences on *functional* behaviour. In other words, we are interested not only in what aspects of family life are important for the development of deviant teenage drinking, but also in what aspects of family life are important for the development of sensible teenage drinking. Focussing on positive, rather than negative, aspects of behaviour may be a more useful and productive method of health and social education.

Having said this, we first look at the evidence for the association between families and alcohol abuse, a relatively well researched area: the transmission of problem drinking from parent to offspring is a frequent phenomenon. This discussion sets the scene for the main focus of the chapter: the relationship between family process and teenage drinking.

Families and alcohol abuse

Familial influence on the aetiology of 'alcoholism', or problem drinking, has been well documented. Some of this research focusses on genetic influences - in which familial transmission of 'alcoholism' is hypothesized to involve a substantial genetic component. The evidence for this comes from numerous studies which report links between the problem drinking of a biological parent and offspring's problem drinking.

To briefly summarize these general findings, demographic and clinical studies suggest that a family history of problem drinking (FH+) is predictive of offspring's eventual problem drinking. In adoption studies, FH+ individuals adopted at birth into FH- adoptive families, are more likely to become problem drinkers than adoptive siblings (Goodwin *et al* 1973; Cloninger *et al* 1981). Twin studies have indicated that mono-zygotic twins are more concordant for developing problem drinking than di-zygotic twins (Kaij 1960).

However, contrary results have been obtained with the twin study method. Gurling *et al* (1981, 1984) found little evidence for a genetic loading for alcohol abuse. Furthermore, twin study and adoption study approaches have come in for substantial criticism. Searles, in a comprehensive critique of genetic studies of alcoholism, listed numerous methodological concerns about twin and adoption studies. For example, in a re-analysis of Cloninger's work, Searles (1990, p.20) comments:

> "almost half of the adoptees who were classified as abusers had neither a genetic predisposition nor an environmental releasor. Cloninger et al (1981) investigated an extremely limited set of environmental influences, none of which was directly related to alcohol abuse. Therefore, the causes of alcohol abuse in these cases can probably be found in the environment since there appears to be no genetic linkage."

Of those who misuse alcohol, a large number have developed a drinking problem without any family history of alcohol abuse. On a related note, there is also a large number of FH+ individuals who do not become problem drinkers. It may be that those individuals with a positive family history of problem drinking are more likely to have had a disrupted upbringing, suggesting a non-genetic familial pathway for the transmission of alcohol abuse. These points suggest that a gene for 'alcoholism' should not be over-emphasized as an aetiological factor. In line with most contemporary viewpoints, we prefer to think of problem drinking as aetiologically multi-factorial. As Davies (1983, p.78) comments:

> "Alcoholism cannot therefore be determined solely or uniquely by genes. Consequently, it seems likely that what we are talking about is not a constitution which determines alcoholism, but a continuous distribution of 'predisposition', ranging from 'high' to 'low', which does not make an alcoholic outcome inevitable."

It is not our intention to dismiss the genetic argument for the transmission of alcoholism. Rather we intend to focus on environmental aspects of family life - family process - which might be seen to be protective or contributory for alcohol use and misuse. Some of these factors may be more liable to genetic influence than others. But we have briefly pointed to limitations of evidence for the genetic model, and as Searles (1990) concludes, this suggests that environmental factors have been underemphasized in the aetiology of 'alcoholism'. We are therefore focussing on environmental, specifically familial, factors in understanding alcohol use and misuse.

It is only quite recently that the contribution of family environmental factors in the development of problem drinking have been examined. Bennett and Wolin (1990) note that the recurrence of problem drinking in the children of an alcoholic parent is significantly frequent. In looking for explanations for this pattern, these authors have examined the cultural nature of family life, rather than biological contributions. Their work focusses specifically on *"family culture and alcoholism transmission"*.

Family culture consists of the behaviour patterns and belief systems of a family. These incorporate language, thought, action and material objects, and are conveyed through the socialization of each new generation. Central to this theoretical perspective is the concept of family rituals. Bennett and Wolin (1990) describe family rituals as symbolic forms of communication between family members. Habitual behaviours typify such rituals. The process of sitting down for a meal together, having set meal times, set bedtimes, going out together regularly and routinely as a family, are all examples of ritualistic family behaviour. These ritualistic family processes contribute to the family's sense of cohesiveness and group identity. Wolin, Bennett and Noonan (1979) examined the family rituals of twenty-five families in which at least one parent was, or had been a problem drinker. They found that families whose rituals were most altered during bouts of parental drinking were more likely to evidence transmission of problem drinking to their offspring than those families whose rituals did not suffer. Altered rituals no doubt contributed to reduced family cohesion and confused family identity.

Orford and Velleman, in a series of reports, described recollection of childhood family life by a sample of 170 young adult offspring of parents with drinking problems. This sample were perceived to be at high risk for developing problem drinking due to their positive family history of problem drinking. The most frequently reported effects of life at home were parental moodiness, unreliability, and a tendency to upset or fail to join in with family activities. These young adults were also likely to recall negative childhood experiences, worry and uncertainty, family instability, and being caught between conflicting parental interests. Maternal problem drinking had a greater impact on the recall of negative childhood experiences, and was also more likely to take place in the home (Velleman and Orford 1990).

In another paper, Orford and Velleman (1991) reported that, as adults, these offspring of problem drinkers were more likely than a control group to have started their drinking careers earlier, and were more likely to have reported risky drinking behaviour. Such risky drinking behaviour was more likely among the offspring of problem drinkers if both parents were problem drinkers, and also if the drinking of the parent often took place at home. Wilson and Orford (1978), in a separate study, reported that excessive drinking in the home by problem drinking parents conferred a high risk for the later development of problem drinking. From these studies these authors suggest that greater family disharmony, rather than alcohol specific effects, may be a more salient factor in the transmission of problem drinking across generations.

Other studies support this conclusion. Beardslee *et al* (1986) reported on a forty year prospective study. They examined the effects of a positive family history of problem drinking, and also the degree of exposure to associated family environmental factors on the development of disorders in the offspring of problem drinkers. The sample comprised 176 offspring and 230 control subjects. Two exposure factors were measured and combined - amount of parental drinking and disruption of family functioning. The combined exposure variable contributed significantly and independently of family history to the later development of problem drinking. Reich *et al* (1988) followed up 54 children of problem drinkers five years after the parents had been interviewed. These children were aged between 6 and 17 years, and could be distinguished from a control group by their impoverished home environment, marital and parent-child conflict, poor adaptive functioning, and an increased incidence of physical abuse. DeJong *et al* (1991) investigated 48 polydrug addicts and 91 alcohol addicts with the EMBU, an instrument for assessing parental rearing styles. Compared with a normal Dutch population, the alcoholics in this study had considerably higher scores on rejection, higher scores on over-protection and markedly lower scores on emotional warmth for both father and mother.

The above studies all point to the importance of family environment for the offspring of problem drinkers. The notion of a good home and family life is central to the effective socialization of young people. For many of the offspring of problem drinkers, life at home is difficult, tense, conflictual, and inconsistent. Such environments are contributory to the development of problem behaviour, such as excessive drinking, in later life. On the other hand, a satisfying, warm, loving and consistent family environment should provide a stable platform from which young people mature into a problem-free adulthood. Thus this stable platform is a protective factor against the development of problem behaviour.

The organization and perception of family life in the home is necessarily constrained not only by psychosocial factors, such as those outlined above, but is also structured by physical and temporal factors. We will consider in detail the layout of the home and the timing and temporal pattern of home life events in chapters 8 and 9.

So far, by considering family culture and alcoholism transmission, we have pointed to the importance of family process in the aetiology of problem drinking behaviour. It therefore seems sensible to broaden this outlook, and examine not only the familial aetiology of problem drinking, but the familial aetiology of drinking behaviour in general. The rest of this chapter is concerned specifically with this latter proposition.

Adolescent drinking: alcohol culture and familial transmission

The links between teenage drinking and family life are clear. Most young people are given their first drink of alcohol by parents and family, and much of an individual's knowledge about alcohol (or lack of it) is developed throughout childhood and adolescence by family-oriented interactions with alcohol. As we have emphasized, family process is an important consideration in the socialization of young people, and in this chapter we look specifically at those elements of family process which are influential in the development of adolescent drinking.

Perhaps the most pervasive influence on family theory in recent years has been the family systems approach. One influential contributor to family systems theory is Minuchin, who described the family as *"the matrix of its members psychosocial development"* (1974, p.48). As drinking is predominantly a social behaviour, the case for looking at family system influences on the development of adolescent drinking is well supported. Later on in this chapter we will discuss other theories of family life which have implications for adolescent alcohol use. We will draw on the parent-child relations literature, and also on social control theories of deviance. These theories have been developed within distinct academic and therapeutic orientations, from sociology, developmental psychology, clinical psychology, psychoanalysis, psychiatry, and general systems theory.

There are though, not surprisingly, commonalities between these different perspectives. Indeed, some overlapping perspectives show a common genesis. The integration of these overlapping perspectives has led to the development of a framework for the investigation of family process. We have used this framework to impose order on a range of studies which have looked at the relationship between family life and adolescent alcohol use. The result is a comprehensive meta-analysis of this literature, presented towards the end of the chapter.

Family systems

Systems theory was initially developed by von Bertalanffy (1968), a biologist. He felt that the physical sciences did not provide suitable models for the behavioural and biological sciences. Living systems exchanged energy, nutrients, and information with their environments, and in the process grew and differentiated. To von Bertalanffy, this was contrary to the way inanimate objects dissipated energy and reverted to simpler forms. Thus he proposed a theory of systems. A system consists of a set of elements, the relationships between the elements, and the relationships between the attributes or characteristics of the elements. Going on from this, Ghodse and McCartney (1992, p.1378) stated that:

> *"The systems approach emphasizes wholeness: it encourages us to attend to the constant dialectic between individual processes and the environment; between interpersonal relationships and wider social forces.*
>
> *The total situation is seen as being in a dynamic flux: there is a continuous process of mutual adaptation of members to each*

other resulting in homeostasis or, under certain circumstances, change. Any resultant change will, in turn, affect the whole group or system."

What then are *family* systems? According to Broderick (1990), families are *ongoing, open, social, systems*. As a system, the family is regarded as having emergent qualities. That is, the whole is greater than the sum of its parts, and has qualities that cannot be deduced from the combined characteristics of each of its parts.

As a social system, the main focus is on process - the communications, actions and interactions of the components of the ongoing system - rather than the structural characteristics of family composition. In family systems, linear causality is rejected in favour of a model of circular, reflexive effects. Systems theory therefore includes the notions of feedback - both positive and negative.

As elements of an open social system, family members do not only interact with each other, they also interact with external systems - other people, families and organizations.

As an ongoing, open, social system, interactions are observable in calendar time (days, months, years, generations) as well as in clock time (seconds, minutes, hours). The stability of patterns or sequences of behaviour in an ongoing family system is usually considered in calendar time. The calendar time process of socializing children is, according to Broderick (1990, p.185):

"one example of a family's style of interaction being the prime determinant of the child's behaviour and mental health."

The patterns and regularities that are observed over time can be described by rules that govern the system. A few family rules can govern the major aspects of ongoing personal relationships, and thus address the functions that the family serves.

Minuchin (1974) highlights two functions that the family serves. Internally, the family is responsible for the psychosocial protection of its members, and externally for accommodation to a culture and the transmission of that culture. Adolescent drinking and familial transmission refers to the second of these familial functions. However, if an adolescent develops problem drinking behaviour, then this is a reflection on (the failure of) the first family function - psychosocial protection. Furthermore, when conflict arises between these two functions then both appropriate family behaviour and appropriate cultural behaviour are threatened. Healthy family functioning should cope with such conflicts successfully, whereas unhealthy functioning would lead to tension and poor conflict resolution. The teenager who is caught between conflicting family pressure and general cultural pressures is in a difficult position.

Traditionally, adolescence is seen as the time of 'storm and stress' - of the rejection of parental values and the identification with 'deviant' peers - the so-called youth sub-culture. This perspective regards disturbance and discord during adolescence as a perfectly normal developmental process. All teenagers are said to experience an 'identity crisis' (Erikson 1968). However, there is little contemporary evidence which supports this traditional view. Current research suggests that by far the majority of young people progress through adolescence without serious discord, and without becoming disturbed. Young people, on the whole, successfully and competently negotiate their adolescent years and expanding peer relationships while maintaining close family ties.

Although peer relationships may become more important, parental influence remains a central factor for major socialization issues. Ausubel and Sullivan (1970) refer to the systemic properties of relating through adolescence, first to the family system and then to a peer system, as a process of desatellitization/resatellitization. However, Bloom (1990) suggests that a more appropriate term would be extra-satellitization, referring to the fact that the adolescent does not so much lose one system as gain another. Bloom (1990, p.14) introduced this term because:

> "The growth in importance of peer groups has been viewed as entailing a reduction of parental influence, but evidence suggests that long term influence of the parents over major topics remains."

During adolescence the family remains a central locus for emotional support and guidance. For example, Rosenberg (1979) found that parents ranked higher than peers in interpersonal significance throughout adolescence. Also, satisfaction with support from parents, especially mothers, was a better indicator of adolescent well-being than satisfaction with help from peers (Burke & Weir 1978). Greenberg *et al* (1983) found that age did not appear to be a significant factor in relative parent/peer relationships. Older adolescents were no different than younger adolescents in their report of quality or utilization of relationships with parents or with peers. It seems that throughout the school years parents are highly valued, usually more so than peers, for their support, love, advice, and guidance. As Noller and Callan (1991, p.51) remark:

> "Although peers become more important for adolescents, and they spend a lot of time talking with peers, there is little evidence that the peer group actually becomes more important than the family during adolescence."

One of the reasons for the rejection of the 'storm and stress' model of adolescence is the lack of evidence of dysfunctional relationships between parents and offspring. Yet adolescence is undoubtedly a stressful period for the individual, especially for relationships with parents. Transitional behaviour, negotiating and traversing the boundaries between childhood, adolescence and adulthood, may not be easy for parents to support or control. However, the social and cultural values that young people aspire to are, on the whole, the same values they see in their parents. Furthermore, parents are generally encouraging about their offspring adopting similar values. Even with regard to under-age drinking, parents are overwhelmingly moderating or ambivalent to this behaviour (Hawker 1978; Health Education Authority 1989). Both adolescents and parents tend to regard such age-graded behaviour as a normal transitional step on the path to adulthood - it is part of growing up.

Nonetheless, there are some individuals who do exhibit problem behaviour, alcohol misuse being one facet of this, and there are two alternative familial explanations for this behaviour. Firstly, the individual may not regard such behaviour as contrary to familial and cultural influence and values. In this case, the definitional criteria of the problem behaviour need to be re-examined with regard to social and cultural norms. This is instanced by contrasts between recommended sensible drinking levels, legal drinking age, and socially and culturally condoned actual drinking behaviour. Or, secondly, a dysfunctional family environment leads to the expression of dysfunctional extra-familial behaviour. We shall focus on the latter hypothesis in this chapter.

Minuchin's structural theory of family systems is based on the functional demands of family life, as developed over repeated transactional patterns. This structural theory has formed the basis of a whole school of family therapy, and as such the constructs of the theory have played an important role in treating dysfunctional families. Two main areas of functional demand are outlined, cohesion and adaptation, and each area is characterized and measured by the nature of psychological boundaries within the family system and sub-systems. Cohesion can be understood as the degree of emotional bonding, or togetherness, that exists between family members, and between family sub-systems. Adaptation refers to the ability of the family to moderate internal mechanisms, to change, when faced with stressful and/or new pressures. For normal functioning, the boundaries within these two dimensions of family process should be clear.

Extremes of cohesion are typified by overtly rigid boundaries (disengaged) or diffuse boundaries (enmeshed). Mid-range cohesion (normal) is indicated by clear boundaries. Most families fall within the wide normal range. Minuchin also states that the type of boundary is a function of a particular transactional style, and should not be regarded as a difference between functional and dysfunctional. In some instances an enmeshed boundary is functional, for example between mother and new-born child, but at other times an enmeshed boundary may be dysfunctional, for example between a mother and an adolescent seeking autonomy.

Boundaries should also be flexible for normal functioning. As an adolescent grows, then the boundaries of appropriate and inappropriate behaviour change. In childhood, drinking alcohol is not an appropriate behaviour but, as an individual progresses through adolescence, alcohol use becomes more acceptable and appropriate. Family systems therefore need to be able to adapt to the changing internal and external environments. Adaptability can also be depicted in terms of a range of appropriate and inappropriate levels. Families which are inflexible and rigid have difficulty adjusting to the changing environment. Conversely, families which are over-flexible fail to guide their members through the assimilation of new behaviours and the acceptable and appropriate limits to such behaviours. Mid-range adaptability is therefore important for normal family functioning.

In an attempt to clarify and operationalize Minuchin's concepts, along with related concepts from other family theorists (notably the work of Hill), Olson and his colleagues (1979, 1983, 1986, 1989) have developed their Circumplex Model of family functioning. They have also designed and developed a family assessment instrument (the Family Adaptability and Cohesion Evaluation Scales - FACES) to measure the constructs of cohesion and adaptability.

In the Circumplex Model (Figure 5.1), cohesion and adaptability are each classified into four groups, or levels of functioning. Enmeshment and disengagement form the extremes of the cohesion dimension, with separated and disengaged families the two intervening groups on the continuum. Rigid and chaotic adaptability are extremes of adaptability, with flexible and structured adaptability on the intervening continuum. Interactions of these eight groups give rise to sixteen family types. These sixteen types can then be reduced to three general levels of family functioning - balanced, which is the combinations of the two central groups on each dimension; mid-range, which is the combination of an extreme group on one dimension and a central group on the other dimension; and extreme, which combines an extreme group from each dimension (see Figure 5.1).

A balanced level indicates more adequate family functioning. However, such families may not always operate in a balanced manner. They may, occasionally, exhibit extremes of family behaviour but, for most of the time, they do manage to operate on a balanced level. Also, a balanced family does not always necessarily equate with moderate extra-familial behaviour. If a family purposefully socializes an individual into 'deviant' extra-familial behaviour, there is no reason why the family should not function in a balanced manner. This, as we suggested earlier, is one of the alternative familial explanations for such behaviour. An extreme family type indicates less adequate family functioning. According to the Circumplex Model, individuals in extreme family types are more likely to develop problem behaviours, such as problem drinking.

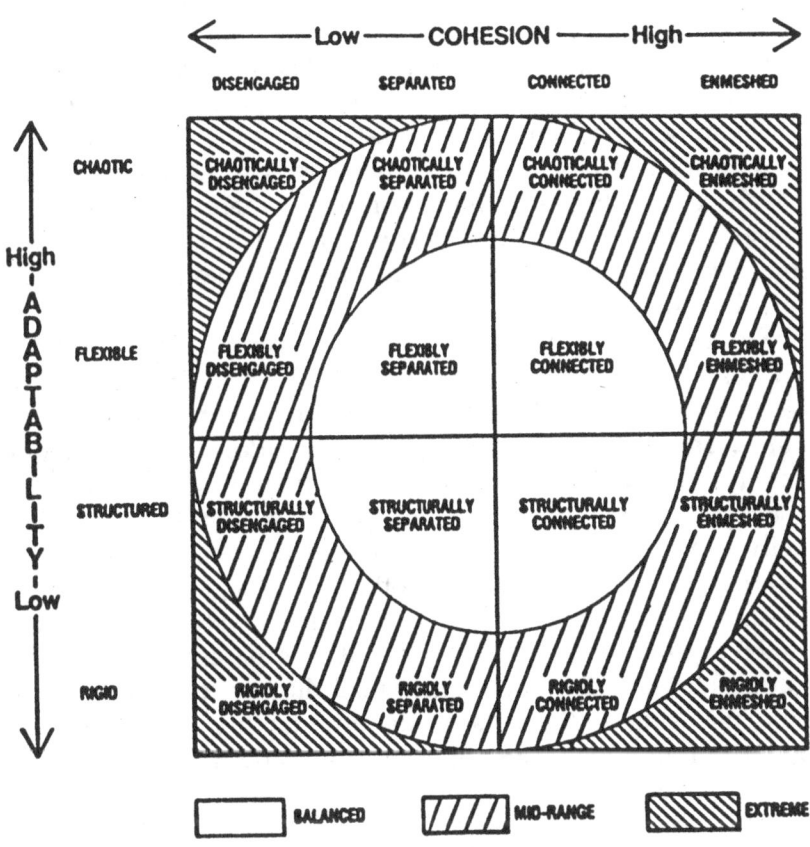

Figure 5.1: The Circumplex Model
(reprinted with permission from Olson *et al* 1989)

For the adolescent, the family is at a particular stage in its life cycle. The family life cycle is made up of several stages, including young married couples without children, families with pre-schoolers, families with school-age children, families with adolescents in the home, empty nest families, and families in retirement. The adolescent stage is typified by reports from parents and from adolescents of relatively low levels of cohesion and adaptability (Olson *et al* 1983).

Several studies have used the Circumplex Model to examine the family functioning of substance abusers. In a study by Friedman *et al* (1987), a sample of drug abusers reported on their family environment (using FACES II). Most of these individuals depicted their families to be disengaged rather than enmeshed, and to be rigid rather than chaotic on the adaptability dimension. This contrasted with the assessment of family functioning by family therapists for these same substance abusers. The therapists were much more likely to rate these families as enmeshed. This perceptual difference between family members and family therapists may reflect the particular schema imposed on the family assessment procedure. The substance abusers may be more likely to view high cohesion as optimal, whereas the therapists, familiar with systems theory, may view too much cohesion as dysfunctional. Or, the difference may simply be due to the therapist having greater (or perhaps poorer?) insight into the family process.

These results were similar to those found in a more recent study by Volk *et al* (1989). They also examined the perceived family functioning of drug abusing adolescents (using FACES III), and found that these adolescents were three times as likely as non-drug abusing adolescents to report disengaged family functioning (60 per cent compared to 19 per cent). Contrary to their predictions, hardly any of the drug abusers reported an enmeshed family type. When the drug users were divided into soft users (alcohol and marijuana) and hard users (all other drugs, eg. cocaine, heroin, crack), then an incremental effect emerged. Hard users were more likely to report disengaged family types (over 75 per cent) compared to half (50 per cent) of the soft users. They also found only small differences between drug users and non-drug using adolescents on the adaptability dimension, and that the proportion of all adolescents reporting rigid adaptability was quite small - between 15 per cent and 25 per cent.

The results from studies which have examined adolescent substance abuse in relation to perceived family cohesion have found that only one extreme, disengagement, is linked to substance abuse. This suggests that perhaps enmeshed family types may not be dysfunctional in terms of substance abuse. Similarly, only rigid adaptability was linked with substance abuse in the study by Friedman *et al* (1987).

In summary, we have drawn on structural family systems theory and highlighted two major dimensions of family functioning. The family systems model also specifies that extremes of family behaviour are potentially dysfunctional. Other family research and theory has also identified two major dimensions of family functioning, and we look at these next.

Family relationships: support and control

Another source of theory on the implications of family environment for the functioning of individual family members comes from developmental psychology. The parent-child relations literature consistently identifies two dimensions of family life which are important in effective socialization of social competence in young people (Rollins & Thomas 1979; Maccoby & Martin 1983). These two dimensions are family support and parental control. However, the majority of studies focus on infancy and childhood, and there is a relative deficit of studies which look at adolescent development.

One possible reason for previously not extending these two important family characteristics into adolescence is because of the traditional perspective of adolescence - the 'storm and stress' model. In the traditional view, adolescence is a totally distinct life period, separated from childhood by puberty, and from adulthood by the 'generation gap' However, as we mentioned earlier, current evidence does not support the traditional model of adolescence. This leads to a rather obvious reflection - that there is no reason why those aspects of family relationships important in infancy and childhood, such as support and control, should not also be important during adolescence.

We can describe support as those behaviours which foster in an individual a sense of belonging, and that he or she is basically accepted and approved of by the family. Supportive behaviours are warm, loving, responsive, and are integral to the development of emotional bonds with each other. In the parent-child relations literature the most effective level of support in adolescent socialization is usually conceptualized as high support (Rollins & Thomas 1979; Maccoby & Martin 1983). Control can be described as consisting of behaviours within a family which are concerned with guidance and flexibility in the power hierarchy. Contributing to the control dimension are behaviours such as rules and rule negotiation, discipline, power, punishment, permissiveness, authority, and guidance.

Maccoby and Martin (1983) proposed a four-fold classification of parenting patterns. Their four-fold scheme describes the interaction between the two major dimensions of parent-child behaviour - support and control (Figure 5.2). In this typology, optimal behaviour in the parent-child relationship is seen as the interaction between high support and high control. This relationship is regarded as authoritative and reciprocating, and these children should be independent, able to control aggression, socially responsible, self-confident, and high in self-esteem (Maccoby & Martin 1983).

	Support	
Control	Accepting Responsive Child-centered	Rejecting Unresponsive Parent-centered
Demanding, controlling	*Warm-directive Authoritative and reciprocal*	*Authoritarian Power assertive*
Undemanding, low in control attempts	*Indulgent*	*Neglecting, ignoring, indifferent, uninvolved*

Figure 5.2: A two-dimensional classification of parenting patterns (adapted from Maccoby & Martin 1983, p. 39)

The three other patterns of parenting in this typology are not viewed as positively. High control and low support indicate an authoritarian and power assertive parent-child relationship. These children tend to have poor social competence with peers, lack social initiative and spontaneity, and they tend to withdraw. They are also less likely to show evidence of a 'conscience', or moral orientation. Low control and high support indicate an indulgent and permissive relationship. These children tend to be impulsive, aggressive, lack independence and the ability to take responsibility. Finally, the fourth pattern of parenting in Maccoby and Martin's typology is the combination of low support and low control. At its worst, this pattern is one of indifferent parenting, typified by uninvolvement, rejection, and neglect. According to Maccoby and Martin, these children are more likely to exhibit 'delinquent' behaviour. They are also impulsive, moody, and their friends are often not liked by the parents.

Level of parental control is also important in Baumrind's (1972) theory of parenting styles. Lax and strict control equate with permissive and authoritarian parenting styles, and moderate levels of control are closely related to Baumrind's concept of an authoritative parenting style. According to Baumrind, the authoritarian parent values obedience and favours coercive measures to induce compliance. Permissive parents do not place demands or restrictions on behaviour, and are generally accepting and benign about the behaviour of their offspring. Authoritative parents, however, employ firm, but fair and less overtly punitive, methods of control. They generally try to direct their child's behaviour in a rational, issue-oriented manner (Baumrind 1972).

The influence of control processes for the internalization of social norms and values has received some attention in the social psychological literature. Aronson and Carlsmith (1963) demonstrated that mild as opposed to severe threat of punishment for a transgression was more effective for the internalization of acceptable behaviour. Children who received less severe threats proved more likely on later testing (over several weeks) to express negative evaluations of the activity and to avoid carrying out the previously forbidden behaviour, even in later situations when the prohibition no longer applied.

Thus, methods of social control are much more likely to foster the internalization of behavioural values if they successfully produce compliance and, at the same time, are subtle enough (or are mutually agreed rather than outrightly coercive) so that the individual does not view his or her compliance purely as a consequence of the coercive process. In Baumrind's study these effects were clearly seen. Children with authoritative parents showed much greater social responsibility in later years than children with authoritarian parents, and also than children with permissive parents.

Inconsistent control techniques may also contribute to poorer socialization. If parents fluctuate between lax and strict control the lack of consistency can contribute to poor internalization and subsequent lower adherence to socially and culturally accepted modes of behaviour. In a longitudinal study of children in New Zealand, Feehan et al (1991) found that inconsistent discipline (but not strict discipline) was associated with time 1 (age 7-9) behaviour problems, as measured by the Rutter Child Scale A (Rutter et al 1970). Prospectively, both inconsistent and strict discipline techniques at time 1 were associated with externalizing disorder at time 2 (age 15). According to DSM-III (A.P.A. 1980) externalizing disorder incorporates behaviours such as attention deficit disorder, aggressive and non-aggressive conduct disorders, and oppositional disorder. Internalizing disorders, on the other hand, incorporate anxiety and depressive disorders. Interestingly, externalizing disorders in youth have been linked with problem drinking in adulthood (McCord & McCord 1960). Supporting this, inconsistent and strict discipline in childhood was found to be associated with alcohol abuse in adulthood, in a retrospective study by Holmes and Robins (1987). Also, Vicary and Lerner (1986) reported from the New York Longitudinal Study on the relationship between parental control processes and adolescent drug use. They found that both strict and inconsistent discipline in childrearing were associated with alcohol (and marijuana) use in older adolescents.

Two major dimensions of family life are also outlined in social control theory, which we discuss next.

Social control theory

Seydlitz (1991) refers to the centrality of the family in social control theory, and outlines modes of parental control as major elements in the effect of the family on adolescent delinquency:

> *"Direct control is control imposed by discipline, restriction and punishment, whereas indirect control is the attachment or affection between the parents and child."* (p.175)

Direct and indirect controls were originally described in Nye's (1958) study of family relationships and delinquency. Relationships with parents, according to Nye, contribute to conscience formation. Indirect control refers to the affectual relationship with parents, and is an important factor in teenage conformity. Nye goes on to state that although parent-child relationships are important for forming and maintaining social control *"they cannot explain all conformity"*. Direct control is also a contributory factor, and consists of parental restrictions and rules about time allowed away from home, choice of friends and type of activities. Direct control is accomplished by keeping children and teenagers

> *"within the home, allowing and forbidding behaviour outside the home, and by promising and delivering punishment for infractions of parental or societal rules."* (p.7)

Nye also points to a limitation of direct control, in that it can only be achieved if the teenager is under the supervision, or in the presence of, their parents. As teenagers become involved in more and more activities outside the home, direct control cannot therefore be effective by itself.

Parental attachment is also a distinct construct in Hirschi's control theory (Hirschi 1969). Higher levels of attachment are theoretically linked with less deviant behaviour. Hirschi assumes that humans are naturally antisocial and deviant, but that they usually conform to social norms. Therefore, with this conceptualization, it is important to understand why people conform, and not why they deviate. Traditionally referred to as a major sociological theory of deviance, in fact Hirschi's formulation is a theory of non-deviance, or conformity. In the present context, why do young people conform to appropriate drinking behaviour, rather than deviate with excessive drinking?

In social control theory, conformity depends on the nature of attachment between an individual and the social environment. A positive attachment between an individual and significant others within a society leads to the adoption of the social norms and behaviour displayed by those significant others, in the form of a bond to society. There are four separate elements which contribute to the social bond: attachment to parents; religious attachment; educational attachment; and belief in conventional values. Without this social bond which emphasizes conformity, individuals are free to deviate. Social control theory also suggests that a poor social bond encourages identification with a deviant group, to which an alternative social bond is established.

Marcos *et al* (1986) have examined adolescent drinking within the framework of social control theory. They found a significant positive association between parental attachment and lifetime alcohol use. They defined and measured attachment to parents in terms of affective ties to parents. Individuals who reported less affectional ties and distant bonds with parents were likely to have a higher lifetime alcohol use score.

Overlapping perspectives

We have briefly described above three major theories of family relationships. Although these theories were developed somewhat independently, there appears to be similarities in the way important theoretical constructs are described. Control and adaptability can be viewed, and have been operationalized, as similar concepts. Bloom (1985) reported on a factor analysis of several different family functioning scales completed by the same individuals, and found that FACES II adaptability scales were redundantly correlated ($r=0.8$ or higher) with a separate measure of control from the Family Environment Scale (FES) (Moos & Moos 1986). According to the FES manual, the FES control sub-scale measures:

> "the extent to which set rules and procedures are used to run family life." (p.2)

Olson *et al* (1983) defined adaptability as:

> "the ability of a marital or family system to change its power structure, role relationships, and relationship rules in response to situational and developmental stress." (p.70)

Olson and his colleagues go on to state that concepts mainly from family sociology make up this dimension. Such concepts are family power (assertiveness, control, discipline), negotiation styles, role relationships and relationship rules. These concepts are very similar to those we outlined earlier as contributing to a family control dimension. Strict and lax control attempts might respectively equate with Olson's rigid and chaotic adaptability. A curvilinear property of the control dimension does find limited support in Rollins and Thomas's (1979) review of the parent-child relations literature, and also in Baumrind's conceptualization of parenting styles.

There is also a significant overlap between the concepts of support and cohesion (Bloom 1985). In a factor analysis, Bloom found that questionnaire items which measured support (FES) were redundantly correlated with items which measured cohesion (FACES II).

These concepts have sometimes been used inter-changeably, and it is apparent why when one considers the description of support we gave earlier (p.61) and the definition of cohesion given by Olson et al (1983):

> "*the emotional bonding that family members have toward one another.*" (p.70)

There are also clear similarities between the concepts of support and control on the one hand, and indirect and direct controls on the other. Indirect and direct controls are the dimensions of family functioning specified by social control theories, which were developed to explain the development of deviant behaviour.

Meta-analysis

So far we have attempted to pull together several similar perspectives on family functioning. We proceed now to a review and combined analysis of numerous individual research studies. Studies of adolescent alcohol use/misuse and family process variables vary in their theoretical base, and thus in the measurement of constructs. By pointing out commonalities between such theoretical orientations we have facilitated the combination of these studies in a comprehensive meta-analysis (Foxcroft & Lowe 1992). In this meta-analysis we have used the terms support and control to label these two major dimensions of family process.

We attempted to identify all family behaviour variables investigated in previous adolescent drinking research, and subsumed these variables into either a support or a control dimension. Although this was a subjective categorization, variables were sorted along the lines of the precedent set by Rollins and Thomas (1979) in their meta-analysis.

It soon became apparent that *three* factors recurred throughout the literature. As expected, variables which could be subsumed under the dimensions of support and control were frequently reported as an important correlate of adolescent drinking behaviour. We also found that family structure (i.e. the extent of parental intactness) was also quite often reported as an important correlate of adolescent drinking behaviour.

From 30 published articles, we were able to locate 28 variables which measured support, sixteen variables which measured control, and eight variables which assessed family structure. In these studies, sample sizes ranged from 57 up to 10,579; ages from 9 to 22; and the studies were all published between 1973 and 1990. Tables 5.1 and 5.2 show the drinking behaviour variables that were identified in these studies (Table 5.1), and the family environment variables for support, control and structure (Table 5.2).

Drinking behaviour variables
Frequency of use (10)
Quantity-frequency index (7)
Problem drinker status (3)
Combined substance use index (3)
Non-users or habitual users
Frequency of drinking problems
Transition to drinker status
Initiation and frequency of use
Onset of "hard liquor" use
Lifetime alcohol use
Alcohol abusers
Ever had an alcoholic drink
Previous week's consumption
Control of drinking

Table 5.1: Drinking behaviour variables identified in the meta-analysis (Identified frequency in parentheses)

The three dimensions we extracted from the literature - support, control and structure - were subjected to meta-analysis. A sorting method was used (Glass *et al* 1981), with each study's results being classified on the appropriate dimension as either positively related, negatively related, or non-significant with respect to drinking behaviour. For example, in a study by Budd *et al* (1985), family conflict (a support variable) was found to co-vary positively with adolescent drinking, but as family conflict is negatively related to family support, then this finding provides evidence that family support is negatively related to drinking behaviour. Table 5.3 shows the results of the meta-analysis.

Support	Control	Structure
Parental Support (5)	Parental Control (6)	Parental intactness (3)
Conflict (5)	Parental discipline (2)	Family structure (2)
Closeness to Family (2)	No. of parental rules	Family intactness
Cohesion (2)	Parental permissiveness	Father absence
Family attachment (2)	Parent-youth power	Who raised child
Parental love (2)	Adaptability	
Emotional climate	Parental willing involvement	
Parental warmth	Strictness	
Trust & concern	Organization	
Family involvement	Overall parental autonomy	
Family commitment		
Acceptance-rejection		
Parent-youth sentiment		
Warmth, support & interest		

Table 5.2: Family variables identified in the meta-analysis
(Identified frequency in parentheses)

	Relationship with drinking behaviour			
	+ sig	n.s.	- sig	
Support	0	5	23	(χ^2= 31.36, df=2 p<0.001)
Control	1	6	9	(χ^2= 6.13, df=2 p<0.05)
Structure	0	1	7	(χ^2= 10.75, df=2 p<0.005)

Table 5.3: Total significant and non-significant results for the relationship between drinking behaviour and family environment

A criticism sometimes levelled at the sorting meta-analytic technique is that individual sample sizes are not taken into account, and that it is a slightly crude method which gives weight to differing quality of research. Bearing this in mind, Table 5.3 clearly shows that the majority of studies reach similar conclusions, especially for support and structure. In fact, the Pearson r between sample size and result is non-significant for each dimension, enabling us to discount sample size as a confounding factor (Foxcroft & Lowe 1991).

Differences between the outcomes for each dimension were statistically significant, and we concluded that the meta-analysis showed that the family dimensions of support, control, and structure were all negatively related to adolescent drinking behaviour. In other words:

- Adolescents from less supportive families tended to drink more
- Adolescents from less controlling families tended to drink more
- Adolescents from non-nuclear families tended to drink more

In the meta-analysis there were six non-significant results and one significantly positive report of the relationship between control and adolescent drinking, compared to ten significantly negative results. Although this produced a significant effect in the chi-square analysis, this effect is not as clear cut as in the structure and support dimensions. Why is this effect not as clear cut? It may be that the control dimension is less important in the socialization of drinking behaviour. Or, one possibility is that the relationship between adolescent drinking behaviour and control is not a linear one, thus confounding the results from previous studies. In fact, earlier in this chapter we pointed to both lax and strict control as potentially dysfunctional, and one study, although with a small sample, did indeed find this pattern.

Barnes et al (1986) looked at the influence of support and control on the incidence of adolescent problem drinking. They used a random digit dial telephone procedure to select a representative sample of adolescents and their families in an area of New York state. Their final analysis consisted of interviews with 124 families. Generalizing from Rollins and Thomas's (1979) meta-analysis, they predicted that effective socialization (into non-problem drinking) would be associated with high support and moderate levels of control. Their results were consistent with this hypothesis, as there was a clear (though non-significant) curvilinear trend in the relationship between control and problem drinking. Moderate control was associated with a much lower incidence of problem drinking than both lax and strict levels of control, especially when associated with high support. This is in line with our earlier comments about the relationship between parental control and outcome behaviours, when we pointed to both lax and strict control as potentially dysfunctional socialization behaviours. This pattern is also consistent with the family systems perspective, in which extremes of adaptability may be dysfunctional. Interestingly, Barnes et al (1986) developed their concepts of support and control from Parsons and Bales's (1955) instrumental-expressive functions of the family. Olson et al (1979) also developed their Circumplex Model using Parsons and Bales's instrumental-expressive concepts. This common genesis for two individual theoretical perspectives of the family lends support to the integration of these perspectives carried out earlier in this chapter.

If this curvilinear hypothesis is correct, why did other studies in the meta-analysis not find this? Firstly, many research analyses rely on linear statistical tests, and any curvilinear pattern may not have been apparent. Secondly, this curvilinear pattern may be a particular function of certain family behaviours or of certain social behaviours. For example, Barnes *et al* (1986) used measures of control and of problem drinking which may be different from more usual measures of family life and adolescent drinking behaviour. Or, it may be that those studies in the meta-analysis which reported a linear relationship between control and adolescent drinking, although in the majority, may suffer from a problem with 'thin' variable ranges. That is to say, the range of behaviour which a variable assesses is not sufficiently wide to allow a true picture to be obtained. For example, if control does indeed have a curvilinear quadratic association with adolescent drinking, but a particular variable only taps the downward slope, or only taps the upward slope, then a linear picture will emerge. Many of the present studies may ask questions which consider only part of the range, and it is possible that a false picture may build up of a linear relationship between control and adolescent drinking.

These measurement considerations therefore beg the question: If, generally, control scales tap only a linear component of the dimension, how can we explain the overlap with adaptability described by Bloom (1985)? One problem with the definition of adaptability in Olson's Circumplex Model is that it has been criticized as inferring a linear relationship between adaptability and family functioning, i.e. families *more* able to change are optimal. This has led to consequent confusion in the items of the test battery (FACES I to FACES III), designed by Olson and colleagues to measure this dimension[1] (Lee 1988; Anderson & Gavazzi 1990).

Systems theory specifies that extremes of family cohesion - enmeshed and disengaged families - can be dysfunctional, with the mid-range of cohesion optimal for family functioning. This is not the picture obtained from the meta-analysis of adolescent drinking behaviour, where support is linearly related to drinking behaviour. However, other family theorists have found that cohesion is essentially a linear function: they suggest that higher cohesion is indicative of better family functioning; and lower cohesion of poorer family functioning (Beavers & Voeller 1983; Lee 1988; Anderson & Gavazzi 1990).

---

[1] The problems with operationalizing the curvilinear properties of the Circumplex Model in FACES I to FACES III have caused Olson and his colleagues to state that in FACES III the scales of cohesion and adaptability should now be treated as related in a linear manner to family functioning. High cohesion and adaptability constitute balanced family types, and low cohesion and adaptability measure extreme family types (Olson 1991; Olson 1991, personal communication).

Or, as outlined for family control in the previous section, there may be a measurement deficiency which explains the preponderance of findings of a linear relationship between family functioning and family support. Furthermore, family systems theorists usually work with dysfunctional families, and it may only be in problem families that high support is considered dysfunctional (Olson *et al* 1983).

Conclusion

Adolescent drinking should be regarded as a normal developmental process, given that the adolescent's social and cultural environment condones such behaviour. Thus effective socialization should lead to controlled and sensible drinking behaviour. If a family is deficient in support and control, then deviant or excessive drinking behaviour may result. In the meta-analysis we found that low support and lax control were associated with heavier drinking in adolescents. But, if an individual remains abstinent in an environment which condones and encourages drinking, then this too is deviant drinking behaviour. Thus high levels of support and control are also important for drinking behaviour. High support and high control might be associated with **non-drinking.** Moderate amounts of support and control would therefore be the most functional for the socialization and development of **sensible drinking** in an individual. This hypothesis is also amenable to the family systems viewpoint, where extremes of support and control, or cohesion and adaptability, are viewed as dysfunctional. This is an important step because it clarifies the family systems viewpoint on non-problem families. Previously, and presently, research has shown that generally a linear relationship exists between these two dimensions and a target behaviour, for non-problem families, and although these findings may be legitimate, it is the range of normality of the target variable which is important. For example, if the target variable is anti-social behaviour, then a linear relationship may indeed exist between the amount of anti-social behaviour and the two socialization dimensions, with low support and lax control associated with higher levels of anti-social behaviour. But, closer examination would perhaps reveal high support and high control to be associated with poorly autonomous, very socially conforming behaviour. This image is one with which readers of Orwell's *"1984"* will be familiar. In the present climate autonomous individuals with good social skills and independence of thought are viewed as more able and attractive. Moderate amounts of support and control would therefore socialize an individual towards this ideal.

We have also looked at the study by Barnes *et al* (1986) in which problem drinkers reported strictly controlling family environments. If this is a reliable and valid result, how does it fit into the above picture? As outlined above, strict control may be dysfunctional, and individuals from this type of family environment more likely to be non-drinkers, contrary to social and cultural norms. However, there may be an interaction between control and support at the extremes of these dimensions. If there is optimal support for an individual, then they are perhaps more likely to be abstainers if they are from a strictly controlled environment. On the other hand, if there is strict control, but dysfunctional support, then individuals may become heavier drinkers. Also, this pattern might only be reported in families where there is a teenager already with a drinking problem, i.e. heavier drinking might be a contributory factor in that more strict control (attempts) are perceived.

Although in the meta-analysis family structure was extracted from the literature as a separate dimension, the absence of a parent may have profound effects on the amount of support and control provided within such a family. Most studies have found that children and adolescents from divorced families exhibit emotional distress and behaviour disorders, although this can depend on the recency of the parental separation. When quality of the parent-child relationship is controlled, then the effect of family structure is greatly reduced, but may still be significant (Flewelling & Bauman 1990; Needle et al 1990).

Individuals for whom the family socialization process has provided a good psychological adjustment are generally more confident and autonomous, have better social skills, and are more likely to pass on these qualities to their own offspring, than individuals from families who have provided poorer socialization. Support and control are two major dimensions of the socialization process, and are two of the most important factors in familial influence on adolescent drinking behaviour. Individuals from families deficient on these two dimensions are more likely to have less confidence, autonomy, and poorer social skills. Ford (1982) reported that social cognition variables (including social support networks) accounted for a large proportion of the variance in social competence. This accords with recent work by Bagnall (1990), who evaluated an alcohol education initiative, and reports that the way forward in alcohol education lies in an approach which emphasizes social influences and social skills.

In the U.S.A. the level of under-age drinking has generally been found to be much less than in Britain. About 80 per cent of American adolescents aged 16 or over were reported to have consumed an alcoholic beverage (Rachel et al 1980, cited by Plant et al 1985). In Britain the level is nearer 95 per cent (Marsh et al 1986; Fogelman 1978). Bearing this in mind, it is interesting to note the cultural variation in parent-child relations between England and the U.S.A. observed by Devereux (1970), who found lower levels of support and looser control in English families. Intuitively, this accords with the results of the meta-analysis, in which the majority of studies came from the U.S.A. That is, higher support and firmer control were found to be associated with lower drinking levels.

Although the two family process dimensions of support and control are important factors in the family socialization of teenage drinking, another area of potentially important family influence is social learning. In the next chapter we introduce and discuss social learning influences, and go on to present a model of family socialization for teenage drinking which incorporates both family process (non-alcohol-specific) and family social learning (alcohol-specific) factors.

Chapter 6

The family socialization of teenage alcohol use

In the previous chapter we described how family relationships make an important contribution to the socialization of adolescent drinking behaviour. From childhood through adolescence and into early adulthood a person's family is the mainstay of emotional support and guidance, and this is reflected in a wide range of behaviours, including teenage drinking. It is usually only when a young adult leaves his or her family home, and enters close relationships with other young adult(s), that the socialization influence of parents wanes.

Poor socialization by parents and family might lead a teenager to develop inappropriate and unacceptable social behaviour. Optimal family socialization, on the other hand, should lead to the adoption of socially and culturally normative behaviour, behaviour that is acceptable and appropriate for that person. For example, if an individual is brought up in a social and cultural environment that condones sensible alcohol use, either explicitly or implicitly, then optimal socialization should encourage the adoption of such sensible drinking behaviour. Poor socialization, on the other hand, could lead to the development of deviant drinking behaviour, either abstention or excessive drinking, depending on the prevailing social and cultural norms for youthful alcohol use.

So far, we have discussed only non-alcohol-specific family behaviours, such as support and control. But there are also alcohol-specific family behaviours that may be just as important (if not more so) in the socialization of adolescent drinking. Alcohol-related family behaviour is a primary mode of alcohol-specific interpersonal influence. Such behaviour may contribute both independently and interactively (with family process factors) to the socialization of teenage drinking. Research by Barnes and colleagues (Barnes 1977; Barnes *et al* 1986) and by Kandel and colleagues (Kandel 1980; Kandel and Andrews 1987) offer a perspective on the family socialization of adolescent alcohol use that incorporates not only elements of family process, but also of social learning. However, Barnes's work tends to emphasize family process behaviours, but also includes parental modelling influences; whereas Kandel tends to focus on social learning influences, but also includes a measure of family support in her work.

We now go on to describe social learning theory, and discuss how its concepts are important in the family dynamics surrounding teenage alcohol use. To do this we present a review and meta-analysis of over 40 recent empirical studies. We then go on to combine elements of both family process and social learning in a straightforward, but comprehensive, framework for investigating and understanding family socialization influences on the development of teenage drinking.

Social learning theory

Before describing social learning theory, let us first briefly outline the nature of relationships between people and their environment. The typical representation of the relationship between person (P), behaviour (B) and environment (E), is $B=f(P,E)$. Lewin (1951) developed this model in his Field Theory, in which the most important and basic construct is the lifespace. Every person's **subjective environment** forms his or her lifespace, which consists of the person and the environment viewed as one constellation of interdependent factors. The theoretical expression can thus be re-written to acknowledge the interdependent influences between person and environment, $B=f(P \leftrightarrow E)$. However, as Bandura (1977) noted in relation to social learning theory, behaviour is an interacting determinant, and cannot simply be regarded as the end result, or outcome, of a person/environment interaction. To express the truly reciprocal nature of interaction between behaviour, person, and environment, a more complex model is required (Figure 6.1). This model demonstrates the systemic properties of the relationship between behaviour, person and environment. As described by Bandura, the relationships are reciprocal, and as such family social learning is in line with family systems theory. Indeed, social learning behaviours are a particular subset of communicative behaviours within the family system. One would therefore predict, in line with family systems theory, that extremes of social learning behaviours would be dysfunctional for the socialization of teenage drinking.

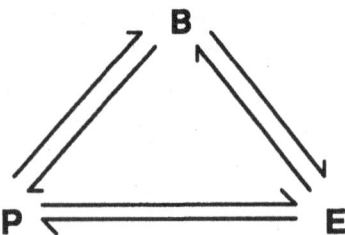

Figure 6.1: The reciprocal relationship between behaviour, person and the environment

Social learning theory (Bandura 1977) describes the adoption of behaviour through **imitation or modelling** as a major source of an individual's learning and development. Individuals observe the behaviour of others, both directly and indirectly. Indirect observation can take place through media such as television, radio, news reports, advertising, marketing, stories, jokes, although direct observation of significant others, especially peers and family members, provide a more influential model. As an illustration of the indirect exposure young people have to alcohol, one recent estimate suggested that by the time young people reach the legal drinking age, they will have seen alcohol consumed on the television alone approximately 75,000 times (Radecki 1986, cited by Coombs *et al* 1988).

This direct and indirect exposure leads to the acquisition of symbolic representations of the observed behaviours. These symbolic representations then serve as a guide, or schema, for subsequent behaviour by an individual. Schemata can be described as cognitive sets for a particular behaviour, perception, or action. They are consistent with the organization of knowledge based on social and cultural experience.

As an example of how schemata relate to behaviour, we have described how an individual's reasons for drinking - reasons for drinking form one part of our social and cultural experience - contribute to a schema for drinking alcohol (Foxcroft & Lowe 1993; see also chapter 3). We found that adolescents who reported drinking more were significantly more likely to say they drink because they like the taste, because they like the effects, to get drunk, and to cheer up. Additionally, those teenagers who reported *more* reasons for drinking were more likely to be heavier drinkers. Thus not only do the types of reasons within a schema for drinking relate to drinking behaviour, but also overall consumption may be a function of the number of reasons for drinking within each person's schema.

In the present discussion, however, we are interested in how alcohol-specific behaviour within the family contributes to the development of an adolescent's drinking behaviour. As we mentioned above, and also in the previous chapter, parents and family are a major source of psychosocial influence throughout adolescence. How, why, what, when and where parents drink alcohol provides a base on which individuals develop their own alcohol use. Thus, perceived parental alcohol use, incorporating observed parental drinking behaviour as well as indirect observation of reported and assumed parental drinking, contributes to a teenager's alcohol use schema.

Bandura (1977) describes a four-stage process which governs social learning. Firstly, attentional processes discriminate and focus on the appropriate stimulus. Secondly, retention processes come into play in the coding, organization and subsequent symbolic rehearsal of the behaviour. Thirdly, motor reproduction processes determine whether or not the observed behaviour is within the capabilities of the observer (this stage is more important in social learning by infants and young children). Finally, motivational processes come into operation. This fourth stage is the most important in determining whether or not observed behaviour is reproduced.

Thus, social learning theory distinguishes between the acquisition of behaviour and performance. People are more likely to reproduce observed behaviour if it has positive consequences, i.e. if they are motivated to carry out the behaviour. Positive consequences of behaviour are those which are rewarding to an individual, and behaviours which are not rewarding, because they are regarded as unpleasant or not worthwhile, will not be adopted.

What, then, are the specific factors which motivate some young people to display behaviour that all have presumably 'acquired', or know how to? Motivational processes, according to social learning theory, are contingent on reinforcement, either from the environment or from self. But which, if any, is the most important process of reinforcement in adolescent alcohol use and misuse? As Bandura (1977, p.10) states:

"there are times when environmental factors exercise powerful constraints on behaviour, and other times when personal factors are the overriding regulators of the course of environmental events."

With regard to adolescent alcohol use, parental behaviour (an environmental influence) usually provides the initial motivation for behaviour change. Although social learning theory posits that unrewarding behaviours should not be adopted, if an individual is encouraged to undertake a behaviour which they initially perceive negatively (unrewarding), and if they persist in that behaviour, then eventually their cognitive set or schema regarding the appropriateness of the behaviour will moderate (the behaviour becomes rewarding). The discrepancy between performing the behaviour and the person's desire (not) to perform the behaviour is known as *cognitive dissonance* (Festinger 1957). To try and maintain consistency between schema and action, individuals are motivated to reduce any conflict or dissonance. This motivation to reduce dissonance can lead to changes made in the schema for the behaviour. (If we regard schemata as a feature of the person and the requirement to undertake a behaviour a feature of the environment, then cognitive dissonance is an example of the reciprocal interactions at play between behaviour, person, and environment - see Figure 6.1).

This is one reason why, in the period from pre-adolescence through early to late adolescence, individuals move from having negative or unrewarding concepts about alcohol, to eventually regarding alcohol as a positive reinforcer. It is during this period that adults, usually parents, begin to introduce their children to alcohol, thus facilitating the dissonance and consequent change in cognitive set. Parents are the predominant providers of first tastes and first 'proper' alcoholic drinks, often in the form of a glass of wine or a glass of beer, though soft drinks are sometimes added to make the taste of these drinks more palatable and acceptable. During the adolescent phase, larger and more potent drinks generally become available within the sanction of the family - a few glasses of wine, a sherry, a pint or a can of beer - usually on appropriate occasions. Thus young people are being 'weaned' on to alcohol.

This process is illustrated by the results of two studies carried out in the U.K. Jahoda and Crammond (1972) found that children between the ages of six and ten had progressively more unfavourable perceptions of drinkers (especially women drinkers). According to Jahoda and Crammond, this seemed to parallel the child's progression through social institutions (eg. primary school and church) which held negative and prohibitive attitudes towards alcohol (these attitudes seemed to be internalized by the children, evidenced by consistency between direct and indirect response observations made in their study). In a separate study Hawker (1978) questioned a large sample of 12-18-year-old teenagers, and found that these teenagers were far more likely to say they were given their first alcoholic drink by their parents and family than by anybody else, and usually between the ages of 10 and 12. Similarly, the location of this first drink was more likely to be at home than anywhere else. Furthermore, Hawker also reported that the teenagers in her study were far more likely to usually drink at home than anywhere else.

So, the transition to drinking, fostered within the family and home environment, is paralleled by changing attitudes and perceptions of alcohol. The family and home provide social reinforcement (motivation) for drinking which, through the mechanism of cognitive dissonance, encourages the change in a young person's schema for drinking. Parental attitudes to their teenager's alcohol use, whether parents encourage or discourage, approve or disapprove, are influential and underlie the social reinforcement of alcohol use within the family. In other words, parental attitudes (environmental change) leads to a change in the schema for drinking (feature of the person) resulting in increased teenage drinking (change in behaviour).

With a slightly different theoretical orientation (from a purely behavioural point of view), Akers et al (1979) describe a mechanism of *differential reinforcement* which underlies this process. Pure behaviourism ignores any possible cognitive mechanisms involved in behaviour - behaviour is seen purely as a function of external motivators, i.e. stimulus and response. In Akers's social learning perspective the reproduction of behaviour is seen to depend on perceived rewards and punishments for the behaviour and the perceived rewards and punishments attached to alternative behaviour - differential reinforcement. If the benefit of engaging in the behaviour (drinking) outweighs its associated cost, and also outweighs the benefit of an alternative behaviour (not drinking), then the behaviour is likely to re-occur. Thus, as parents introduce their children to alcohol, the pattern of reinforcement-punishment changes and subsequently behaviour changes. This operant learning approach is not entirely in line theoretically with Bandura's more cognitive approach, but Akers's social learning perspective has been used in numerous adolescent alcohol studies (c.f. the work by Kandel and colleagues). Both theories provide explanations of the influence of parents on the early development of drinking behaviour in their offspring.

To summarize so far, social learning theory predicts that parents (and older family members) provide salient role models for drinking alcohol. Knowledge of how, why, what, when and where these influential family members drink alcohol is assimilated into each adolescent's schema for drinking, and forms a base and guide for their own drinking career. In addition, the social reinforcement provided by parents and family surrounding the use of alcohol - both initiation and continuing use - contributes to how young people learn to drink. Whether parents approve, disapprove, or are indifferent about their offspring's alcohol use is thus an important motivational process.

Social learning theory therefore contributes two major factors to knowledge and theory of the family dynamics of adolescent alcohol use. These are imitation/modelling and parental attitudes. These two factors may also interact with each other. For example, if parents disapprove of their offspring drinking, but drink heavily themselves, how does this influence the drinking behaviour of their offspring? We now go on to review the empirical evidence for these family social learning factors in relation to adolescent alcohol use.

The drinking behaviour of parents and older siblings provides a model of alcohol use on which individuals may base their own drinking. If parents drink regularly and sensibly, then an individual's schema for alcohol use may develop along the lines of regular, sensible drinking. Or if parents are heavier drinkers, then a model of heavy drinking is provided and could be incorporated into the individual's schema. Alternatively, non-drinking parents provide a model of abstemious behaviour.

If, as we pointed out in the previous chapter, adolescents aspire to adult behaviours rather than to reject adult behaviours, one would expect the drinking behaviour of adolescents within a community to reflect the drinking patterns of adults in that same community. This is exactly what Barnes (1981) found in a study which compared the drinking behaviour of a local sample of adults with that of a local sample of teenagers. The similarity between the patterns of use for beers, wine and spirits was quite striking.

Family based social reinforcement of teenage alcohol use is manifested in parental norms and definitions about their teenager's alcohol use (Akers *et al* 1979). Parental norms and definitions are expressed in the form of attitudes to their offspring's alcohol use (and to alcohol use in general). Social learning theory (Bandura 1977) suggests that adolescents internalize the norms and definitions of their parents and that these internalized referents (part of the individual's schema for alcohol use) are reflected in the teenager's drinking behaviour.

If drinking, rather than non-drinking, is the norm in adulthood, one would expect parents to moderate their attitude toward their offspring's alcohol use as their son or daughter grows older: from a prohibitive attitude in pre-adolescence, through prescriptive and controlling stages to more tolerant and approving attitudes in later adolescence. As such, parental attitudes at any one time may be directly reflected in teenage behaviour only in the short term.

Meta-analysis

In a second meta-analytic study, we looked at published research which detailed the relationship between adolescent drinking and family social learning. Using a similar selection and inclusion criteria to the first meta-analysis, which we reported on in the previous chapter, we identified over 40 separate research studies. In these, sample sizes ranged from 74 up to 15,000; ages from nine to 21; and the studies were all published between 1967 and 1991. Many of these studies reported both imitation/modelling and social reinforcement variables in relation to adolescent drinking. We used a sorting meta-analytic technique (Glass *et al* 1981), with each study's results being classified on the appropriate family social learning factor as either positively related, negatively related, or non-significant with respect to drinking behaviour.

We included in this meta-analysis 38 recently published empirical studies which measured the relationship between teenage drinking and parental drinking. Thirty studies reported a positive relationship, with more frequent and heavier parental drinking related to more frequent and heavier adolescent offspring's drinking. The majority of studies were cross-sectional, and tended to report relationships which contributed to only a small part of the variation in teenage drinking. Eight studies found no relationship between parental drinking and offspring's drinking, and no studies reported a negative relationship between parental and offspring's alcohol use (see Table 6.1).

In a previous review, Bucholz (1990) stated that heavier drinkers were more likely than moderate drinkers or abstainers to report parents who approved of their drinking. We reached a similar conclusion in a further meta-analysis of 24 recently published separate research studies. Of these, 18 studies found a positive relationship between adolescent drinking and parental attitudes, with heavier teenage drinking linked to parental approval of their offspring's drinking. The other six studies did not find any association (Table 6.1).

	Relationship with adolescent drinking			
	+ sig	n.s.	-sig.	
Parental drinking	30	8	0	(χ^2=38.31, df=2 p<0.001)
Parental attitudes	18	6	0	(χ^2=18.0, df=2 p<0.001)

Table 6.1: Total significant and non-significant results for the relationship between adolescent drinking behaviour and family social learning factors

In summary, the results of this meta-analytic study show that:

- Adolescents drink more if their parents drink more
- Adolescents drink more if their parents approve of their drinking

We discuss below parental drinking and parental attitudes, discussing in more detail the results of some studies which we included in the meta-analysis.

Parents as models

There is a clear theoretical rationale for implying that such modelling is largely unidirectional. Parents are likely to have developed a fairly consistent pattern of alcohol use, which is unlikely to be influenced by how their offspring begin to use alcohol. Longitudinal studies which measure the relationship between parental drinking at time 1 and offspring's drinking at time 2 show a pathway of positive influence. Almost two thousand teenagers in Grade 7 (age 12) were followed up by Ellickson and Hays (1991) three months and 12 months later. They found that alcohol use by parents or a close adult was significantly related to initiation of drinking; to continuing alcohol use; and to the development of heavy drinking. Johnson and Pandina (1991a) followed up over thirteen hundred students aged 12, 15 and 18 over three years. They found parental alcohol use was significantly related to the future frequency of drinking in their offspring (but not to the development of problem drinking). Kandel and Andrews (1987) followed up 345 secondary students over six months. Frequency of alcohol use by the interviewed parent was significantly related to initiation of alcohol use in their offspring. Further, initiation into hard liquor use was predicted by parental use of hard liquor measured six months previously, in an earlier study by Kandel *et al* (1978).

Pointing to potential sex differences, Thompson and Wilsnack's (1987) results from a 4-year follow-up study involving 839 students (aged 12-17) showed that father's drinking predicted male offspring's alcohol use, and mother's drinking predicted female offspring's alcohol use. And, in a cross-cultural comparative study, Adler and Kandel (1982) reported that in the U.S.A. frequency of drinking by both parents was linked to son's and daughter's frequency of drinking. In Israel, mother's use only was influential, and in France mother's use predicted only daughter's use.

Other studies, predominantly cross-sectional, have also found sex differences, although no clear patterns are apparent. For example, Barnes *et al* (1986) found that adolescent drinking was significantly related to frequency of drinking of mother, but not father. However, the father's drinking did show a marked trend - adolescents with heavier drinking fathers were twice as likely as those with low/moderate drinking fathers to be heavier drinkers.

Donovan and Jessor (1978) found that family models of drinking were significantly related to problem drinking in girls, but not in boys. Forslund and Gustafson (1970) found that mother's drinking was associated with drinking without parental supervision by both sons and daughters, but paternal drinking was only related to daughter's unsupervised use. Conversely, Wilks *et al* (1989) reported that paternal drinking was related to drinking by both sons and daughters, but mother's drinking was linked only with son's drinking.

Most studies in our second meta-analysis reported significant associations between the drinking behaviour of both parents and that of sons and of daughters. In those studies where sex differences were found, these may reflect genuine differences, perhaps cultural, in the inter-generational transmission of drinking behaviour. Or, as with several studies which used multiple regression techniques to analyse data, it may be a statistical artifact. For example, if there is a notable positive correlation between the drinking of mothers and the drinking of fathers, as there generally is (eg. Wilks *et al* 1989), then statistical techniques which partial out such co-variation and contribute such overlap in the relationship with offspring's drinking to either maternal or paternal drinking, may be inappropriate (eg. Kandel *et al* 1978; Smart *et al* 1978). Indeed, it may be the co-variation between the drinking of each parent which is the salient influence - the drinking behaviour model of both parents rather than one over the other. Of course, there may be some sex differences, but probably not of the order suggested by those studies reporting a stepwise multiple regression which indicates, for example, that father's drinking is significant but mother's is not significant.

Parental attitudes

As we stated above, most of the studies examined in the second meta-analysis were cross-sectional in design. And as with parental drinking, there is a clear theoretical rationale for supposing that the direction of effect is largely from parents to offspring. However, one could imagine the situation when heavy teenage drinking may cause parents to moderate their attitude to their offspring's alcohol use. If, for example, a teenager comes home drunk from a party, or gets into trouble with teachers or with police for alcohol-related behaviour, then parents will probably become less approving or tolerant towards their son's or daughter's future alcohol use.

The longitudinal studies we looked at tended to be less consistent than the cross-sectional studies. Donovan *et al* (1983) followed up 593 high school students and college freshmen six years later when they were young adults. There was no relationship between parental approval of drinking at time 1 and problem drinker status at time 2. However, in Johnson and Pandina's (1991a) longitudinal study, tolerance by parents to their teenager's drinking was significantly related to both son's and daughter's frequency of drinking three years later.

Kandel and Andrews (1987) measured parental beliefs that alcohol use is harmful. These were not related to initiation of alcohol use in their offspring six months later, but were related to their offspring themselves having a negative attitude to alcohol use. In an earlier study Kandel *et al* (1978) reported similar results: parental tolerance of child's potential hard liquor use was not related, six months later, to initiation of hard liquor use. However, parental approval of alcohol use *was* related to initiation of alcohol use (but not continuing alcohol use) 12 months later in a longitudinal study by Ellickson and Hays (1991) of almost two thousand grade 7 students.

In summary, cross-sectional studies tend to report a significant relationship between parental attitude and offspring's alcohol use. The picture from longitudinal studies is less clear: some report a clear association, others no association. Longer term influence of a particular parental attitude could be a function of the ordinal nature of change in parental attitude - those parents who soften their attitudes earlier may reinforce more frequent earlier drinking which could, in turn, lead to heavier future drinking. However, the evidence for earlier drinking leading to later heavier drinking is poor and inconsistent (Davies 1992), as is the evidence for earlier heavy drinking predicting later heavy drinking (Bagnall 1991). It seems that, on the whole, parental attitudes are more influential in the short-term, and this is supported by the consistency in the cross-sectional studies in the meta-analysis of parental attitudes and teenage drinking.

Peer influence

Although the majority of studies in the second meta-analytic study were cross-sectional in design, there is a clear rationale for positing that parental drinking is more influential for offspring's drinking than vice-versa. Adults who are parents of teenagers will probably have developed an established and stable pattern of drinking, which is unlikely to be influenced to any extent by the way their children begin to drink. On the other hand, teenagers are likely to be influenced by the way they perceive their parent's established drinking patterns. The same cannot be said for the process of peer influence.

Modelling the drinking behaviour of peers is frequently depicted as the major mode of psychosocial influence for teenage drinking, especially for older teenagers. This 'peer pressure' hypothesis has formed the basis of much alcohol- and drug-related alcohol education, and 'resistance to peer pressure' underlies many such initiatives. Peer influence is often found in cross-sectional studies to be a better statistical predictor of teenage drinking than other, including parental, influences. However, association does not imply causation. Many young drinkers drink with their friends. Their close social network is made up of friends with whom they share their behaviour (Eiser *et al* 1991). The argument that peer drinking is more influential for own drinking than own drinking is for peer drinking is obviously flawed. Both peers and self are learning to drink and are developing patterns of alcohol-related behaviour, and influences are reciprocal.

So, longitudinal studies which demonstrate that peer drinking at time 1 predicts own use at time 2 should also measure how own use at time 1 predicts peer use at time 2. Two studies which did just that came up with interesting and illuminating results. Britt and Campbell (1977), in a follow-up study of 1420 high school seniors in their college freshman year (i.e. one year later) found that baseline respondent alcohol use had a slightly stronger effect on follow-up peer influence than baseline peer influence had on follow-up respondent alcohol use. Similarly, Downs (1987) followed up over one year 100 adolescents between the ages of 13 and 17. Drinking by a close friend at time 1 was related to self-drinking at time 2. But, reciprocally, self-drinking at time 1 was related to close friend drinking at time 2. In this study also, the self→peer path was slightly stronger than the peer→self path. This suggests that as well as individuals drinking like their peers, they also choose to mix with friends who share their own drinking preferences and aspirations.

These results are one reason why 'resistance to peer pressure' as an alcohol education paradigm is generally ineffective in modifying behaviour (Moskovitz 1989). Peer drinking cannot be clearly separated out as a distinct aetiological mechanism, as the influence of peers is complex and reciprocal. Therefore, encouraging adolescents to resist peer pressure to drink, when they themselves are already drinking like their peers, is obviously a weak and flawed alcohol education strategy. It is an insufficient attempt to deal with only part of the problem.

However, if we do not regard peer pressure as an aetiological factor but merely as a mechanism through which behaviour can be changed (resistance to peer pressure) then we are also in trouble. This is a form of cognitive-behaviour intervention, a method common in clinical psychology. But there are a couple of problems in using this technique with young drinkers. Firstly, this method relies on the recognition by young people that their friends' drinking influences the way they themselves drink. In a recent study however (Foxcroft & Lowe 1993; see also chapter 3), we found that only a small proportion of older teenagers (approximately 1 in 8) said that they drink because their friends do. Secondly, and perhaps more importantly, this technique requires that individuals see their own drinking as a problem which needs to be modified. Most young people drink because it is enjoyable and because it is a normal social behaviour, not a problem one, and as such do not wish to modify their behaviour.

Moreover, given that many teenagers want to drink, then if they are told by alcohol educators that they drink because of peer influence, and that they should resist such influences, teenagers may reject the incorporation of peer influence into their alcohol use schema. This would then reduce dissonance, and the young people would feel comfortable about carrying on drinking. This could also help explain the low number of individuals who cite friends' drinking as a reason for own drinking in the study mentioned above (Foxcroft & Lowe 1993).

Modelling and social reinforcement

We predicted, and have found in a meta-analytic study, that parental models of alcohol use and parental attitudes to their teenager's alcohol use are two important mechanisms in the socialization of adolescent drinking behaviour, and should always be considered together in the relationship with teenage drinking. Social learning theory clearly outlines these two factors, and also points to the potential additive and interactive effects of modelling and social reinforcement. Parental attitudes are particularly important in that they provide social reinforcement which may encourage or discourage the modelling of parental drinking. For example, parental disapproval provides little or no reinforcement for modelling parental drinking. On the other hand, parental approval directly reinforces modelling of parental drinking. Thus it is the combination of parental approval and heavy parental drinking which may result in heavier teenage drinking.

This pattern of influence was indeed demonstrated by O'Connor (1978). She reported on the relationship of parental drinking and parental social rules for their offspring's drinking (parental attitude) with their offspring's light or heavy alcohol use. The data were analysed using logistic regression, and although confidence limits were not reported, the pattern of the results is illuminating nonetheless (Figure 6.2). The results of the logistic regression are presented in the form of odds ratios of the teenager being classified as a light or heavy drinker. For example, if odds of 3 to 1 are found for drinkers with approving and heavy drinking parents, this means that individuals with these parents are three times more likely to be heavy drinkers. The actual results (Figure 6.2) showed that adolescents whose parents were heavier drinkers and also approved of their drinking, were most likely to be heavy drinkers. Even if parents were light drinkers, providing they approved of their teenager drinking, then their teenager was more likely to be a heavy drinker. As predicted by social learning theory, parental disapproval was associated with light drinking by offspring, regardless of level of parental drinking.

In Figure 6.2, parental approval seems to be a more important influence than parental drinking per se, but it is the combination of heavy parental drinking and an approving or tolerant parental attitude which provides the most risk for heavy teenage drinking.

Although O'Connor's analysis is a step in the right direction, the classification of parental drinking and parental attitudes into light/heavy and approve/disapprove may be too general. In the previous chapters we have pointed to the normality of sensible teenage drinking, reflecting the alcohol use of most adults in the social and cultural environment. Teenagers who are heavy drinkers *or* non-drinkers are, we suggested, socially deviant. The same argument applies to parental drinking. If parents do not drink *or* drink heavily then they too may be socially deviant. Thus, rather than light/heavy categories of parental drinking, classification should distinguish non-drinkers from sensible/moderate drinkers and from heavy drinkers.

Parental attitudes should also be classified more distinctly. Parents may approve of their teenagers drinking, providing they drink sensibly and appropriately. This moderating attitude to teenage drinking is clearly different from unlimited parental approval or indifference, and also from parental disapproval of drinking.

To summarize, adolescent drinking is influenced by social learning in two respects. Parental drinking and parental attitudes provide models and social reinforcement through which young people develop their own drinking. The combination of parental approval of drinking and heavier parental drinking seems to be a serious risk factor for heavier teenage drinking. However, the relationship between these parental behaviours and teenage drinking is complex, and examination of the relationship should involve at least three levels within each behaviour. Nil, sensible and heavy levels of parental drinking need to be considered, as do parental disapproval, approval, or moderating attitudes to their teenager's alcohol use.

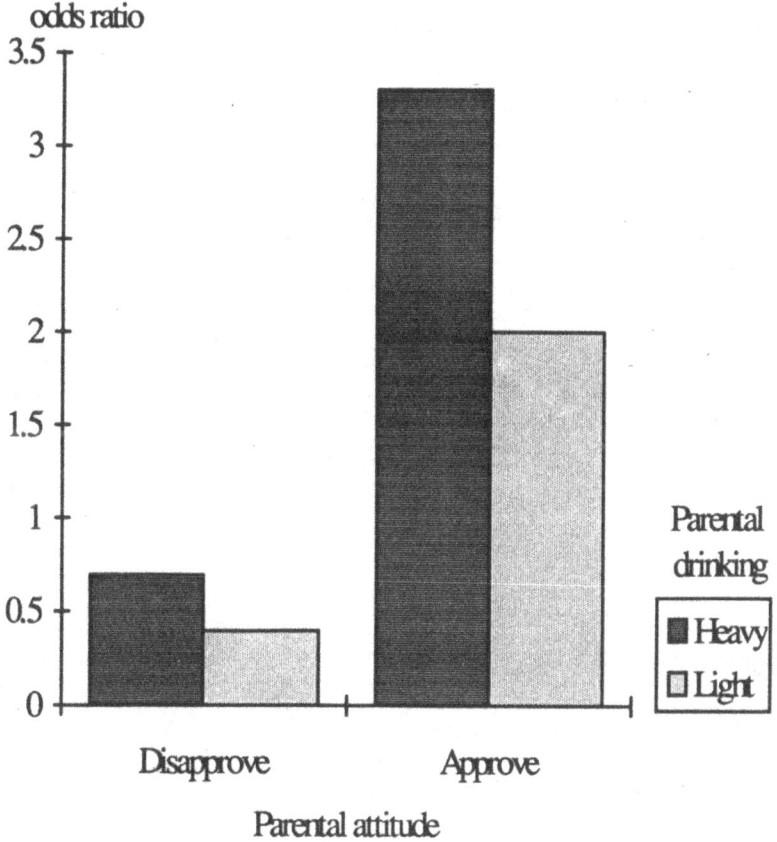

Figure 6.2: Odds of being a heavy drinker according to parental attitude and parental drinking (adapted from O'Connor 1978)

Family process and family social learning

Barnes (1990) produced a model of teenage drinking in which family socialization is the central and most important influence. This is also a major theme of this book, and we have developed further the specifics of this model, by detailing the elements of family dynamics which are important in the socialization of teenage drinking.

In the previous chapter and in the early part of this chapter we have gone into some detail about family socialization influences on teenage alcohol use. These family socialization influences are non-alcohol-specific and alcohol-specific. Family process underlies non-alcohol-specific family influences, characterized by levels of supportive and controlling behaviours. Social learning is the alcohol-specific mode of family influence, characterized by modelling of parental drinking behaviour and by parental attitudes to their teenager's actual or potential alcohol use.

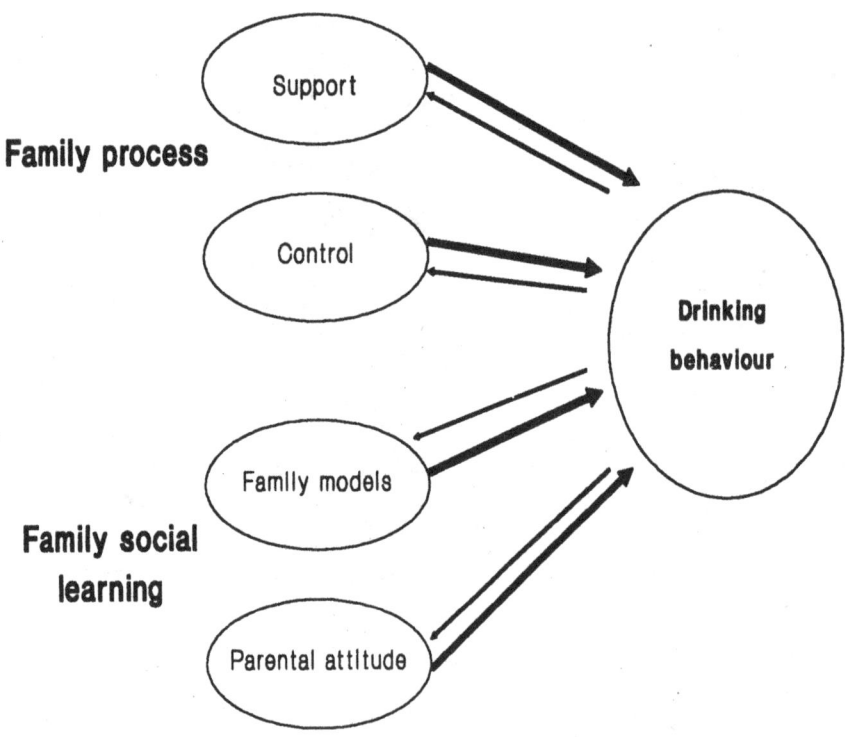

Figure 6.3: Family socialization factors which influence the development of teenage drinking

These four factors make up a framework for the investigation and understanding of family influences on the development of adolescent drinking behaviour (see Figure 6.3). Insofar as this framework encourages the generation of testable hypotheses then it also constitutes a theoretical model. This model specifies causal relationships, but prediction of the direction or magnitude of the hypothesized relationship with drinking behaviour may not always be possible, especially with the more complex interactions between the factors. Although to a certain extent this is a post-hoc framework or theory, the organization which the theory brings to present knowledge and understanding (largely a product of atheoretical research) is important. This demonstrates the iterative research-theory process involved in most theory development. The full causal model of family socialization influences on teenage drinking is specified in Figure 6.4. Demographic factors include age, sex, family structure, SES, etc. Shaded arrows indicate direct influences, and unshaded arrows indirect, moderating influences. (If we were to include peer socialization influences in this model, they would be depicted as having a reciprocal and equal relationship with the teenager's drinking behaviour, and also influenced by family socialization factors).

Furthermore, our conceptualization of family socialization theory goes beyond the organization of knowledge of family influences on teenage drinking. Previous research has focussed mainly on heavy or problem drinking adolescents, and classified non-drinkers and sensible drinkers as one indistinct group. Problem drinking adolescents are the most important focal group for many research programmes (researchers are often most interested in the practical implications of the research for treating and educating individuals with problem drinking or problem substance use behaviour). However, this focus may neglect a more global view of family influences and teenage drinking, one which incorporates non-drinkers as a socially deviant group. This is an important point. If we, as parents and educators, strive to socialize teenagers into behaviour which will prepare them best for adulthood, then the goal must surely be sensible drinking, rather than non-drinking. Optimal family socialization should be those family behaviours which lead to sensible and normative levels of drinking. It is therefore important for researchers to examine and specify such family behaviours, as well as family behaviours which may lead to non-drinking and heavy drinking.

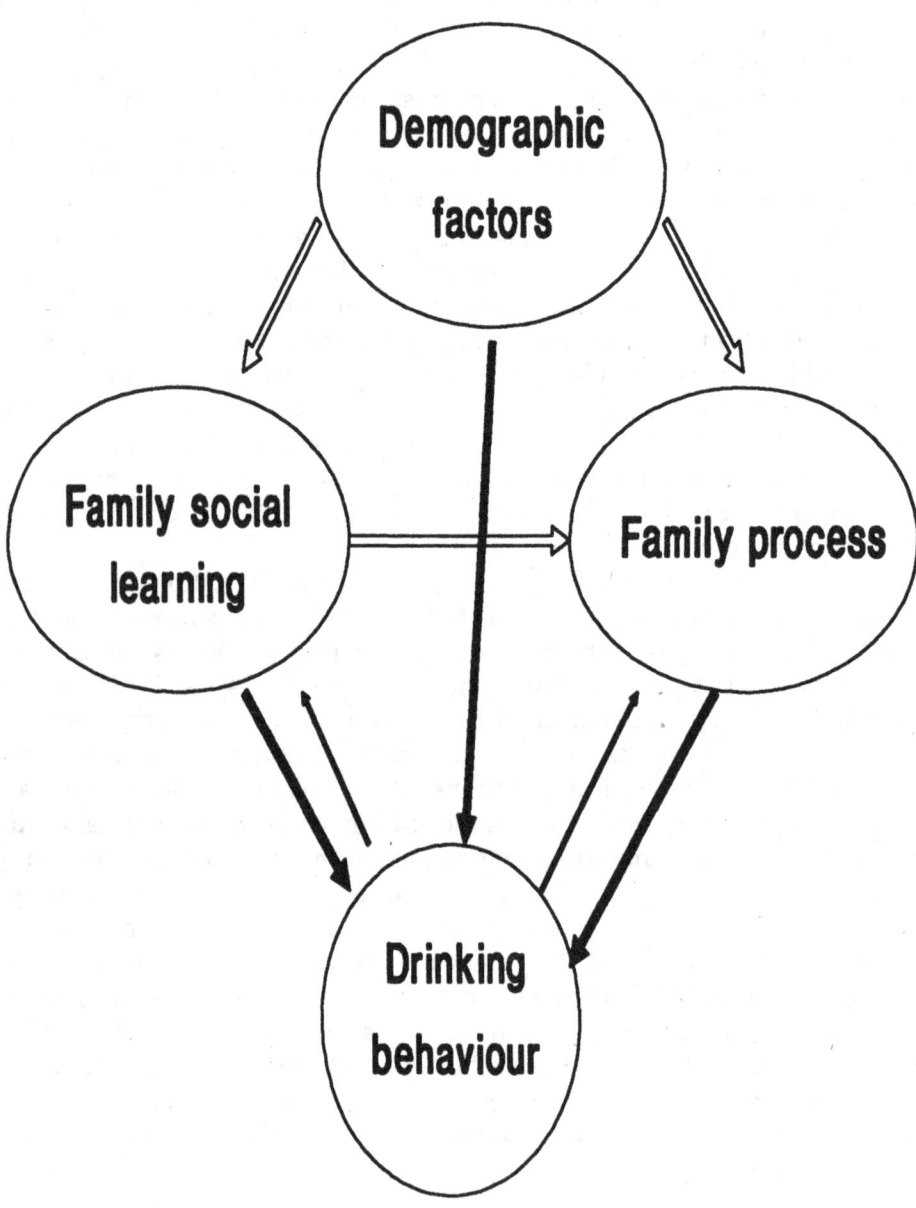

Figure 6.4: Family socialization: a model for teenage drinking

Non-drinking teenagers

Most adolescent drinking research distinguishes heavy drinkers from non-heavy drinkers. Few studies have looked specifically at non-drinkers, and unfortunately this distinction has not been carried forward into subsequent research studies by others. In one study that did look at teenage non-drinking, Davies and Stacey (1972) examined teenagers' perceptions of heavy drinkers and of abstainers along two dimensions - tough/rebellious and attractive/sociable. They found that these perceptions represented two contrasting stereotypes. The non-drinking teenager was seen by most people as lacking in toughness and rebelliousness, whereas heavy drinkers were seen as tough and rebellious. In terms of attractiveness and sociability, heavy drinkers were on the whole viewed by all sex/age groups as unattractive and unsociable, whereas the non-drinker was perceived as falling midway between the extremes of attractive/sociable and unattractive/unsociable. For further insight and clarification, it would be interesting to look at the perception of a sensible drinker in terms of toughness and attractiveness, and to compare this with the perception of the heavy drinker and of the non-drinker.

A report by Demone (1972) also distinguished non-drinkers from moderate and heavy drinkers. Demone reported characteristics associated with abstinence in his sample of 3256 young male adolescents. These characteristics included living with both real parents, a non-drinking father and a non-drinking mother, parental refusal to grant permission to drink under any circumstances, feelings of strong obligation to parents, and agreement with parents on fundamental issues, such as agreeing that the teenager may make his own decision about drinking when he is supporting himself.

Contrast this with the profile of the pathological drinker. Among the characteristics highlighted were a broken home, father or mother who were abstainers, father or mother who reportedly drank daily, father or mother with a drinking problem, failure to confide in parents, commitment to peers in parent-peer conflict about excessive drinking, and parental indifference to their son's drinking. In describing this contrast in family characteristics between non-drinkers and heavy drinkers, Demone points to the rejection by heavy drinkers of formal adolescent activities and adult sanctioned behaviour, whilst non-drinkers overreact in the opposite direction - emulating all models and behaviours defined for adolescents by adults.

The above profiles support the conclusions we made at the end of the previous chapter that non-drinking, as well as heavy drinking, is viewed as a 'deviant' behaviour, and that extremes of family process behaviours lead to extremes of teenage drinking behaviour. The non-drinkers in Demone's study felt a strong obligation to parents, whereas heavy drinkers failed to confide in their parents. In the last chapter we reported that low support and low control were associated with heavy adolescent drinking, and that high levels of support and control may be associated with non-drinking. These observations clarified the family systems perspective, which suggested that extremes of family behaviours would be associated with dysfunctional outcome. Most previous research, however, has not confirmed this hypothesis, because the dysfunctional outcomes typically examined referred only to problem (heavy) drinking or problem substance use.

What we also see in the above profiles is the relevance of the non-drinker, sensible/moderate drinker and heavy drinker distinction for social learning influences. Non-drinkers were more likely to have non-drinking parents and parents with a disapproving attitude to their teenager's drinking. On the other hand, heavy drinkers were more likely to have non-drinking *or* heavy drinking parents and parents with an indifferent attitude to their teenager's drinking. The interactions between these social learning influences and family process influences may also help explain why heavy drinkers might have heavy drinking parents or parents who abstain. Both influences are inadequate models for normative socialization, and it may be that different levels of support and control in the family environment provide positive or negative reinforcement of parental models and attitudes.

However, regarding family process as a social reinforcement factor in the modelling of parental drinking creates a theoretical problem for family socialization theory. This problem appears when parents provide inadequate models of drinking behaviour, leading to alternative predictions from social learning theorists and family theorists. For example, if parents are heavy drinkers, social learning theory predicts that a good family environment would reinforce the modelling of parental drinking. However, family process theorists would argue that an optimal family environment would protect against the adoption of dysfunctional behaviour. In reality though, heavy parental drinking is more likely to be associated with a poorer family environment, but nevertheless the possibility of a good family life and a problem drinking parent does produce competing predictions within family socialization theory.

These competing hypotheses have been examined in a study of the offspring of problem drinking parents (Orford & Velleman 1991), and some support was found for both hypotheses. The authors concluded that the transmission of problem drinking occurs through a variety of mechanisms of differential importance in different sub-groups. This interesting problem merits further examination, preferably using a matched control group of offspring of non-problem drinking parents. How family process moderates modelling of parental drinking could depend on the level of parental drinking: a good family environment could foster social reinforcement of normative parental drinking, but may protect against the modelling of heavy parental drinking behaviour. Figure 6.4 shows how family social learning has a direct effect on teenage drinking (shaded arrow) and also an indirect effect through family process (unshaded arrow).

Consistent and inconsistent family socialization

The results of the meta-analyses in this and in the previous chapter suggest that family behaviours which consistently socialize an individual towards heavier drinking behaviour are a combination of low support, low control, heavy parental drinking and condoning parental attitudes. These complementary behaviours provide the most risk for the development of heavier adolescent drinking. Consistent behaviours may also underlie adolescent non-drinking: high support, strict control, parental non-drinking and disapproving attitudes. These were linked with non-drinking in the study by Demone (1972).

Inconsistent behaviours may also pose a risk for deviant drinking behaviour. The discussion above about moderating influences and competing hypotheses generally highlights inconsistent socialization behaviour. Such inconsistent socialization may be due to different behaviours from different parents, but another important influence is likely to be inconsistent socialization practices between distinct family socialization factors. For example, the inconsistency between heavy parental drinking and disapproving parental attitude, or the inconsistency between low support and high control and an indifferent parental attitude (and perhaps abstaining parents thrown in for good measure), is not a complementary pattern of family behaviour, and is probably not optimal family socialization behaviour. In terms of communication theory, such inconsistent family behaviours are not optimal in terms of adolescent socialization because they provide disjunctive messages and meta-messages to the maturing teenager (Bateson *et al* 1956).

In essence, the issue here is one of additivity or interaction. Do the two family process and two family social learning factors combine independently and additively in the socialization of teenage alcohol use? Or is there an interactive effect between these factors? If the effect is independent and additive then the prediction of teenage drinking behaviour from both consistent and inconsistent patterns of family socialization behaviour is quite straightforward. For example, a disapproving parental attitude towards a teenager's drinking in a family environment which otherwise socializes towards heavier drinking (low support, low control and heavier family drinking) would reduce that teenager's alcohol use behaviour. This teenager is therefore less likely to drink heavily than those individuals whose families consistently socialize towards heavier alcohol use.

Alternatively, there are two types of possible interaction effect. Ordinal interaction can be described as the potentiation of an outcome (drinking) by the combination of predictors (family socialization factors). An ordinal interaction effect is clearly shown in Figure 6.2 in which the likelihood of being a heavy teenage drinker is synergistically related to the combination of heavy parental drinking and an approving parental attitude. With disordinal interaction the rank order of the predictor variables changes. For example, there is a disordinal interaction in the situation where heavier drinking is linked with low support and low control, and also with low support and strict parental control.

From the patterns of socialization we have described so far, the optimal pattern for the socialization of sensible teenage drinking behaviour seems to be a pattern of moderation - moderate levels of support and control, a moderating attitude to offspring's drinking and a model of sensible parental drinking. This pattern of socialization is most likely to have positive consequences for sensible teenage drinking, and could therefore be described as a pattern of positive or functional consistency.

Semi-structured interviews

To investigate the relationship between family socialization factors and teenage drinking, we interviewed, in depth, teenagers who volunteered to talk about about their perceived family life and also their own drinking behaviour (Foxcroft and Lowe 1992c).

Following the interview with each teenager, the interview transcripts and notes were written up as individual case studies. Each case study report was subsequently examined and confirmed as a true account by the interviewee, increasing the validity of the study. The protocol for the interviews specified the design of the case study (Yin 1989), and involved five components:

(1) *The research question:* How does family life influence the development of adolescent drinking behaviour?
(2) *Propositions:* From family socialization theory, incorporating family process and family social learning behaviours.
(3) *Units of analysis:* Q. What is the case? A. The perception of family life and of family's and own drinking behaviour by an adolescent.
(4) *Linking data to propositions:* Use of 'pattern matching' (Campbell 1975). Several pieces of information from the same case are related to the theoretical proposition.
(5) *Interpreting the findings:* How good a 'match' is the case study?

In the remainder of this chapter we report in detail two example case studies, one from a teenager who was a heavy drinker, and one from a teenager who reported drinking sensibly. We intersperse these case study reports (italicized) with comments. Of course, the names of these two individuals have been changed to preserve their anonymity.

Tony

Tony is an 18-year-old apprentice joiner. He stated that he recently went through a period when he was drinking a litre bottle of vodka every day.

> *When he was five years old Tony's parents split up. Tony stayed with his mother, and even though his father lived in the same town, he lost all contact with him. In fact Tony's mother prohibited him from seeing his father. She told him stories about how she had been beaten up by his father. Tony knew that at least one of these stories was a lie, because he had been there at the time his mother said the incident had occurred.*

There was considerable animosity from Tony's mother to his father when they separated. Tony's feelings and loyalties were clearly confused. He lived with his mother, as his father had moved out and left them, and his mother was telling lies in order to paint a bad picture of his father. Tony was conscious and sensitive to the possibility that his mother's stories were untrue, and that his father was probably not the "ogre" he was made out to be.

> *For the next 10 years Tony lived with his mother. He had two older sisters. One sister never lived with them, and the other "left home as soon as she could". Tony's mother never married again. In fact she never went out, and never dated anyone else. Tony's mother was very strict. She didn't like him to go out with his friends, she preferred him to stay at home with her, and when he objected he was frequently sent to his room. Tony says that his mother really worried about him all the time. When he was in the third year of secondary school (age 13-14) she would still meet him from school. Tony found this quite humiliating, and was teased by his school friends. Tony says that his mother wouldn't let him have a life of his own. He wasn't allowed to get a job, and she didn't let him have an allowance.*

That Tony's sister was described as leaving home as soon as she could suggests that she was not happy at home. Tony describes his mother as being very over-protective and strict, and it seems that she withdrew from the outside world into the relative security and stability of her own family - herself and her son. That both her husband and her daughter had left her perhaps made her fear that Tony would do the same, and that was why she was over-protective and controlling. The fact that Tony was not allowed to have a life of his own made Tony feel that he was not getting the sort of support and independence he wanted from his mother.

> *At the age of 14-15 Tony started rebelling. He stayed out all night, at friends', without telling his mother. When he did go home he was punished severely and grounded. When Tony was introduced to cigarettes, by the following week he was smoking twenty a day. He said it was to relieve the pressure. Tony was occasionally drinking a few cans of beer. His mother didn't let him drink, she was scared in case he got caught for under-age drinking. His mother drank little and rarely - only on special occasions. By this time Tony had got a part-time job. He said his mother had eased off a bit by now because he was physically bigger than her. However they were still constantly arguing. After one argument Tony told his mum that he was leaving, that he was going to live with his dad. His mother "went wild", and threw him out.*

As Tony approached his mid-teenage years he clearly began to feel hemmed in and controlled by his mother. He began to assert his independence from her when he started to disobey her. This transitional period was obviously one of great conflict - with his mother trying to slow down or prevent Tony's individuation by being controlling, and Tony feeling very stressed at his mother's inadequate support and excessively controlling approach. This came to a head and Tony left home to find his father.

> *His father, even though there had been no contact for ten years, was happy to see him. It turned out that he had tried to contact Tony, but that Tony's mother had blocked all his efforts. Tony's father gave him a large allowance, and alcohol was freely available in the house. His father was a "big drinker", sometimes drinking "13 pints and then driving home". However Tony didn't feel any real pressure to drink, and at this time only drank moderately and socially. His father found Tony a job at the factory in which he was the manager. But Tony found it difficult arriving with the boss every day, being "the boss's son". The other workers gave Tony a hard time, so he moved back with his mother. Tony then started to go out socially with his workmates. He joined a darts team, and by this time was drinking 2 to 3 pints most nights.*

Initially Tony seemed to settle in well at his father's. He might have been indulged because of the long separation between them. Tony was found a job in his father's factory, but this set up another area of conflict - he was the boss's son - and there was antagonism between his peer role and his family role during this period. To try and resolve this antagonism Tony went back to live with his mother. This resolved the antagonism by placating his peers, and he became one of their group. However, this may have distanced him from his father. Tony also described his father as a big drinker, which provided a model of excessively heavy alcohol use. That alcohol was freely available suggests that Tony's father had an approving, perhaps indifferent, attitude towards Tony's drinking.

> *At home Tony's mother was still trying to control him - she would take 70 per cent of his wages for rent, and she was "always telling [him] how to behave". Tony said that he took no notice of her.*
>
> *Tony decided to pack in working at his dad's factory. He said he wasn't big enough to manage the heavy manual work, and he was fed up with the early mornings. A week later, after a party in which Tony had drank a lot of vodka (he'd never really had any spirits before), he stole a car. Tony was caught and arrested. He was bailed over providing he stayed at his mum's house. However, after another big row, his mother kicked him out. Tony had to move to a bail hostel in another town, organized by the probation service. He said his mother hated the 'stigma' of having a 'criminal' for a son. Tony lost all contact with his mother and father after he moved to the bail hostel.*

Conflict still existed between Tony and his mother - it was still not a healthy supportive environment. However, although Tony's mother was still attempting strict control, this for the most part was ineffective. A week after Tony had left his father's factory he got into trouble. Many teenagers at some time or other get drunk and some even get into trouble with the law. However, what is important in Tony's case, is the lack of support and lack of direction he received from his mother and his father during this crisis period. It seemed that both Tony's parents did not want anything to do with him - he overtly states this about his mother and it is suggested covertly by the lack of contact with his father.

> *In the bail hostel Tony and the other residents started drinking heavily. Gradually, as the other residents were tried and sent to prison, Tony became more and more isolated and worried. His drinking increased until he was having a litre bottle of vodka every day. Tony said that he was just becoming a wreck, that if he*

> didn't have a drink inside him he would just lie on his bed and cry. There was nobody he could talk to, to confide in. This carried on for a couple of months (Tony was in the bail hostel for 6 months in all). When Tony finally got to court he was sentenced to 2 months imprisonment. While in prison he had no visitors at all, even though he wrote to his mother. On release the first thing that Tony did was buy a bottle of vodka. He went back to his mother, who initially welcomed him back with open arms. However, she couldn't talk about Tony's time in prison, and he was made to feel like an outcast. After three days of arguing, Tony's mother kicked him out again, and he came back to the town where he had stayed at the bail hostel. The first night he bought a litre bottle of vodka and slept rough in the park. Then he booked into a cheap hotel.

Tony's isolation from his parents and subsequent involvement with a deviant peer group probably contributed considerably to Tony's drinking problem. There was a clear lack of support from his mother, the person who brought him up, and also from his father, who had initially made him so welcome after all those years. Because of the nature of this relationship (or lack of it) with his parents Tony was not in a position to be influenced by their control attempts. We have already seen that previously his relationship with his mother resulted in ineffective control, and his father, when he played a part in Tony's life, was probably indulgent. The lack of family contact while Tony was in prison probably emphasized his feelings of being an outcast. This was not helped on Tony's return to his mother's after he completed his jail term.

> By now Tony was 17, and he came into contact with a worker from a local youth organization. This worker was very supportive, encouraged Tony to lay off the vodka, and found him a job and a place to live.
> Tony is now 18, and has stopped drinking the vodka. He still has a full bottle in his room, from an occasion when he nearly relapsed. With the help of the youth worker Tony realized it wasn't worth it. He realized that if he drank the vodka he would pass out - only to wake up in 12 hours and nothing would have changed. Tony has re-established contact with his father. However, he doesn't want to see his mother again. He resents her for not supporting him, and blames her for getting in the way of him and his father. He feels that if his father had been there to help, then he would never have ended up at the bail hostel, or in prison, and would never have started drinking so heavily.

The supportive youth worker helped Tony regain some organization and structure in his life. The youth worker took on the role that Tony's parents should have done. Although not in a position to exercise control in the way a parent could, the youth worker performed a skilful job in negotiating the parameters of Tony's drinking behaviour. The role of Tony's family in the development of his drinking behaviour is emphasized by Tony himself. He seems to be saying that if, during his teenage years, his mother and his father had provided better support and guidance, then he would not have got to the stage where he was drinking a litre bottle of vodka every day.

Darren

To contrast with Tony's history, we describe below the development of Darren's drinking behaviour - which could be regarded as 'sensible'.

> *Darren is a 17-year-old apprentice welder. He was adopted at 6 months of age and lives at home with his adoptive parents, younger sister (also adopted), and younger brother. Darren speaks warmly of his family, and expresses no desire to find his 'natural' parents. Darren's father is a crane driver, and his mother has had various part-time shop assistant jobs. They met when they were both in the army, but were both back in civvy street when Darren came along. Darren's father has never been out of work, and his mother stayed at home to look after the children. Darren's mum and dad get on well, and there have never been any major family upsets - not to Darren's knowledge anyway. Darren's mother is quite religious - she goes to church regularly. No-one else in the family is religious though, and there is no pressure to conform to any religious viewpoint.*

Right from the outset we can see that Darren described his family in a positive way. He speaks warmly of his family, his parents get on well, and there is no pressure to conform to his mother's religiosity. This immediately suggests a family environment with good levels of support and control.

> *Darren was never in any serious trouble at school, he never played truant. When asked why not, he replied that he didn't want to be caught and punished. He didn't feel that any punishment would be excessive, he just didn't want to be in the position where he had done something wrong and have to be punished at all. He describes a couple of instances when he was naughty - at age 10 he was caught swearing, and also disobeyed his father on another occasion. At times like this the usual form of*

> *punishment was to be grounded for a couple of nights or to have his pocket money stopped.*

In the above paragraph it is clear that Darren has a healthy set of internalized norms for behaviour. In their extensive review of the parent-child socialization literature Maccoby and Martin (1983) reported on the importance of good levels of support and moderate levels of control (not too lax or too strict) for the process of internalization of norms. When Darren did break the rules he was suitably punished, indicating that his parents operated control mechanisms, but this control was not excessive. That Darren's parents were optimally supportive and moderately controlling is therefore an important factor in Darren's normative behaviour.

> *Darren feels closest to his mother, but is also reasonably close to his father. He feels however that he couldn't give his father a cuddle, as it isn't the "done" thing. Darren is quite happy with his family situation, and wants to carry on living at home for the time being. He has one or two minor grumbles - he has to share a room with his brother - but the loft is being converted so he will soon have a room of his own. Also Darren sometimes wears his hair in a pony tail, and his dad thinks this is scruffy. When his father first saw it, he went out and had a short hair cut - to show Darren what a "proper haircut" looked like!*

Again, the impression of warmth is conveyed in the above description. Darren recognizes that his father would feel uncomfortable if he tried to cuddle him, but seems to realise that it is not because his father does not love him, but is because of the nature of the masculine role in society - especially his father's generation. The fact that Darren's father had a "proper haircut" in response to Darren's pony-tail suggests that his father disapproves of the pony-tail, registering his disapproval in a quite humorous good-natured way, but would not insist that his son should immediately change his hairstyle. This suggests a responsive democratic family environment.

> *Darren had planned to go into the army, but then decided against it. Looking back, Darren says that when he left the army cadets he thinks his father was disappointed, but didn't say so. His dad was outwardly supportive and respected his decision.*

> *When Darren was younger [age 15] his parents used to set a deadline for Darren to be in at night. This was quite early compared to Darren's friends, and they teased him about this. Darren was unhappy about this, so he decided to sit down and have a talk with his father about it. He asked his mum to put a*

> good word in first, and then approached his dad. This discussion was quite sensible and fruitful - they agreed on a more flexible deadline. Darren says that his father then started to "loosen out", and Darren became more and more independent - he got his own set of keys.

When Darren felt restricted by parental control he felt able to sit down and negotiate the control parameters with his parents. His father seems to be the authority in the family, but he is authoritative rather than authoritarian. That the family were able to achieve a successful compromise is an important factor in the maintenance of the warm regard Darren has for his family. Bearing in mind the optimally supportive and moderately controlling family environment described above, the development of Darren's drinking behaviour is outlined below.

> Darren's parents have "never been big drinkers". His father would have one or two cans of beer a couple of nights a week. There was always beer in the fridge. In the past couple of years Darren's parents have started to enjoy the occasional bottle of wine. Darren was introduced to alcohol by his parents. At the age of 9 or 10 he was given an occasional glass of wine on special occasions. When out for Sunday walks with the family they would often stop at a pub, and Darren would have a glass of shandy. At 12 years old Darren shared a can of beer when out with his father at a friend's house. At 14 or 15 he occasionally shared a bottle of cider with friends on the street. Darren first got drunk one New Year just before he left school. He was in Scotland with his family visiting relatives, and says that he was so drunk he slept all through the next day, and missed the party the following evening!

Darren's first interactions with alcohol took place with his family. He was gradually introduced to alcohol, from quite an early age, but his parents were sensible drinkers and were sensible in the amount of alcohol Darren was given. Although Darren was allowed to get quite drunk one time, this also was with his family, and in the context of a celebration.

> Darren first went into a pub without his family when he was 16. It was at Christmas, and he went at lunchtime with some friends from college. He had two pints. He didn't drink again for a while, until his parents moved house, and there were lots of kids his age living nearby. They frequently went out on Monday nights, and Darren would have 3 or 4 pints. Darren has recently started going to clubs to watch bands play - he goes perhaps a couple of

times a week - and has a couple of pints each time. He tries not to get drunk - "When you're drunk you're prone to be a troublemaker - shoot your mouth off". Darren says that he never goes into a pub just to have a drink, although several of his friends drink a lot more than he does.

Darren does now drink regularly. His drinking is sensible, i.e. not more than two pints (four units) on not more than four occasions per week, and he feels no need or pressure to drink more, despite the fact that some of his peer group are heavier drinkers than he is.

Conclusions from the case studies

Family process

Tony's mother was clearly not supportive, and her control attempts were strict and latterly unsuccessful. The difference between control attempted and control achieved may help explain why some studies find a curvilinear relationship between control and drinking, and others a linear relationship. Strict control attempted but lax control achieved could be linked with heavier drinking. In both linear and curvilinear relationships lax control is associated with heavier drinking. If a study measures control attempts rather than control achieved then a curvilinear relationship may be found. Barnes *et al* (1986) used questions which seemed to assess control attempts rather than control achieved, and did find such a curvilinear relationship. This point needs to be borne in mind in future research.

Tony's father had no input for most of Tony's childhood, and when he most probably should, and could, have been there to provide support and direction, he was not. By contrast, both of Darren's parents provided good levels of support. His mother was less strict than his father, who was the power base in the family. His father, however, was flexible in his control and important issues seem to have been negotiable.

Although Darren lived with adoptive parents he regarded them as his natural (nuclear) family. Tony's parents separated when Tony was a lot younger, and Tony was raised by his mother. This supports the indication from our first meta-analysis that adolescents from non-nuclear families are more likely to be heavier drinkers.

Family social learning

Through social learning influences, parents are models and reinforcers of their children's behaviour. Tony's mother was an infrequent light drinker -

perhaps a glass of sherry at Christmas. She did not let Tony drink at all. His father, though, was a heavy drinker, and he let Tony drink what he wanted to. Darren's mother and father were both sensible drinkers. They initiated Darren into alcohol use in a gradual and sensible way.

To Tony, his parents comprised two extremes of drinking behaviour and attitude - infrequent/intolerant and heavy/tolerant - and neither are good models/attitudes for the development of sensible drinking behaviour. Darren's parents, on the other hand, were both sensible drinkers, and they provided good models and a moderating attitude towards the development of Darren's sensible drinking behaviour.

In summary, these two contrasting case studies support the findings from the meta-analyses we reported on earlier. For Tony, poor perceived parental support, poor perceived parental guidance, a heavier drinking father, and an apparently indifferent paternal attitude to his drinking were dysfunctional socialization factors in the development of Tony's drinking behaviour. Furthermore, the inconsistency between the extreme parenting style of his mother on the one hand, and the indulgent but mostly absent paternal input on the other, may also have been a contributory factor in the development of Tony's heavy drinking. In Tony's case, dysfunctional family dynamics seemed to be an initial key factor in his deviant behaviour: when he needed parental support and guidance it was lacking, inappropriate parental drinking models and social reinforcement for drinking suggested the development of a similarly inappropriate alcohol use schema, and Tony subsequently became involved with a heavy drinking peer group.

This picture contrasts with the family socialization of Darren's more sensible pattern of alcohol use. Darren perceived his family in terms of consistent socialization behaviours. He saw his family as optimal in terms of support and control - neither too low or too high - and he also reported sensible parental drinking and a moderating parental attitude to his own drinking.

These case studies, although rich in data and meaning, may not be representative of young people as a whole, and the conclusions from the case studies should be examined with a much broader sample. Also, these example case studies have not thrown any light on the family dynamics of young non-drinkers. We have suggested that non-drinkers would also have extreme family socialization behaviours, given that non-drinking is a 'deviant' adolescent social behaviour. In the next chapter we try and address these issues by reporting the results of a large general sample survey of teenagers.

Chapter 7

Family profiles of teenage drinkers

So far we have talked in some detail about family behaviours which are influential in the development of teenage drinking. Taking leads from family systems and social learning theories, we have put forward an integrated model of family socialization of teenage alcohol use, which includes non-alcohol-specific family behaviours (family process) and alcohol-specific family behaviours (family social learning). We bring to this model, from the family systems perspective, the notion that extremes of family behaviour are potentially dysfunctional, and as a consequence may lead to deviant teenage drinking behaviour. Although this idea is intuitively appealing, the evidence for extreme family behaviours being associated with problem drinking and substance use in adolescence was not very good. We have clarified this perspective by suggesting that deviant substance use behaviours are not necessarily confined to only one end or extreme of the substance use behaviour continuum. This is especially the case with adolescent alcohol use, which in most western cultures is a normal transitional behaviour. Those individuals who do not follow the normal developmental path because they do not drink, or do not begin to drink, are also behaving in a deviant fashion, albeit a generally non-harmful deviant behaviour. Thus extremes of family behaviours would be associated with extremes of drinking, and balanced family behaviours would be linked with the development of sensible and normative levels of adolescent alcohol use.

In this chapter we present the results of a large survey of teenagers from Humberside, England. Previously known as East Yorkshire, Humberside is a county in the East of England. Recent statistics indicate that the adult population of the Yorkshire and Humberside region has the highest weekly alcohol consumption of any region in England and Wales (Goddard & Ikin 1988; Goddard 1991; Regional Trends 1990). This region also had the second highest per cent increase in overall alcohol consumption in a ten year period (23% increase between 1978 and 1987). Statistics about the drinking behaviour of adolescents in this region are broadly in line with the adult pattern. Regional studies (eg. Foxcroft & Lowe 1993; Greer 1989; Sharp 1992;) have typically found higher levels of adolescent alcohol use than national studies (eg. Goddard & Ikin 1988; Marsh *et al* 1986)

In this study we examined perceived family behaviours and their relationship with self-reported drinking behaviour in a region of England noted for relatively high levels of alcohol use. The particular family behaviours we wished to measure in relation to drinking were those we have discussed in the previous chapters. These are family process influences (non-alcohol-specific) characterized by family support and control, and family social learning influences (alcohol-specific), characterized by modelling and social reinforcement. The sample (N=4369) was made up of secondary school students from over thirty randomly selected secondary schools in Humberside. Ages ranged from 11 to 18 (school years 7-13), and the sample was divided approximately equally between males and females. We state below the expected relationship with adolescent drinking for (i) school year and sex of respondent; (ii) family support and control; and (iii) modelling and social reinforcement variables. Following on from this, we describe how the family socialization variables and the drinking behaviour variables were measured, and then go on to present selected results from this study.

(i) School year and sex

For most adolescents, level of drinking increases as a function of age. Although an individual's age is an important consideration when looking at the development of drinking behaviour, it is perhaps more appropriate to consider the school year (grade) of the individual. Young people tend to regard level of maturity and age-related status more as a function of school year than their actual age. In the U.K. teenagers in year 11 (aged 15-16) are in their final year of compulsory education, and these teenagers have a higher status than those in younger year groups, and this is reflected in their level of alcohol use. Indeed, in the present study, school year was a much better predictor than age of respondent of reported drinking behaviour. In this chapter we therefore refer to the school year rather than the age of the respondent.

Alcohol use by teenagers who have left school also seems to be more a function of status than age. In 1991 we carried out a study of 430 young people aged 16-19 in youth training in Humberside (youth training is a U.K.

Government training initiative for those people unable to find employment after leaving school), and the reported alcohol use of 16-17-year-olds was closer to the 18-19-year-olds than to 16-17-year-olds still at school (school years 12 and 13). We found that male 16-17-year-olds reported drinking on average 21.4 units of alcohol in the previous week, and male 18-19-year-olds reported drinking on average 27.8 units of alcohol in the previous week. The equivalent levels for females were 8.4 and 8.9 units respectively. Goddard and Ikin (1988), in their national sample survey, found that for male 16-17-year-olds the average previous week's consumption (using a similar retrospective diary technique) was 6.5 units. The equivalent figure for females was 4.6 units. In the 18-24 age group males reported drinking on average 21.4 units and females 8 units in the previous week.

The youth trainees, with the exception of older females, clearly reported a much higher average consumption than Goddard and Ikin's national sample. Although this is in line with the overall heavier drinking in the Yorkshire and Humberside region, comparisons with national sample studies should be viewed cautiously because of different methods. Although a 7-day retrospective diary technique was used in both these studies, the participants and context varied. First, in Goddard and Ikin's study, questionnaires were administered to teenagers still at school and also to teenagers who had left school. However, in another national sample study, Marsh *et al* (1986) broke down their weekly drinkers into those still at school and those who had left school. Those who had left school were more likely to be weekly drinkers than those still at school. Secondly, the national sample participants were 'interviewed' in their own home, and parents may have been present, perhaps introducing a bias into the way questions were answered. Such contextual biases have been shown to have an important effect on the actual answers respondents give (Davies & Baker 1987).

Nevertheless, the status associated with having left school and entered the job market seems to be a more important factor for drinking behaviour than the actual age of the individual. This important point was noted by Parker (1974, p.125) in his sociological study of down-town adolescents:

> "In short, no-one really saw under-age drinking as wrong in itself. If you were old enough to work, you were old enough to drink and spend your earnings as you wished."

Although we might expect some sex differences in alcohol use if adult patterns are anything to go by, there are two considerations which might lead us to modify this expectation. Firstly, sex differences in adult alcohol use are not as marked as they once were, and secondly, younger adolescent patterns of alcohol use are not as marked by sex differences as older adolescent and adult patterns of alcohol use.

Wilsnack and Wilsnack (1978) reviewed recent trends in male and female drinking and pointed to the reduction in differential alcohol use between the sexes, saying that this was associated with an increase in the drinking behaviour of women rather than a decrease by men. According to Wilsnack and Wilsnack (1979) this change in alcohol use by women is a function of the change in sex roles in recent times, and sex roles influence how young people drink in a variety of ways:

- by creating different opportunities for male and female teenagers to drink
- by affirming norms that obligate male and female teenagers to behave differently towards alcohol
- by arousing different needs and motives for using alcohol
- by making drinking behaviour a way to symbolize the sex roles that male and female teenagers try to adopt

By rejecting traditional models of femininity, women nowadays are much more likely to adopt sex role behaviour which has traditionally been regarded as male behaviour. In terms of teenage alcohol use, there are now equal opportunities for male and female teenagers to drink. Indeed, it is probable that females have more opportunities to drink outside of parental influence because of their earlier pubertal development and ability to look older than they actually are, enabling them to 'cheat' the drinking age laws earlier than males of a similar age. Also, because females reach puberty earlier than males, differential alcohol toxicity between males and females due to physiological differences may be less marked. Wechsler and McFadden (1976) described sex differences in alcohol use as a disappearing phenomenon when they found few consistent sex differences in patterns of alcohol use in a study of teenage drinking in two communities in the United States. The differences which were found were largely confined to beer drinking by students aged 12-13 (males were more likely to be beer drinkers). Also, in the 14-17 age group, females drank more wine and spirits than males (but no sex differences in beer drinking were found). In a more recent study with over 1500 11-16-year-old school pupils in Humberside, U.K., Sharp (1992) found that sex of respondent was not a significant predictor of alcohol use in a multiple regression which also included school year, age of first drinking experiences, drinking behaviour of significant others, reasons for drinking, and expectancies about the effects of drinking.

However, although sex differences in alcohol use may be narrowing, as we indicated in chapter 2 the bulk of the research evidence still points to some sex differences in teenage drinking. There are several possible reasons for this. Sex roles still differ quite markedly in some respects and heavier drinking norms, especially in older teenage groups, are predominantly male characteristics. There is a sense of bravado and machismo about going out and getting drunk with a group of friends, and this is a frequent behaviour of some young males in the U.K. Attitudes towards female drinking are quite different. From quite a young age, drunken females are viewed more negatively than drunken males. Jahoda and Crammond (1972) reported in their study of 6-10-year-olds that both boys and girls had a more negative attitude to women drinkers, and this finding has been replicated more recently by Fossey (1993).

The fact that males are able to tolerate more alcohol than females may also contribute to the maintenance of sex differences in alcohol use. Indeed it is probable that sex differences in alcohol use will not decrease beyond the limits of differential alcohol toxicity. Thus it is not the absolute level of alcohol consumption we should consider when comparing male and female drinking, but the level of consumption adjusted for differential alcohol toxicity. In the present study we use a measure of teenage alcohol use which attempts to adjust for sex differences in sensible and heavy drinking by drawing on recommended sensible drinking limits for males and females put forward by the Royal College of Physicians (1987).

One possible consequence of this 'ceiling effect' for female alcohol use relative to male use, brought about by sex role and physiological differences, is that females may feel discriminated against in their alcohol use. An interesting thought is that females may turn to other, less discriminated substances, as a reaction to the discrimination they face with alcohol. This may be one reason why young females are more likely to be smokers than young males - a trend which seems to be growing (Lader & Matheson 1991; Smyth & Browne 1992). Females who are heavier drinkers are stereotypically portrayed negatively, whereas males who are heavier drinkers may be stereotypically portrayed positively. Thus, for females, cigarettes may offer an alternative substance which is not restricted socially or physically in the same way that alcohol is. Smoking by younger females could be an important, although potentially harmful, 'equal opportunity' substance use strategy.

In this study we expected teenagers in older year groups to be heavier drinkers. Also, given the recent decrease in sex differences in drinking behaviour, and that we were using a measure of alcohol use which adjusted for differential alcohol toxicity between males and females, we expected that within each school year group any sex differences would be relatively small.

(ii) Family support and control

The results of the meta-analysis of recent research which we presented in chapter 5 suggest that low support and low control would be linked with higher alcohol use, and that high support and high control would be related to lower alcohol use. Therefore, in the present study we expected to find a similar pattern of results in the relationship of the family process variables support and control with self-reported teenage drinking. Specifically, we predicted that moderate levels of perceived support and control would be important for the socialization of sensible teenage drinking. However, we were also aware of the study by Barnes *et al* (1986), in which, as we reported in chapter 5, low and high control were linked with problem drinking. Although this curvilinear pattern was not statistically significant in the Barnes small sample study, it was possible that this pattern would be significant with a larger sample, as Barnes *et al* (1986) concluded. But why should high control be linked with problem or heavier drinking? Remember that in chapter 5 we adopted a family systems perspective for the family dimensions of support and control, in which extremes of behaviour are viewed as dysfunctional. Although we suggested that high support and high control might be linked with non-drinking, it is also possible that strict family control might lead to rejection of parental authority by the teenager and the subsequent adoption of heavier drinking. This relationship might possibly be typical of inconsistent family behaviours which involve, for example, strict control but low support, and social learning influences which encourage the teenager to drink.

However, the present study differed from the earlier Barnes *et al* study in several respects. Firstly, the questions used by Barnes and her colleagues to measure control primarily addressed control attempts within the family rather than control achieved. In our study the questions we used to assess level of control primarily reflect the *actual* control environment rather than the attempted control environment. Secondly, the outcome criterion used by Barnes *et al* was problem drinking rather than any drinking behaviour as in the present study. Also, in the earlier study, subjects were interviewed in their own homes whereas, in the present study, respondents completed an anonymous and confidential questionnaire at school.

(iii) family modelling and social reinforcement

Early in the previous chapter we reviewed the evidence for the relationship between teenage drinking and family social learning influences. This led us to predict that individuals who reported that their family drank more frequently would also report higher alcohol use, and similarly that those who said their parents approved of their drinking would drink more. However, in pre-study discussions and pilot studies carried out with young people in Humberside, we found that parental approval of their offspring's drinking could take different forms.

Parents may approve of their teenager drinking in a variety of ways. If parents permit their teenager to drink only on special occasions and only with parental supervision, then this is a form of prescriptive approval. Also, teenagers may report that their parents do not mind them drinking as long as they drink sensibly and behave sensibly. This is a form of authoritative approval. On the other hand, if teenagers report that their parents are not bothered or do not care about their offspring's drinking then this suggests parental indifference. Parental indifference is regarded by teenagers as tacit approval of their alcohol use, in that no drinking restrictions whatsoever are applied. Parental indifference is thus one extreme of parental attitude towards offspring's drinking, and the other is disapproval. Of course, parental attitudes probably vary as a function of the age (school year) of the respondent. In the socialization of alcohol use parental attitudes may be initially more prescriptive but moderate as the teenager matures.

From this basis we made the prediction that teenagers who reported parental indifference towards their offspring's alcohol use would drink more, because no restrictions or suitable guidance as to what constitutes sensible or appropriate alcohol use would be available from parents. Teenagers who reported parents with a moderating attitude to alcohol use would have such guidance and therefore we expected these individuals to be sensible drinkers. We expected parental disapproval to be linked with lower alcohol use, especially for the younger respondents. It is possible that a disapproving parental attitude may be linked with heavier drinking if the teenager is rebelling against family values, but this would probably be more apparent in older age groups, when the individual is more autonomous and peer groups may have more influence. Supporting this, we have previously found some evidence for a curvilinear relationship between parental attitude and older teenage heavy drinking. In the study of youth trainees we mentioned earlier (Foxcroft & Lowe 1993), over a third of those teenagers who reported parental disapproval were heavy drinkers; similarly, over a third of those teenagers who reported parental indifference were heavy drinkers; whereas less than a quarter of respondents who reported a moderating parental attitude were heavy drinkers.

Extremes of behaviour

In the general sample of young English adolescents in this study we were especially interested in how extreme forms of family behaviour might link with extremes of drinking behaviour, or conversely, how moderate family behaviours might relate to sensible and moderate teenage drinking. One of the difficulties involved in looking at extremes of behaviour is that the prevalence of such extreme behaviours in the general population is relatively low. For example, we have already mentioned that most teenagers drink sensibly. Those who do not drink or those who drink heavily (i.e. extremes of drinking behaviour) are in the minority. Similarly, most teenagers do not go through an identity crisis which involves rejection of family links and family identity. Most teenagers tend to report satisfactory family relationships throughout adolescence, as we indicated in chapter 5.

In the previous chapter we used a qualitative case study approach to examine extremes of behaviour. This is one accepted method of analysing and presenting information and data which are not common in the general population (eg. individuals with a family history and drinking history like Tony). Alternatively, one could use selective sampling, perhaps from adolescents in treatment, but these methods have a drawback because of the probable change in perception/behaviour brought about by entering the counselling or treatment process. Another method is to obtain as large a sample as possible from the general population, so that those few individuals who do perceive extremes of family behaviour, or who do report extremes of drinking behaviour, are randomly selected and included in the sample.

For example, if we were to ask 100 teenagers about their family life, probably only a handful would report extremes of support and control, family drinking and parental attitude. Furthermore, it is likely that even fewer would report extremes of behaviour which were inconsistent with each other, such as heavy parental drinking but parents who disapprove of their teenager's drinking. This is especially so with the socialization of alcohol use. As we have emphasized throughout this book, drinking alcohol is positively regarded by most adults and is also viewed as a normal adolescent developmental behaviour. Parents therefore are more likely to be consistent in their behaviour and attitude towards this accepted and condoned teenage behaviour. The same could not be said for cigarette use. Regular smoking is almost universally perceived as a damaging activity, and even though parents may smoke, it is more likely that they would discourage their offspring from starting to smoke cigarettes - a "do as I say and not as I do" attitude. We will return to this point in the concluding chapter, when we discuss family socialization theory and other substance use behaviours. In the present study we went some way towards addressing the problem of small proportions of individuals with extreme behaviours by questioning over 4000 young teenagers.

Thirty-two schools from throughout Humberside took part in the study. All the schools were chosen at random and represented a broad cross-section of all schools in the region. Respondents were drawn from each year group (from years 7 to 13; ages 11 to 18) although the focus was on those students in years 7 to 11 (ages 11 to 16). Participants completeted an anonymous and confidential Adolescent Drinking and Family Life Questionnaire (ADFLQ), which included a retrospective 7-day drinking diary, questions about usual alcohol consumption, frequency of own, parental and older sibling's (if applicable) drinking, questions about supportive and controlling family behaviours, and also parental attitude to the respondent's alcohol use.

Measuring drinking behaviour

In the present study, and in much of the research into adolescent drinking behaviour, adolescents' self-reports are relied on as an indicator of actual drinking behaviour. Such self-reports are seen, at the least, as being reasonably valid. In fact, such self-reports go beyond being just an indicator of actual drinking behaviour: they also reflect each individual's attitude to alcohol. As such, self-reports can comprise elements of social, cultural and stereotypical attributions and aspirations regarding alcohol use. For example, a young person who reported drinking in excess of the recommended safe levels, but actually did not, may perceive such levels of alcohol use as desirable. Thus self-reports may reflect actual or intended drinking behaviour and, viewed in this way, provide information about each individual's alcohol use schema.

For analysis of the data our aim was to use a measure of alcohol use which encompassed several separate but overlapping characteristics of drinking behaviour. One measure often used in alcohol research is the retrospective drinking diary - typically over a one-week period. This involves each respondent indicating what and how much they have drunk for each day of the last seven days. This information is then used to calculate how many units of alcohol that individual has consumed in the previous week. One unit of alcohol is approximately equal to one half pint of normal strength beer, one glass of wine or one measure of spirits. Strictly speaking, one unit is 10 millilitres of pure alcohol.

Recommended sensible, moderate and heavy (dangerous) levels of alcohol use are based on the number of units of alcohol consumed by a person over a one week period (Royal College of Physicians 1987). These limits are, for *adults*, depicted in Table 7.1(a). In the present study, however, the majority of respondents (97 per cent) were aged between 11 and 16 and were at varying stages of physical and psychological (im)maturity. The recommended sensible limits for adult drinkers are probably not appropriate for this younger and less mature age group. In this study we have therefore redefined these recommended drinking limits for this younger age group (Table 7.1(b)). Of course these are arbitrary criteria. Sensible and safe teenage drinking levels should be linked to age and physical and psychological maturity. These factors vary considerably from pre-adolescents to young adults. As such, we do not suggest that the sensible drinking levels we have applied here be extended beyond this study and applied generally. Their purpose is merely to facilitate comparison in the present study between levels of reported drinking in the previous seven days.

The 7-day retrospective drinking diary, however, provides only a snapshot of each individual's drinking behaviour, and does not describe their overall, long-term pattern of alcohol use (although it may approximate it). Yet the recommended levels of sensible alcohol use put forward by the Royal

College of Physicians (1987) apply to average drinking behaviour over a period of time. Therefore, in this study we also asked each individual how often they drank, and also how much they usually consumed. This quantity/frequency information is another often used method of measuring drinking behaviour, and gives a picture of drinking patterns over time. Together with previous week's consumption, this information combined to give a composite measure of drinking behaviour which incorporated both of the more usual and useful measures of alcohol use - a Q/F index *and* a 7-day drinking history.

(a) adult levels	Drinking behaviour	(b) teenage levels
no units	*nil*	no units
females 1-14 units males 1-21 units	*sensible*	females 1- 7 units males 1-11 units
females 15-25 units males 22-35 units	*moderate*	females 8-14 units males 12-21 units
females 26-35 units males 36-50 units	*heavy*	females 15-25 units males 22-35 units
females over 36 units males over 50 units	*very heavy*	females over 25 units males over 35 units

Table 7.1: Drinking behaviour according to weekly consumption for adult drinkers (R.C.P. recommendations); and teenage drinkers (this study)

Table 7.2 shows how individuals in the present study drank according to the 7-day diary, frequency, and usual consumption criteria. We have also in this study conceptualized usual level of consumption in a new way (see Table 7.2 and chapter 3). Usually researchers try and gain some measure of number of drinks on each drinking occasion. However, there are notable differences in how a given quantity of alcohol affects different individuals. Important factors in this respect are sex, body mass and drinking experience. We addressed this problem by asking each individual what effect they usually liked to achieve from alcohol - i.e. whether they usually drink enough to get merry or drunk (or only have one or two drinks, a few sips, or do not usually drink at all). By asking about usual level of consumption in this way we overcame the difficulty of differential alcohol toxicity, and also gained a deeper qualitative insight into each individual's usual drinking outcome.

We can also see in Table 7.2 that the proportions of males and females reporting each drinking behaviour were very similar, and in fact there were no significant sex differences in previous week's drinking, frequency of drinking, or in usual level of consumption. As we suggested earlier, this shows that male and female patterns of alcohol use were very similar, given the differential alcohol toxicity between males and females.

Drinking behaviour	n	%	n	%
	M		F	
last 7 days				
0 nil	1035	46	1025	49
1 sensible	864	38	731	35
2 moderate	183	8	183	9
3 heavy	86	4	91	4
4 very heavy	95	4	76	4
frequency				
0 do not drink	305	14	300	14
1 every few months; special occasions	1104	50	1109	53
2 few times a month	618	28	548	26
3 more than once a week	198	9	135	7
usual consumption				
0 do not drink	291	13	281	13
1 few sips	479	21	512	24
2 one or two drinks	879	39	742	35
3 enough to get merry	385	17	393	19
4 enough to get drunk	219	10	173	8

Table 7.2: Drinking behaviour - secondary school students

There are a couple of methodological points worth mentioning. We can see that there was a small difference (1 per cent of the sample) in the number of people who said that they did not drink in answer to the frequency of drinking and the usual consumption questions. This may reflect a lack of consistency, but more likely this slight response difference was due to the options available when answering the question. Some people who very occasionally have a few sips of alcohol, for example at Christmas, when choosing between 'do not drink' and 'drink every few months' are likely to prefer the 'do not drink' option. However, they would be likely to prefer the 'drink a few sips' option rather than the 'do not drink' option when reporting their usual consumption. This is known as a *comparison shift* in questionnaire responses.

We mentioned above that we combined these three separate but overlapping alcohol use measures - 7-day diary, frequency and quantity of use - into one composite drinking behaviour variable. This was done simply by summing each individual's response or score on the three measured variables to give a combined drinker score, which ranged from 0 to 11. For example, an individual with a drinker score of 0 would be a non-drinker; a person with a low drinker score might have consumed no alcohol in the past seven days, drink only on special occasions, and only have a few sips each time (drinker score of 2). A heavy drinker (high drinker score) would perhaps have consumed 12 units of alcohol in the past seven days, drink more than once a week, and usually drink enough to get drunk (drinker score of 9).

Measuring family behaviour

Family process

There are numerous ways of looking at family process behaviours. For example, one could try and gain an overall picture of family functioning from the perspective of each member of the family; or, some researchers have employed participant observation techniques to study families; or alternatively, one could focus on one individual and assess their perception of family life. This is an important approach if one is interested in the consequences of family life for that individual. In this study we were looking at the self-reported drinking behaviour of adolescents, and it was therefore a logical step in this study to look at an adolescent's perception of his or her family. This approach though is one which has not received much attention, as Amato (1990, p.614) points out:

> "...relatively little attention has been devoted to how children perceive parent-child relations. Instead, the dimensions of support and control have largely been formulated by researchers and theorists and 'imposed' on family interaction as a way of organizing observations...a pertinent question is whether or not children themselves experience and interpret the family environment in such a fashion."

Amato goes on to report that, for his sample of children, perceptions were indeed organized into two broad dimensions - support and control. But if perceived support and control can be considered salient constructs, a relevant question is how to assess or measure these dimensions. The work that has been carried out in this area has tended to rely on questionnaire scales whose properties have been shown to vary according to the nature of the sample. The Family Environment Scale (FES) (Moos & Moos 1986) is probably the most used and most cited family self-report measure in the U.S.A. and U.K. Fowler (1981) factor analysed the FES subscale items and elicited the two constructs support and control, but Oliver *et al* (1988), in a study which superceded Fowler's report, found that the resultant factors of the FES were specific to the heterogeneity v homogeneity of the sample and also the age of the sample. Furthermore, family functioning has been shown to vary cross-culturally. For example, Devereux (1970) reported on the different normative family socialization behaviours between England, Germany, and the U.S.A. This has no doubt contributed to the ongoing debate about the FES and its measurement properties and underlying constructs (Roosa and Beals 1990; Moos 1990; Waldron *et al* 1990). In the U.K., Sloper *et al* (1988) reported FES subscale internal reliabilities (α) which were all lower than those reported in the FES handbook, and the majority were less than 0.70; several considerably so.

Our aim in the present study was to examine perception of family process in a regional sample of adolescents in the U.K. As outlined above, the FES is arguably not suitable for this task. Therefore we constructed an adolescent family functioning questionnaire, which comprised items purporting to measure aspects of support and control. These items were taken from an item and subscale pool of two established family functioning questionnaires, the FES and the Bloom Family Functioning Scales (Bloom 1985), the latter measure itself derived from several family assessment scales (including FACES and the FES). Both the FES and the Bloom scales describe Relationship (support) and System Maintenance (control) meta-concepts, each made up of several subscales. For example, the FES subscales cohesion, expressiveness and conflict make up the Relationship dimension, and the subscales control and organization make up the System Maintenance dimension. Additionally, we also included in the questionnaire several items from FES subscales other than those mentioned above. This was because Waldron *et al* (1990) report a different factor structure for the FES, one which included items from other subscales of the FES loading on support and control factors.

We undertook exploratory factor analysis of the questionnaire responses in a large pilot study (N=430), with the intention of elucidating two aspects: first, items loading onto subscale factors; and secondly, determining whether the dimensions of support and control would be revealed as salient constructs. The factor analysis proved successful in both these respects, and we derived both a useful support scale and a useful control scale for use in the main study. The family support measure was made up of 20 separate items, with a high internal consistency in the present study ($\alpha=0.86$), and the control scale comprised 15 items (with $\alpha=0.73$). In another preliminary study (N=99), we also found high test-retest reliabilities for support and control (r=0.95 and r=0.86 respectively).

Each questionnaire item consisted of a statement about family life, and respondents indicated whether they 'strongly disagreed', 'disagreed', 'agreed' or 'strongly agreed' with each statement, scored 1-4 respectively. Examples of family support questionnaire items are: *'We really get along well with each other'*; *'We hardly ever fight in my family'*; *'We don't tell each other about our personal problems'*; *'My family always does things together'*; and *'In my family we really help and support one another'*. The following are examples of the control scale items: *'There is strict punishment for anyone breaking the rules in my family'*; *'There are set ways of doing things at home'*; *'In my family you can get away with almost anything'*; *'There are very few rules in my family'*; and *'In my family we are severely punished for anything we do wrong'*.

For the purpose of analysis we split the support and control scores into three groups. The potential range of the support scores was from a score of 20 to a score of 80, and we divided this into five equal categories (20-32, 33-44, 45-56, 57-68, and 69-80), labelled very low, low, moderate, high and very high support respectively. The potential range of the control scores was from a score of 15 to a score of 60, which was also divided into five equal categories (15-24, 25-33, 34-42, 43-51 and 52-60), labelled very low, low, moderate, high and very high control respectively. Subsequently, for both support and control, the two low groups were collapsed together as were the two high groups because of small numbers of respondents reporting very low or very high support and control. In the final analysis we therefore used three categories or levels for both support and control, labelled low, moderate and high.

Family social learning

In measuring non-alcohol related family influences (family process), we used a broad range of questions about family life to assess the broad range of non-alcohol-related family behaviours. On the other hand, with alcohol-specific family behaviours, we asked much more specific and to the point questions. Alcohol-specific social reinforcement was assessed simply as the reported attitude of parents towards their teenage son or daughter drinking alcohol. This scale ranged from parental disapproval through two moderating categories - drink only with parental permission and drink only if it is sensible - to parental indifference to their teenager's drinking. In the final analysis we used three discrete levels of parental attitude - disapproval, moderating (the two mid-categories combined) and indifference.

Level of family drinking, for this analysis, was measured as a function of each parent's (and closest older sibling's if applicable) alcohol use as reported by the respondent. Level of family drinking was classified into three groups - non-drinkers, drink less than once a week, and drink more than once a week. We were unable to probe parental drinking further in the questionnaire because of reservations by school health education advisers about the sensitivity of this issue.

If parents were both non-drinkers, then family drinking was nil. If both parents drank regularly (more than once a week) then level of family drinking was also regular. If both parents drank less often (less than once a week) then family drinking was also classified as less than once a week. In cases where each parent had a different reported drinking pattern, then in this analysis we took the average drinking behaviour of both parents. For example, if one did not drink and the other drank regularly, then overall family drinking was classified as the combination of each parent's drinking - i.e. the composite family drinking level was the middle group (labelled as 'less than once a week').

To summarize, we had a dependent variable which was a composite score of drinking behaviour, based on the respondent's self-reported alcohol consumption in the last seven days, frequency of drinking and usual alcohol consumption. Six independent variables are reported here. School year and sex of the respondent were demographic variables; family support and control were family process variables; and family drinking and parental attitude were family social learning variables. Sex had two levels or categories (males and females) and the other independent variables had three levels (eg. low, moderate and high).

Results

For the whole sample (N=4369), the drinker score was approximately normally distributed. Most teenagers had a mid-range drinker score, and although there were a number of non-drinkers, which did produce a slight bi-modal distribution, this was not sufficient to compromise the statistical analysis.

The sample was split fairly evenly between the sexes, just over half the respondents were male (52 per cent). Most respondents were in school years 9 and 10 (44 per cent), with just over a quarter of the sample in each of the school year groups 7-8 and 11-13.

Most respondents reported moderate levels of perceived family support and perceived family control. One in 10 respondents were classified as low perceived family support, and 1 in 8 as low perceived family control. Just over half were classified as moderate support, and just over two-thirds as moderate control. The remainder were classed as high support and high control (37 per cent and 17 per cent respectively).

Most respondents reported moderate parental drinking behaviour. Only 1 in 16 respondents reported that neither parent (or older sibling if applicable) drank, and 1 in 5 reported that both mother and father drank more than once a week. The rest (72 per cent) were classified as mid-range (composite family drinking of less than once a week).

Four out of five respondents reported that their parents held a moderating attitude towards their drinking. One out of every six reported parental disapproval towards their actual or potential drinking, and very few (less than 3 per cent) reported parental indifference.

Analysis of Variance (ANOVA)

Sex of respondent and school year were significant independent factors in the ANOVA with drinker score as the dependent variable. The two family process variables, support and control, were also significant, as were the two family social learning variables, family drinking and parental attitude.

Variable	S.S.	d.f.	F ratio	probability
Sex	27.09	1	6.54	0.01
School year	2106.26	2	254.39	<0.0001
Support	395.17	2	47.73	<0.0001
Control	226.31	2	27.33	<0.0001
Parental attitude	1203.96	2	145.41	<0.0001
Family drinking	885.97	2	107.01	<0.0001

Table 7.3: ANOVA of drinker score and family socialization factors

The ANOVA results are outlined in Table 7.3 above, and are elaborated on in sub-sections (i) through (iii) below. In the ANOVA, parental attitude was the most important variable. Family process variables were less important, and sex differences were significant, but only slight. A large general sample was taken so that a good number of respondents with more extreme behaviours could be included, but the size of the sample should be taken into account when interpreting significance levels. Some two-way interactions were significant at $p<0.05$, but on examination these interactions were very slight, and are thus not commented on in detail. In fact the most important finding in this present study of a large general sample is the additive nature of these family factors in the relationship with drinking behaviour. These are detailed in sub-section (iv) below.

(i) School year and sex

Respondents in older year groups reported drinking significantly more than those in younger year groups, as expected (Figure 7.1). After adjusting for differential alcohol toxicity between males and females, we can also see that males drank more than females in years 7-8, that this sex difference levels out in years 9-10, and that males in years 11-13 also report drinking slightly more than females. However, the sex differences in all year groups are only minor. A more important factor is the school year of the respondent. The mean drinker score[1] ranged from just over 2 (year 7-8 females) to just over 5 (year 11-13 males). Therefore, male and female respondents from all year groups reported, on average, sensible levels of alcohol use.

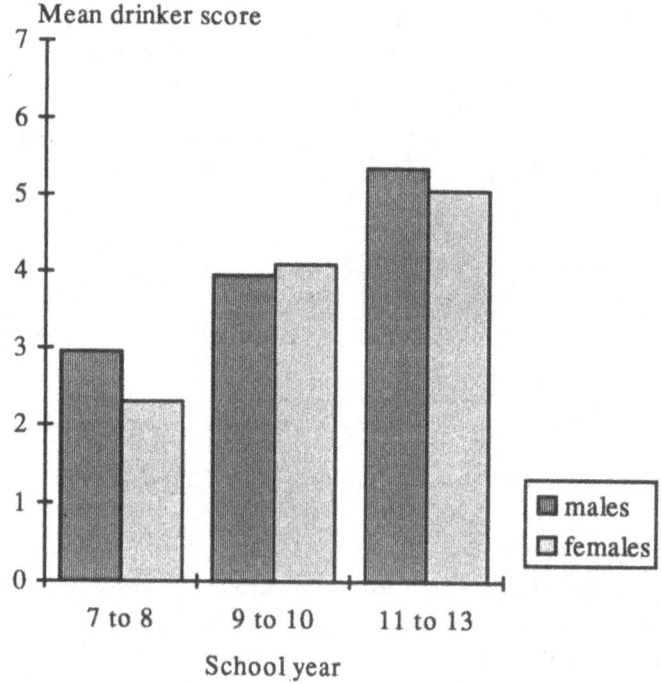

Figure 7.1: Mean drinker score : school year and sex

---

[1] Drinker score: a composite measure of 7-day diary, frequency and usual consumption variables (see p.115).

(ii) Family support and control

Figure 7.2 shows that those individuals who perceived low support and low control had the highest mean drinker score. Alternatively, high support and high control were linked with the lowest mean drinker score. Moreover, the additive nature of support and control in relation to teenage drinking seems to be especially important. There is also a slight ordinal interaction between support and control, with low control a particularly salient influence. In the ANOVA this interaction was significant at the 1% level (F=3.23, df=4, p=0.01).

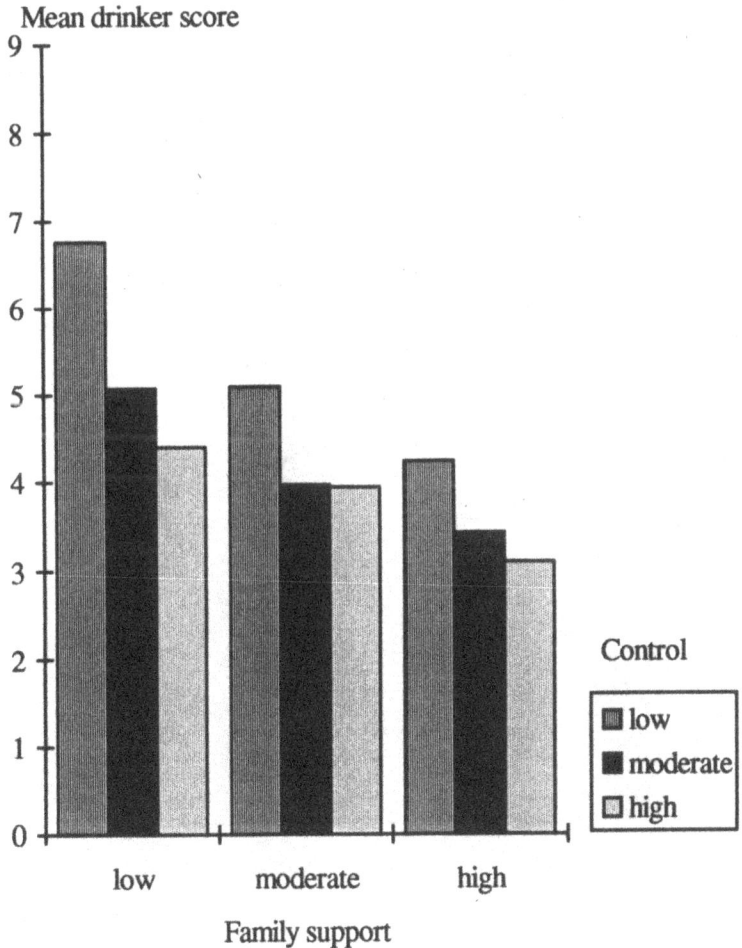

Figure 7.2: Mean drinker score: family support and control

(iii) Parental attitude and family drinking

Respondents who reported non-drinking parents and parental disapproval of their own drinking had the lowest mean drinker score (Figure 7.3). Those whose parents disapproved of their teenager's drinking and whose parents drank more than once a week had the highest mean drinker score (but there were only five respondents who reported both these parental behaviours). Other individuals who also had a high mean drinker score were those whose parents were not bothered about their teenager's drinking and who also drank more than once a week. As we suggested earlier, those five individuals with the highest mean drinker score might have been particularly influenced by the inconsistency in parental messages. This disordinal interaction was significant in the ANOVA at the 1% level ($F=3.87$, $df=4$, $p<0.01$).

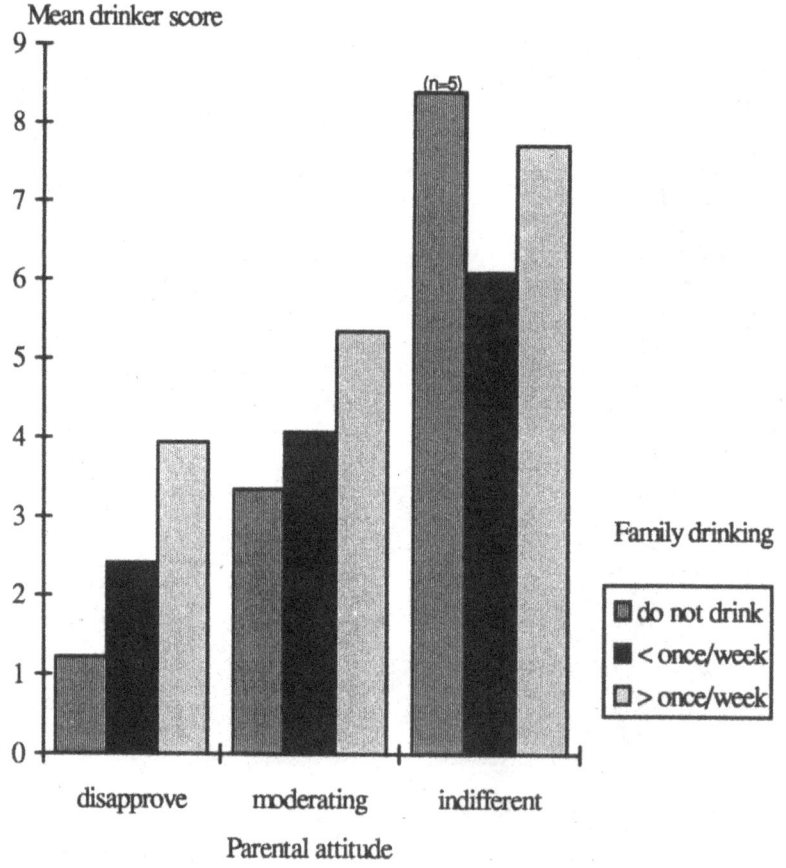

Figure 7.3: Mean drinker score: parental attitude and family drinking

The results from sub-sections (ii) and (iii) clearly point to the importance of family socialization behaviours, incorporating family process and family social learning factors, for teenage drinking behaviour. As suggested by the magnitude of the F-ratios (Table 7.3) family social learning factors, particularly social reinforcement (parental attitude), were stronger statistical predictors of drinking behaviour. Bearing in mind the cross-sectional limitations of this study, these factors might be more important factors in the family socialization of drinking behaviour than the family process factors support and control. Thus, in this general population sample, alcohol-specific family behaviours were more directly related to drinking behaviour than non-alcohol-specific family behaviours. This pattern, however, may only be a function of the social acceptability of alcohol. With less socially acceptable substances (eg. cigarettes; solvents) the role of parental models and parental social reinforcement may be less salient an influence than levels of family support and control.

But one must not disregard the factors which seem less influential. There is no family situation in which family process does not exist as a socialization influence. It is the combined effect of all the family socialization influences which is important in the socialization of children and teenagers.

(iv) Selected family profiles

To illustrate the additive nature of the four family socialization factors we have looked at in this study (support, control, family models and parental attitude), we examined the drinking behaviour of seven groups of respondents with distinct family profiles. By family profile we mean that particular set of family behaviours specified by combination of the levels of each specific family socialization behaviour. In this study we classified each family socialization variable into three discrete levels - eg. low, moderate or high. With the four family socialization factors this gives a possibility of 4^3, or 64 separate family profiles. Of these, we have selected seven distinctive family profiles, and these are described in Table 7.4 below. Bearing in mind the low level of reported inconsistency in perceived family behaviours, we have highlighted seven distinct family profiles which show some consistency in family socialization patterns. These seven family profiles were chosen to reflect a range of different perceived family socialization environments, from consistent socialization of non-drinking to consistent socialization of heavier drinking.

Key	Parental attitude	Family drinking	Family support	Family control
(a)	disapprove	do not	high	high
(b)	disapprove	do not	moderate	moderate
(c)	moderating	< once/week	high	high
(d)	moderating	< once/week	moderate	moderate
(e)	moderating	< once/week	low	low
(f)	indifferent	> once/week	moderate	moderate
(g)	indifferent	> once/week	low	low

Table 7.4: Seven distinct family profiles

For the adolescents in the study the relationship between family behaviours and drinking behaviour is clear (Figure 7.4). Patterns of family behaviour which socialize a teenager towards non-drinking (eg. family profile (a)) were clearly linked to very low adolescent alcohol use. On the other hand, patterns of family behaviour which socialize an individual towards heavier drinking (eg. family profile (g)) were clearly linked with heavy adolescent drinking. The family behaviours which combine to socialize teenagers towards sensible alcohol use are those which are characterized by moderate family process and moderate family social learning influences. In Figure 7.4 family profile (d) - a moderating parental attitude, family drinks less than once a week, moderate family support and moderate family control - is linked with a mean drinker score that suggests sensible alcohol use.

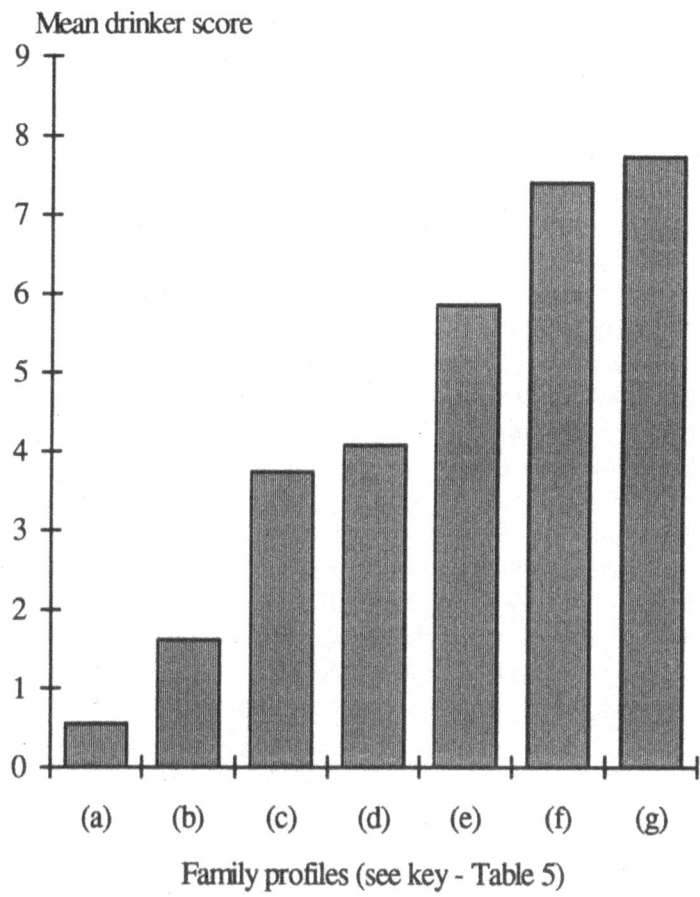

Figure 7.4: Mean drinker score: selected family profiles

Consistent and inconsistent behaviours

In the last chapter we mentioned that families may provide inconsistent as well as consistent socialization of alcohol use. Let us now return to that discussion. Consistent family socializaton, we said, is a pattern or family profile of complementary behaviours. For example, a family profile of complementary socialization towards non-drinking would be parental non-drinking and disapproving parents, with high family support and control (see Figure 7.4, family profile (a) above). We suggested that the optimal pattern of family socialization towards sensible drinking was one of functional consistency, namely complementary and moderate levels of family behaviour - moderate parental drinking and a moderating parental attitude, and moderate levels of support and control (see Figure 7.4, family profile (d) above).

In the previous chapter we suggested that inconsistent or uncomplementary patterns might pose a risk for deviant drinking behaviour because of disjunctive messages and meta-messages between parent-child socialization behaviours. If this is so, such disjunctive behaviours would manifest as disordinal interactions when linked with teenage alcohol use. If there were no interactions then family socialization factors would contribute independently and additively - regardless of consistency or inconsistency.

The present results primarily support the latter picture. On the whole there was a pattern of additivity of effect. However, in Figure 7.2 we saw that those teenagers who perceived low support and low control were especially likely to be heavier drinkers. In an ordinal interaction, the combination of these two family process factors slightly potentiated the risk for heavier alcohol use. Figure 7.3 also reveals an interesting, if slight, disordinal interaction effect. Here we can see that those few individuals (n=5) who reported that their parents did not drink but had an indifferent attitude were, on average, the heaviest drinkers. However, the low number of respondents in this category precludes any inferences being drawn. As we said earlier, it was not possible to test/profile more elaborate inconsistencies because few respondents reported such unusual comninations of family behaviours.

Conclusions

In this chapter we have presented results from a large survey of teenagers in Humberside, England. Both family process and family social learning were significant family influences. The four family socialization behaviours investigated in this study were on the whole independently and additively related to teenage drinking. Parental attitude was the most salient socialization factor in the present study, according to the statistical analysis. Whether teenagers said their parents disapproved, were moderating towards, or were indifferent towards their offspring's alcohol use was quite markedly related to their offspring's reported drinking behaviour.

The results from this quantitative study support the earlier predictions we made about family socialization behaviours and teenage drinking. Importantly, we have found that extreme family socialization behaviours are linked with adolescent low and non-drinking, as well as heavier drinking. Furthermore, these results are in line with the conclusions we drew from the qualitative analysis of the case studies in the previous chapter. These separate studies have enabled us to test the family socialization model we specified earlier, but there are some questions which still need to be addressed. We pointed earlier to the role of inconsistencies in family behaviours. These need to be assessed more fully on two levels. Firstly, inconsistencies between different family members and sub-systems in their socialization behaviours should be considered. From the case studies we reported the potential problem of conflicting family messages (eg. father is a heavy drinker, mother a non-drinker; father is indifferent, mother disapproves of offspring drinking). These inconsistent family behaviours may be particularly important for the many individuals who are offspring of a problem drinking parent. It may be that these adolescents would identify with the parent whose behaviour more nearly matches their own desires, or with whom they have the better relationship.

Secondly, research is needed which supplements the present results in terms of inconsistencies between distinct family socialization behaviours. The low number of respondents in some of the extreme categories and combinations of the family socialization factors was one potential limitation to the generalizability of the present results. One way round this would have been to redefine the cut-off points for the extreme behaviours, increasing the number of respondents labelled as *low* or *high*, thus making the data more amenable to statistical analysis. However, although statistically attractive this option would have been theoretically inappropriate. A main aim of this research was to assess how extremes of perceived family behaviour relate to extremes of reported drinking. If we had redefined these extremes of behaviour the ability of the analysis to address the theory would have been compromised. Having said this, by taking a large sample we obtained in most instances a useful number of respondents who reported extremes of behaviour. The large sample and the general robustness of ANOVA suggest that the results do provide a reasonable basis on which to draw inferences.

In the next two chapters we broaden our perspective from one which looked at family socialization, incorporating family process and family social learning, to look at how the use and definition of space within the home and home environment might influence teenage drinking behaviour. In this sense, the social geography of the home offers a perspective on adolescent alcohol and substance use which both complements and supplements that covered in the chapters so far. The multi-factorial nature of adolescent drinking and family life needs to be taken into consideration. So far, we have seen how socialization factors play a role in the development of alcohol use and misuse. We next turn our attention to the social geography of the home before examining possible connections between domestic space, modes of control, and problem drinking.

SECTION 3:

Domestic Space and Family Dynamics

So far, patterns of teenage drinking have been described and set within the family context. We have argued that socialization in the family is an important influence on adolescent behaviour and an analysis of family systems and family processes serves to identify associations between teenage drinking and aspects of family relationships, particularly parental attitudes.

In the next section, we broaden the contextual basis of the study to include the home as a physical space, a place to which family members relate. Thus, we review research on the home by environmental psychologists, geographers and anthropologists and develop a schema for understanding the family's relationship to domestic space. This involves combining models of family systems and a model of spatial organization in the home. The family-space schema is then used to explore the childhood and adolescent experience of adult problem drinkers with a view to identifying factors in their home life which may have contributed to their drinking behaviour. In moving from section 2 to section 3, there is also a shift in method, from a primarily quantitative to a more qualitative assessment of reported experiences of the home and family.

Chapter 8

Home environments

In an attempt to understand the drinking patterns of teenagers, it may be illuminating to examine a number of environments - the principal locales associated with socialization, including the home, the school, and those places where adolescents associate with their peer group. However, as we implied in the preceding account of family dynamics, the home is arguably the most important environment because it is where children spend most of their time in long-term relationships with adults and, often, with other children. It is clear that the nature of these relationships is quite variable within normal families but the normal grades into the problematical, signalled by anxieties, tensions and conflicts which might be reflected in teenagers in practices such as excessive drinking. By focussing on the home, we would hope to isolate features of family life and the domestic environment which could contribute to oppression and conflict.

The study of family dynamics as a means of identifying problem behaviour and providing appropriate therapy is now well established but what is missing from this research is any consideration of the material environment of the home, the home as a complex set of spaces and objects. Homes can be characterized as 'signed' spaces - material forms which assume symbolic importance in relation to their use by family members. The naming of spaces within the home, like dining room or front room, implies rules about their use and these rules are a part of the set of controls which influence relationships within families. Thus, in this chapter, we will try to identify those aspects of home environments which are intrinsic features of family control systems. We will discuss those uses of space in the home which are ordinary and usually taken-for-granted in order to identify those spatial behaviours which could contribute to behavioural problems.

Making connections between families and domestic space can be seen as one instance of the general problem of defining what Soja (1980) called the 'socio-spatial dialectic', the continual interplay of people and places and the consequent reconstitution of social space. Social groups are constrained by the spaces they occupy because built forms - buildings (the containers of activities) and channel spaces (the routes which connect activities) - are relatively fixed. However, people act on the built environment and attempt to transform it in order to accommodate their activities more satisfactorily. Most people have very little power to modify the larger-scale features of their material environment; others, primarily the major owners of capital and decision makers in state institutions, have the capacity to transform space and their transformations will have positive or negative consequences for the majority. Thus, the transformations of space can be seen as an expression of power relations, constraining or enabling different groups of actors and creating environments of inclusion and exclusion. Much of the time, users of the built environment are unaware of the exclusionary nature of some developments because their daily or weekly routines are unaffected. Thus, shopping malls or indoor shopping centres in Europe and North America have created ambiguous public-private spaces which can be 'enjoyed' by most consumers but which exclude groups like the homeless and teenagers who may be ejected by security guards because they are not seen as consumers - they do not fit the acceptable image of the model consuming nuclear family (Shields 1989). For the majority, the policing of these spaces does not limit their movements in the city but, for targetted minorities, the boundaries erected by the owners of capital can be strong and oppressive. Clearly, part of the problem is a lack of awareness on the part of the majority who contribute to the construction of adolescents or the homeless as problems, with stereotypes persisting because of a failure to recognize the environmental constraints on the lives of others.

We will argue that these questions of conflict and exclusion are characteristic of domestic space as much as they are features of large-scale elements of built form. Generally, homes come off the peg but these fixed assemblages can be manipulated and controlled by those with power and authority, usually one or two parents. Parents may control domestic space by allocating different activities to different rooms and by determining the timing of activities in different spaces. Alternatively, they may choose not to dictate who does what where and when but to negotiate uses of space in the home with other members of the family. In practice, domestic regimes tend to reflect a mixture of these two as strategies. As Putnam and Newton (1990, p.7) have remarked:

> "*Household choices are not made without difficulty; objectives necessarily clash with each other, with constraint, expectation and memory. The re-ordering of space, time and resources as*

circumstances change involves a negotiation with oneself and others in the household."

Some conflict is inevitable. As individuals act to secure space, to create some degree of autonomy for themselves by making their own space, territorial control will lead to other members of the family suffering some degree of exclusion and dependency. The problems associated with contested space can be observed in little acts, like reserving a chair in front of the television. This requires power, it may reinforce authority and it reduces the options of others. Some families may be characterized according to a consistent set of practices of this kind, relating to arrangements for meals, bedtimes, play, house cleaning, and so on.

However, the opportunities for the control or manipulation of domestic space will be affected by the 'geography' of the house or apartment - the number and spatial arrangement of rooms and the density of occupation. As with other features of the built environment, the interior spaces of the home have a permanence which is usually accepted. Change, through knocking out walls, building extensions or moving house is often prohibitively expensive, so families tend to adapt to the given space. The scope for adaptation varies considerably. If a family lives in one room, controlling the activities of children in space and over time will usually be more difficult than in a home where a number of rooms provide obvious physical boundaries.

There is no single way in which families adjust to the physical constraints imposed by the dwelling. This can be demonstrated by pointing to cultural differences in the use of domestic space, particularly cultural interpretations of the home which are very different to those which are often assumed to characterize the mainstream in western societies. To give one example, Kalderas Gypsies in Paris or Oakland, California, knock down the interior walls of houses in order to create a single space for the family because the frequent coming together of the extended family group is an important cultural characteristic (Sutherland 1975; Williams 1982). Thus, the single space for the Kalderas is an asset, not a problem. For comparison, we can note the concern expressed by an English woman having to manage an open-plan living room:

"The overall impression is one of a very cluttered room. It does get tidied up when visitors are expected. Having lived in homes with separate rooms and this one with a through room, I have come to the conclusion that I much prefer dining and sitting rooms to be separate." (Mass-Observation, People's Homes, Autumn, 1983)

While recognizing that the family and the home environment are crucial socializing influences on adolescents, the home should not be isolated from the neighbourhood within which it is situated. Homes exist in localities which vary in design and socio-economic status. Values like conformity and liberalism attach to neighbourhoods where they may be articulated by residents, particularly through protest movements objecting to socially challenging developments like Gypsy sites or half-way houses for the mentally disabled. Values can also be expressed symbolically in the detailed design of suburbs, with manicured lawns and security systems expressing status but also giving messages of not belonging to various 'others'. Conceptually, we recognize that the reciprocal conditioning of these spaces should be investigated. Neighbourhood values may affect the nature of domestic regimes and the kinds of families living in a place will bestow character on the neighbourhood, although families will not necessarily conform to local norms. Similarly, the values embodied in the state and in capitalism invade the home, particularly through the visual and written media as well as indirectly through the schooling of family members. It may be the case, for example, that a television commercial for soap powder reinforces 'family' values as they are projected in the attitudes of a mother towards her children or a commercial may project racial stereotypes. Thus, the home has to be seen as a permeable environment, enmeshed in other social and physical environments which have some effect on domestic life and which are themselves affected by the behaviour, attitudes and values of families.

The house as haven

We have introduced this chapter by sketching in the elements of an ideal analysis of home environments, one which situates homes in appropriate social and cultural contexts and one which would form part of a larger study of socializing influences on adolescents. The empirical research around which this study is constructed, however, relates rather more narrowly to home environments in Britain from the 1950s to the late 1980s, so some of the other important influences on family life and teenager behaviour remain unexamined. In order to put our own approach to the problem in perspective, we will first review some research on the home, the self, and the family, particularly that which explores the theme of 'the house as haven'. This theme appears to dominate environmental psychological accounts of the home and it contrasts strongly with our analysis. Clearly, homes do have aesthetic qualities and they may provide an anchor in people's lives as storehouses of artefacts and memories. Homes can evoke positive feelings, feelings of well-being, and the home environment is often contrasted with the hazardous, uncertain external environment of the city or the workplace. Home is where you can put your feet up, relax, play your kind of music and feel good. Beyond the home, there may be problems of noise, litter, atmospheric pollution and threatening people but at home you are in control and it is possible to insulate yourself from these external hazards.

Most studies of domestic interiors produced in North America and western Europe have depicted the home in these terms. There has been a rather singular concern with middle-class homes where *individuals* restore themselves and reconnect with a symbolically rich environment. The French psychologist, Korosec-Serfaty, who has written extensively on this issue, characterizes the home with this quotation from Marc (1972, p.137):

> "...each one creates ..a clearly evidenced universe...it is only in this spontaneous [sic] architecture that a few signs of authentic living may be gleaned."

Korosec-Serfaty sees "authentic living" in the opportunities provided by the home for self expression. Thus, the living room "bespeaks the dweller" and is a part of "the being's mode of anchoring in space" (Korosec-Serfaty 1984, p.304). Dovey (1985, p.46) similarly stresses the security and anchoring provided by the home, contrasting it with the outside world as the opposition of security and doubt, familiarity and strangeness, sanctity and profanity. She argues that, because the domestic interior is dialectically related to the outside, the positive experience of the home, by contrast with the negative experience of the wider environment, gives home life greater intensity and depth. This gratifying intensity is expressed particularly well in the following passage (Cooper 1990, p.37):

> "Homes are made up of histories and possibilities. So, the empty house is full of spaces for the imagination, of hopes and opportunities. There is a dreamlike quality in the momentary associations of things in the process of change, the accidental relationships of light, space and clutter. Endless alternatives exist in walls almost without traces. The empty space slowly fills...and a kind of order is imposed, disciplining, choosing, fixing. The wide view becomes a picture on the wall, a backdrop for the content of the room - we look increasingly inward, toward the detail. But while the limited possibilities in empty, pristine space are lost, these changes are the acquisition of a history, a mirror to lives, activities and uses, and a measurement of time. The home is a space replete with pasts and memories."

Such lyricism is inspired by Bachelard's representation of the home as a happy memory, recalled in dreams, "giving access to the initial shell which shelters the being" (Bachelard 1981). Thus, we can talk of a "happy phenomenology of the home", as Korosec-Serfaty puts it. The experience of the home is not necessarily bounded by the physical shell of the house because it can be dreamt anywhere, but Bachelard's *Poetics of Space* does convey strongly an image of home as comforting and restorative, the intellectual equivalent of *Homes and Gardens* or a Laura Ashley catalogue.

It is not only phenomenologists who have argued this way, however. Engels, from a materialist perspective, saw the need to create a domestic sphere separate from the world of work to compensate for the alienation created by capitalist relations of production. The idea of the protective shell is suggested also by some psychoanalytical thinking, following Freud and Erikson, that the home serves as a boundary of the self. The home secures privacy and

> *"privacy mechanisms define the limits and boundaries of the self. When the permeability of those boundaries is under the control of a person, a sense of individuality develops."* (Altman 1975, p.50)

Certainly, people do derive a sense of well-being from the fabric of the home and from domestic objects. Space and objects together can provide aesthetic experience and, as Rochberg-Halton (1984, p.352) recognizes, they form a gestalt for those who relate to this material environment. The gestalt communicates something, *"the placing of objects in rooms shows how different rooms in the house reveal different conceptions of self"*.

The home according to these accounts is unproblematic and positively valued. This may accord with the experience of childless professional couples living in oast-house conversions in Kent but such phenomenological interpretations convey far too cosy a picture. At least, for many people, it would not sound like a familiar portrayal of home life. As generalizations, these accounts fail because they neglect the obvious fact that the home also constitutes the setting for violence, child abuse, depression and other forms of mental illness, as well as less serious but routine tensions and conflicts. The focus on the individual and individual satisfactions is peculiar because homes are occupied in most cases by families, who do not always enjoy harmonious relationships. The home for some evokes memories of unhappy experiences, isolation or frequent rows. What is missing from the 'house as haven' thesis is a recognition that there are tensions surrounding the use of domestic space, tensions which reflect patterns of domination in families and which are expressed in attempts to control the use of space in the home.

The home as a site of conflict

Because homes generally comprise fixed assemblages, fixed spatial configurations which are not designed by their users, they have to be appropriated by the occupants. Someone has to decide how the space will be used and we can anticipate that the use of space will be strongly influenced, if not determined, by one or two dominant adult members of the family. Power can be expressed in the partitioning of space. Thus, several writers have suggested a front/back division, with domestic routines - cooking, washing up, and so on, comprising a female sphere associated with the back area of the house and the front area of the home being appropriated for leisure and rest, the front being an essentially male sphere (Putnam and Newton 1990; Lawrence 1987). This front/back dichotomy derives from Goffman's thesis on the presentation of self in everyday life (Goffman 1959). Using a theatrical metaphor, the front (stage) becomes an area of display: the back (stage) is private, hidden, associated with women's work. This division expresses patriarchy - a power relationship in which the male is dominant. Two points should be emphasized here, however. First, the design of the home and particularly the spatial arrangement of work and 'living' areas may reinforce or counteract patriarchy. Secondly, the boundary between front space and back space may be contested so that the allocation of male and female spheres becomes a point of tension. This argument, based on a simple division of domestic space to which patriarchy is connected, clearly neglects cultural variations in male-female relationships within households, the complicating effect of children in interactions in the family, social change in western societies which has tended to weaken the boundary between male and female spheres, and diverse geographies of the home. However, it does point to a potential source of conflict which mirrors gender-based conflict elsewhere in society.

A further reservation about the 'house as haven' thesis concerns the separateness of the home from the outside world. The idea of the home as a place of escape from social ills, from the tensions of city life, and so on, is difficult to sustain given that the outside world invades domestic space via television and other media. Also, people interact with neighbours and may feel pressure to conform to neighbourhood values in relation to the exterior and interior of the home.

Media influences could be significant in that advertisements project images of desirable domestic styles, inviting people to consume - fitted kitchens, carpets, and so on. These messages have sub-texts, however, concerned with cleanliness and order. Dissatisfaction with used and soiled goods encourages consumption but this dissatisfaction may translate into a general concern with spatial order and hygiene (Sibley 1988). However, there may be disagreements within families about necessary or desirable levels of spatial order or cleanliness. Young children, in particular, do not recognize boundaries imposed by adults and have different conceptions of dirt and disorder, so from an adult perspective, children may be seen as disorderly, a nuisance requiring control. Thus, the symbolic order of the home, reflecting adult preferences or choices and reinforced by the images of consuming home-makers produced by the advertising media, can be a source of conflict within families, and particularly between parent and child.

Neighbourhood values, similarly, have implications for domestic life styles and conceptions of order. A suburban community may be boundary conscious, with residents generally concerned about spatial order and social homogeneity, so that behaviour which departs from the norm may be judged deviant by the majority. Attitudes to suburban order and niceness are likely to be expressed in the internal organization of the home, with suburban order and domestic order reinforcing each other. As Hillier and Hansen (1984, p.267) characterize such areas:

> "...*everyday life is strongly conformist to g-models of behaviour* [genotype models, representing an externally imposed sociospatial order] *including spatial behaviours, like the maintenance of a certain type of order in the front garden, and a certain standard symbolic configuration within the household."*

Such a spatial arrangement is illustrated in Figure 8.1 where an ordered pattern (of land-uses in a city, or of the uses of rooms in a home) is represented as a series of non-overlapping sets (c) and a discrete hierarchy of elements, forming a tree graph (d). Only conforming uses are permissible under this arrangement. By contrast, the intersecting sets in (a) and the graph (b) describe many combinations of activities or uses, which could be anathema to those who value a highly ordered environment. This connection between home and locality has been identified in an essay by Taylor and Brower (1985) on the "near home environment", which appears to mean what it says. They outline the benefits to be derived from controlling territory immediately adjacent to the house, including the lawns of fenceless North American suburbs, sidewalks and alleys. They recommend that *"noisy or rambunctious children* [should be] *shooed off the lawn"*, that loiterers should be threatened with police action if they refuse to get off the front steps, and so on. By reducing noise, unwanted intrusions and unregulated activity in these outdoor spaces, they argue that:

> "*the sense of security, orderliness, and the quality of life inside the house is enhanced...Worry is reduced. To put it simply: life inside the home is better and less intruded upon."* (p.190)

This concern about order accentuates the deviance of children and loiterers. The authors ask rhetorically:

> *"How does territiorial functioning contribute to the functioning of the immediate society? First, and perhaps most obviously, attempts to exert territorial control are part of the deviation-countering and vetoing mechanisms of a block-behaviour setting."* (pp.192-193)

The deviant to be countered include "*rowdy teens*" and vetoing includes "*reprimands where the offending person (eg. a street bum* [sic] *sitting on a curb) is asked to leave*". This view of social space and of 'other' people assumes ideological dominance in some suburban and rural communities. For example, in Belle Terre, New York, the Supreme Court ruled in the 1970s that the community had a legitimate interest in excluding households whose members were not linked by "blood, adoption or marriage" in order to preserve "family values, youth values, the blessings of quiet seclusion and clean air...and a sanctuary for people" (Sager 1978, p.1420), 'people' presumably meaning people like them. The comment by the Supreme Court sums up the closed community which, as Douglas (1966) has argued, is preoccupied with external boundaries and questions of who does and who does not belong. This association between social attitudes, domestic design and suburban landscape, all of which emphasize boundary maintenance, social homogeneity and spatial order, is nicely expressed in *Edward Scissorhands* (1990), a cinematic allegory of intolerance in a southern California suburban community, where the look-alike pastel tinted homes have correspondingly uniform interiors and house predictably uniform social attitudes. The community is threatened by the Gothic eccentricity of Edward, who is marked as different, and deviant, because he has scissors instead of hands. His ultimate expulsion to the Gothic castle beyond the suburb is a consequence of his difference which is accentuated by the sameness of the expelling community. What we are suggesting through these examples is that there are close links between home and locality, society and space. Messages associating virtue with order, newness, cleanliness and sameness penetrate both homes and localities, while self-selection through the residential migration process creates receptive audiences for these messages. These ideas about boundaries, spatial order and social order can now be used to develop a more systematic account of the organization and control of domestic space.

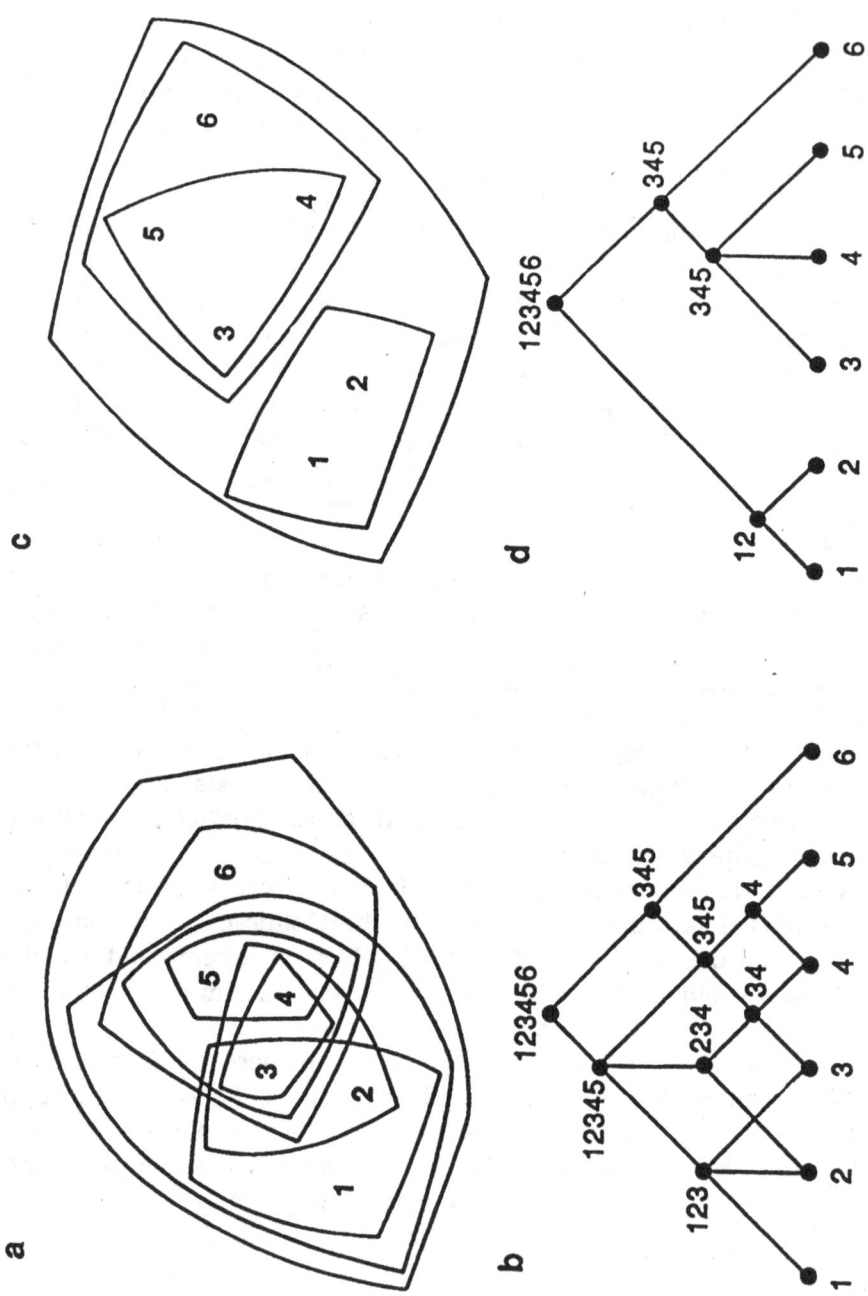

Figure 8.1: Mixed and homogenous spatial arrangements
(adapted from Alexander 1966)

Contested space: boundaries in the home

We will first outline a few models of the spatial and temporal organization of domestic space, then look more closely at the boundary question. Of particular interest here is the problem of anxiety and abjection in relation to people's responses to domestic disorder. We will suggest that the way adults in particular react to 'matter out of place' can be interpreted in terms of Kristeva's (1982) concept of abjection.

The partitioning of space; the segmentation of time

Beyond simple dichotomies, like Goffman's front stage and back stage, we can propose a conceptual scheme which captures the detailed organization of domestic space, that is, answers the question: who does what, where?, and which also can be used to analyse the timing of activities in the home. This space-time schema is then reintroduced in the next chapter in an elaboration of models of family dynamics, such as that proposed by Minuchin.

The spatial model is an adaptation of one of Bernstein's schemata which describe the organization of the school curriculum. This appeared in a paper written in 1970 on the "classification and framing of educational knowledge". *Classification* and *framing* are terms used by Bernstein to describe curriculum structure. Where there is strong classification, the contents of subject areas are clearly bounded and kept separate; strong framing means that there are clearly defined rules about what knowledge may be transmitted within subjects, as, for example, in the national curriculum in France and Britain. Conversely, with weak classification, subject boundaries are weakly defined, the compartmentalization of knowledge is considered undesirable and, thus, boundary maintenance is not an issue. Because the mixing of ideas is viewed positively, weak classification and weak framing usually go together. In regard to power relations, strong classification and framing express authority and hierarchy, with the vertical organization of institutions and control exercised by those at the top. Maintaining subject identity, with clear boundaries, is then a means of retaining power in a particular academic field. By contrast, weak classification and framing reflect a democratic view of knowledge, where power is diffuse. Ideas are communicated laterally rather than vertically so, for example, student contributions are valued as well as those of teachers. While there may be core areas of interest, the system is fluid with weak and permeable boundaries. To give an academic example, strong and weak forms could be represented respectively by geography, a conventional, long-established discipline, where practitioners are concerned about subject identity in competition with other social and physical sciences, and environmental studies, where the boundaries between conventional disciplines are removed in order to explore interconnections.

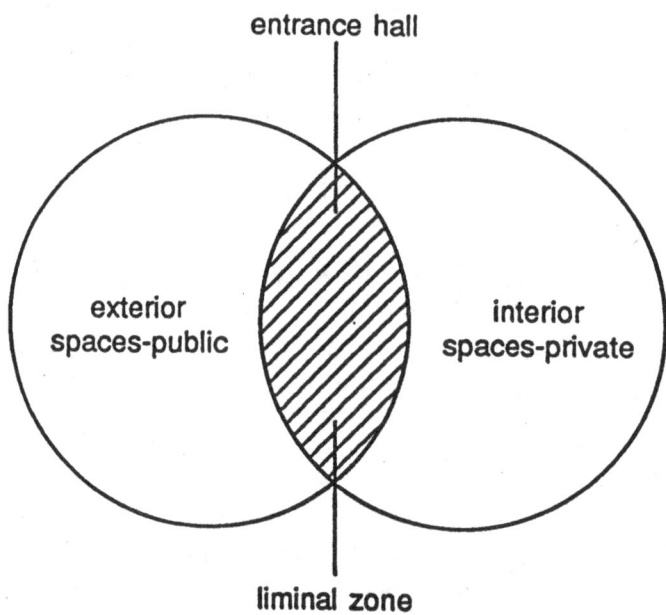

Figure 8.2: Private and public spaces in the home environment (adapted from Lawrence 1987)

There is in Bernstein's model an explicit relationship between structure and ideologies of control. Translating the educational scheme into a socio-spatial one, we can similarly define a structure - a set of bounded spaces comprising the home - and a control system which is operated by family members according to particular ideologies. A space within the home such as a 'front' room is one that can be given a singular identity by a person or persons controlling the use of space in the home, that is, it can be strongly classified. In a strongly classified environment, a person may feel uncomfortable about *liminal* zones - ambiguous areas where conflicting ideas about appropriate use are unresolved. Thus, in Figure 8.2, illustrating the boundary between the home and the exterior, the entrance hall is liminal in the sense that it signals a shift from public to private and, thus, for the occupant, it may create problems of admission and exclusion - who should be invited past the front door, who into the hall and who into the private spaces of the home? In order to signal the intention of the controller to maintain the space as one which serves a single function, there will be a concern with boundary maintenance, rules about use. When the boundary is strong, any activity which does not correspond to the designated use will be seen as non-conforming and may be viewed as deviant. For example, there may be sanctions against children who eat meals in the front room or play with their toys there. In a home where homogeneity, spatial order and strong boundaries are valued, children may be quite inhibited in their play if boundary violations are punished. The children may be alienated or may themselves be socialized into valuing neatness, order and homogeneous spatial categories. Strong framing, similarly, indicates that objects within rooms will have single, unambiguous functions and improvized uses will be frowned upon. Conversely, in a home characterized by weak classification and weak framing, there will be multiple uses of rooms, mixing of activities and the multiple use of objects. Generally, there will be a lack of concern about spatial boundaries; boundary violations will be fewer because there is little to violate. The former, strongly ordered home suggests domination by one or more members of the family, usually a parent. The latter suggests more equality and a tendency to reconcile the competing claims of family members on space through negotiation.

The contrast between strong classification and framing and weak classification and framing, as outlined here, suggests that the former is problematic, associated in the extreme with authoritarianism, rigidity and obsession, while the latter is positive, associated with open and egalitarian relationships within families. While anxiety about maintaining boundaries and creating 'pure' spaces in the home may contribute to behavioural problems, there are also problems associated with very weak classification and framing. In particular, it will be difficult to secure privacy and autonomy when boundaries are not recognized. Children may feel that parents are intruding in their lives. This question is one that we consider in more detail in the next chapter.

The value of Bernstein's scheme in interpreting people's experience of home environments is indicated in the following extracts which come from Mass-Observation surveys during the 1980s. The first describes a strongly framed space in which objects are clearly located. It suggests one person's preferred arrangement of objects in a room and the respondent implies that the room is a part of a strongly classified home:

> *We always call it the lounge. The ceiling is papered and emulsioned in sunshine yellow and the walls have embossed paper emulsioned white with two single wall lights on the 'long wall' adjoining the kitchen and one double wall light on the wall*

> *adjoining the dining room, all with amber glass shades... The other 'long wall' is almost completely covered by wall units - four in all. All four have cupboards at the bottom and shelves at the top - shelves all full of books of all descriptions and size! The two end units also have cupboards in the middle - one houses our record and cassette collection, and the other holds paperbacks and junk! One of the other units has a cupboard with glass doors, inside of which are our more precious items of glass, china and porcelain. The fourth unit has a cupboard with a drop down door and interior light which houses drinks and glasses - all are mahogany. In front of the books are various ornaments and the goldfish! One large shelf holds the music centre and reel-to-reel tape recorder. The units do not quite reach the ceiling and have on their tops the two speakers, three photos of our daughter... and a large stuffed Humpty Dumpty and a tradescantia plant which trails over some of the shelves and threatens to overtake us soon!... Against the wall which adjoins the dining room are the two chairs of the lounge suite - large wing chairs in dark brown dralon with beige pattern. The settee is along the wall opposite the units...Next to the settee is a large square glass-topped coffee table with a cactus plant on top and a book of Pre-Raphaelite paintings, plus the remote control for the TV and my daughter's homework book. Next to the coffee table, behind the door, there is a nest of occasional tables with a fruit bowl on top, holding apples, oranges and bananas, in front of which is a magazine rack full to bursting with papers, magazines, drawings from school, etc. On the floor, one of my daughter's books not put away last night.*
> (Mass-Observation, People's Homes, Autumn, 1983, woman correspondent)

In this account, there is a suggestion that objects in the room are carefully placed - the coffee table with cactus plant and 'coffee table book', the nest of occasional tables with fruit bowl, the magazine rack. The observation that a book on the floor is out of place - "*one of my daughter's books not put away last night*", is a further indication of strong framing.

People can feel uncomfortable if they have an ordered conception of domestic space and objects are out of place in terms of their ordered scheme. The spatial form of the home may itself encourage this view or make it difficult to maintain boundaries. Actual, or yearned for, order might be compared with the weakly framed space of the flat of a male artist, where there is a general clutter of paintings, artist's materials, cat litter, and books. The mantelpiece is particularly interesting:

> *One large pickle jar with £2.00 in copper coins, one Farrah's Harrogate toffee tin, with circa £2.00 of five pence pieces and twenty pence pieces...one clock with cracked face, one bottle of one hundred Boot's aspirins, a box of matches from Maid Marian food stores, one Queen Elizabeth Hospital menu card, one empty envelope, one Photoquick envelope, one Calotherm record cleaning cloth, and five blank Cambridgeshire library request forms. This lot takes up a third of the space. The other two thirds is taken up with three Revell 1/48th incompleted model kits; a MIG 23, a Herschel 123 and a Voight Crusader. Behind this is a 1983 Tennessee car licence plate. The mantelpiece is rather dusty.*
> (Mass-Observation, People's Homes, Autumn, 1983, male correspondent).

Unlike other writers, this correspondent expressed no concern about dirt or untidiness. On the contrary, his observations suggest that he felt quite comfortable with the mixing of objects in the flat.

Bounding time

Since we are concerned with boundary maintenance in the home as an aspect of the regulation of family life, it is important to identify the temporal dimension of the problem as much as the spatial, the timing of activities and the interaction of time and space. Clearly, daily routines are not determined exclusively in the home. The demands of work outside the home and of school hours, for example, have a regulating effect on meal times and leisure time. However, within a framework partly determined by these external activities, there are considerable variations in the use of time and in attitudes to time schedules, which appear to correspond to attitudes to the use of space.

As with spatial boundaries, we can recognize both relaxed and concerned attitudes to the partitioning of time, either of which could be reinforced by the experience of home life. The following recollections of a Glasgow childhood indicate how the demands of rigid temporal regimes created anxieties and conflict in the home:

> *My brother and I used to race to the bus stop for the 1 o'clock bus back home to travel the mile and a quarter to a too hot dinner, followed by a sprint down the drive to catch the 1.30 p.m. bus back to school. I remember on one of these racings to and from the bus stop falling onto a newly tarred and stoned road but, dead or alive, I had to get to school... Bells, of course, rang between periods (45 minutes or so) to end play time. I remember when my*

> *leg was broken by a girl falling onto it that I was horrified to hear the bell ringing between my wailing, that I could not get up and join the serried ranks of children waiting for the janitor to direct them into the building... My parents were most wonderfully organized in running their hotel. The clock ruled. Its discipline was sacrosanct.*

The same correspondent describes acute problems over bed time:

> *The time I spent over homework caused a lot of trouble between my parents and myself. I realize now that the internalized whip made me anxious about learning and I was too insecure not to work... This rubbed off on my daughter as well. A cruel inheritance which I regret. Father would come back late from a freemasons' meetings and stand by the electric light, demanding that I would stop wasting his money and go to bed. I would not. And when he threatened to take me away from school, I attempted suicide, putting on all the gas rings and howling silently into my school books. I am sure they never forgot this. Our relationship was a very guarded one, though this was never talked about.*
> (Mass-Observation, Time, Summer 1988, woman correspondent).

A concern with temporal, as well as spatial, order may well be a source of personal satisfaction. Thus, the father in the above extract attempted to save money by regulating his daughter's bed time. Another correspondent freed time for a number of activities by having a strict domestic regime:

> *I have worked out ways of saving both time and energy about the house by trying to be very tidy so that cleaning takes up a minimum of time...Time saved I use working in the garden, knitting, sewing, writing letters, doing crosswords, etc.*
> (Mass-Observation, Time, Summer 1988, woman correspondent).

This seems unexceptional. Problems arise, however, when a person's preferred pattern of timing and spacing activities in the home conflicts with another's, *conflict being more likely the stronger the classification of space and the more highly ordered the time budget*. If the uses of space and time are largely determined by one dominant individual, the preferred allocations of space and time of other members of the family will appear deviant or disruptive to the dominant person, or they may be suppressed.

The partitioning of space and time within the home cannot be discussed solely as a question of choice or preference because behaviour is affected by the contexts of family life. In particular, we have suggested that the design of the home is important in relation to the maintenance of spatial boundaries because the more segmented domestic space is, the greater are the options for assigning uses and for creating boundaries. Similarly, temporal routines beyond the control of family members, resulting from the demands of work, and so on, can affect the use of space in the home. For example, if children are seen to intrude on scarce 'adult time', where scarcity is related to patterns of work, the spatial behaviour of children may be regulated so that they do not intrude on 'adult space'.

The accounts of people's home lives recorded in the Mass-Observation archive suggest that some feel comfortable with highly ordered spaces and strong temporal boundaries and anxious about disorder. Disorder, however, is someone else's order. Parent-child conflict, in particular, centres on different conceptions of order. It will be appropriate at this point to review attempts which have been made to explain the problem of boundary consciousness and aversion to disorder. Why do people feel anxious about weakly classified spaces and with those who appear to threaten their ordered home lives? Some of the anthropological and psychoanalytical literature which addresses this issue, focussing on boundary construction in individuals, separation and merging, may also be relevant to the question of transgression and problem drinking, which is the theme of the next chapter.

The boundaries of the self and relationships with the material and social worlds

In associating or demarcating activities in domestic space, Lawrence (1987) suggests that the binary opposition clean-dirty (together with day-night, public-private) provides a meaningful basis for understanding behaviour. Here he follows Douglas (1966) who argues that:

> *"Dirt is a potent term. It signifies not just matter out of place but danger, a threat to the stability and unity of a social system or to an individual's world-structure."* (p.7)

Dirt signifies defilement and provides a metaphor for a wide range of animate and inanimate objects and ideas which are judged out of place. In order to understand its function in determining boundaries in the home, we might first consider the constitution of the self and the way in which the self is bounded from the 'other', because dirt figures largely in the construction of otherness.

In *Civilization and Its Discontents* (1929), Freud argues that in industrialized, urban societies, the erotic pleasures which he associated with the anal phase of development are sublimated and libidinal gratification is transferred to the material environment, this transfer being expressed in a concern for cleanliness and order (Smith 1980). At the same time, pleasure associated with bodily residues changes to fear and distaste. Thus, a boundary between the 'pure' self and the 'defiled' self is constructed. However, object relations theorists, like Mead (1934) and Rochberg-Halton (1984) have suggested that this distaste for bodily residues generalizes into a distaste for any objects or people who are 'out of place', that is things or people who transgress the boundaries of an individual's ordered world. As Mead observed, the other can be "anything - any set of objects, whether animate or inanimate, human or animal". They can all constitute dirt in a metaphorical sense.

Recent writing on the boundaries of the self, for example, by Gross (1990) and Young (1990) draws particularly on the work of Julia Kristeva. In *The Powers of Horror* (1982), she locates the problem of self-definition in the pre-Oedipal phase:

> "[The infant] *must separate from its joyful continuity with the mother's body and acquire a sense of border between itself and the other."* (Young 1990, p.143)

The infant rejects the mother, dissolves the unity of mother and child, so the mother becomes the 'other' and rejection is accompanied by aversion. There is a fear of the other in the form of the mother who threatens a dissolution of the self but also a feeling of loss, a desire to re-establish the pre-Oedipal unity of mother and child. Kristeva, like Freud, recognizes that a sense of border includes feelings of disgust and revulsion towards bodily residues - excrement, urine, sweat, and so on, but she describes the feeling towards residues as one of *abjection*. Abjection is a visceral feeling:

> *"When the eyes see or the lips touch that skin on the surface of the milk - harmless, thin as a sheet of cigarette paper, pitiful as a nail paring - I experience a gagging sensation and still farther down, spasms in the stomach."* (Kristeva 1982, p.2)

Abjection is a desire to expel but powerlessness to achieve it. Bodily residues, along with other abject things and people to whom feelings of abjection are transferred:

> *"hover on the border of the subject's identity, threatening apparent unities and stabilities with disruption and possible dissolution."* (Gross 1990, p.87)

Thus, the subject is in perpetual danger, fearing a dissolution of the borders of the self by abject things and people. Some categories of people and abject things are elided, people are constructed as an abject 'other'.

When considering the role of the abject in boundary construction in the home, it is important to recognize that what enters the catalogue of the abject for an individual is in part a social and cultural question. Ideas about purity and defilement which define the self are embodied in cultures, so the process of boundary definition includes the influence of cultural forms such as media images. Here, it is evident, as Erikson (1959) suggested, that the separation of the self and other is not completed in infancy but continues into adulthood and is subject to reinforcement and redefinition. For example, advertising images which emphasize the new, the pure and the white, in contrast to the (negative) properties of old, used and soiled commodities, promote domestic styles where defilement, or in Bernstein's terms, strong classification, is accentuated. More seriously, British t.v. commercials for detergents (Persil, 1991) and cars (Volkswagen, 1990) have used people, children and the homeless, respectively, to suggest defilement as a threat to the boundaries of the self and the home. Washing powder cleans and 'civilizes' the Persil children who are portrayed running wild in a jungle, so removing the threat of defilement, and the Volkswagen insulates the blonde, well-dressed child of the respectable, middle-class parent from the defiled 'others' on the streets of New York. Thus, consumption in capitalist societies is promoted through images of purification which accentuate the defilement of objects and people. This heightens boundary consciousness both within and outside the home.

The home is the one locale where people have the power to enforce separations. Beyond the home, individual adults are subject to stronger institutional forces and have little effective power except where there is local consensus about social and environmental values which is consistent with the interests of the state and capital. In the home, however, the pure and the defiled may be kept separate and, as Kristeva would argue, the individual with a phobic fear of the abject can continuously engage in distancing him- or herself from things or people which threaten the integrity of boundaries. The abject, hovering on the margins, can be repelled.

Conclusion

This discussion has focussed on boundaries because the partitioning and use of space and time in the home creates boundary conflicts which, we would argue, are a key element of family dynamics. The imposition of boundaries may provoke transgressive behaviour; the neglect of boundaries may also contribute to problem behaviour in children and teenagers through the denial of space for individual development. Otherwise, anxieties and tensions relating to the use of space and time in the home can be seen as normal aspects of family relationships and of individual development. However, these are characteristics of family dynamics which have been largely ignored in the literature.

The argument has been presented here as if it was a general one but it is important to recognize that relationships between individuals in families, in home settings, are culturally specific. The design of the house in itself is an important consideration, constraining family members in their relationships to others in varying degrees. The layout of a suburban home in Los Angeles and of a municipal apartment in Gdansk create different boundary problems. Cultures then adapt differently to the fixed spaces of the home. Similarly, conceptions of the self, the boundaries of the body and relationships with the wider environment, as they have been developed in western psychoanalysis, may be specific to western cultures. Thus, Parekh (1974) has argued that mixing and difference are accepted much more readily in Indian cultures than they are in the west. Similarly, Gypsies, while having an acute sense of boundaries, distinguish differently between what is pure and what is defiled (in Romany *mochadi* or *marime*) to the dominant society in western Europe or North America. This, in fact, contributes to the perception of Gypsies as defiling and threatening. They reverse accepted dichotomies and threaten social and spatial boundaries. Further research could usefully examine other cultural variations in boundary construction as a contribution to knowledge of family dynamics and problem behaviour. For example, there may be differences between Scandinavia and Mediterranean Europe which associate with different levels of problem behaviour, or between social classes in a country like Britain. With these caveats, we would argue that it is important to explore the relationship between the subject and the home environment because they illuminate some of the fears and anxieties which are expressed in family conflicts. The home, as a site of actual or potential conflict, comprises one of several sites which provide the context for a study of teenage drinking, one where boundary enforcement and boundary transgression are particularly important aspects of family relationships.

Chapter 9

Domestic space, modes of control, and problem drinking

The general account of home environments in the last chapter provides the context for a more focussed study of family interactions and domestic space. Here, we examine possible connections between spatial and temporal behaviour within families - the manipulation and appropriation of space in the home - and teenage problem drinking. As we suggested in the earlier discussion, it is necessary to define the normal range of behaviour in the home environment in order to isolate problematic cases. Thus, we will proceed, first, by characterizing family control systems in a general sense, associating typical spatial and temporal behaviours with modes of control. Secondly, these conceptual representations of family and domestic space will be used to categorize recollections of home and family provided by problem drinkers to see if they fall into a distinctive pattern. While in a full account of the influence of home life on behaviour we would acknowledge that "*the alien world organizes life within the house as much as without it*" (Sennett 1977, p.187), we will now consider only relationships between family members as they influence and are influenced by domestic space, as if the family and the home were elements of a closed system.

Family types and modes of control

As a way into the problem, we can focus on power relations and, particularly, make use of Bernstein's distinction between *positional* and *personalizing* families (Atkinson 1985) as a means of identifying modes of control, which will include the manipulation of space and time in the home. In the positional family, there is an assumption that power derives from position and makes the arbitrary exercise of power legitimate. Power is vested in position, particularly in a patriarchal society in the father, and the activities of children are regulated through commands which constitute a *restricted code* of communication, like 'go to bed', 'do this', 'get out of my sight', and so on. Control is explicit in the sense that it is "*manifest in the formal status of parent and child*" (Atkinson 1985, p.150). Physical punishment may also be a means of control within the positional family. For example, one respondent in the Alcohol Advisory Service study discussed in detail later in this chapter, recalled both physical and verbal controls being used by his father in an apparently arbitrary way:

> 'Clive' was hit...at the whim of his father. Verbal put-downs and every tactic to make 'Clive' feel small appear to have been used indiscriminately. Because of his father's behaviour, he tried to avoid bringing friends into the home... 'Clive' agreed that, although his father was a physical presence in the home, emotionally, he kept everyone at arm's length.

In the personalizing family, by contrast, control is exercised through negotiation rather than command and is associated with an *elaborated code* of communication, whereby there is a verbal exploration of motives, feelings and identities and the relationship between parent and child is apparently more egalitarian. For example, the question 'Don't you think it is time to go to bed now because you'll be tired in the morning?' would be more likely than the command 'Go to bed'. However, the personalizing regime may be less egalitarian than this characterization suggests. An apparent concern with the interests of the child may still mask what is essentially a patriarchal form of power relations.

An important feature of the positional/personalizing dichotomy is that each mode of control can be associated with characteristic spatial regimes. Thus, we can suggest that the dominant individual(s) in the positional family will exhibit a low tolerance of ambiguity. This will be manifest in a concern for boundaries, for using the boundary and purified space as a means of regulating the lives of children. In Bernstein's schema, there is a close relationship between the positional mode of control within the family and strong classification, including the strong classification of space. Some of the activities of children and their associated objects, like toys on the carpet, would be seen as 'matter out of place', a source of pollution, by the dominant adult because they did not fit his or her rigid classificatory system. Regulation through the use of a rigid temporal regime would also be characteristic of the positional family. By contrast with this kind of regime, in the personalizing family, where power may be more diffuse, the use of space and time would be negotiated, there would be more sharing of space and, therefore, less concern with boundary maintenance as a means of control. Space would be weakly classified and the child's conception of space and time would not be a source of conflict because different world views can be accommodated in a weakly classified environment.

Clearly, this positional/personalizing dichotomy will fail to capture the complexity of inter-personal relations within many families. For example, positional behaviour is likely in a family which may be generally characterized as personalizing, when a parent decides that negotiations with a child are going to be unproductive and resorts to direction. However, the dichotomy usefully summarizes a cluster of family characteristics, control tendencies and spatial behaviours and, thus, it makes a good starting point for analysis. The positional is associated with a dominant authority, strong boundaries and rigid rules; the personalizing with equality, or at least egalitarian gestures, with negotiation and a relaxed attitude towards spatial and temporal boundaries. The identification with the spatial schema of strong and weak classification and framing, described in the last chapter, provides a direct link between domestic regimes and space.

Reconciling Bernstein and Minuchin

As we have interpreted Bernstein's thesis, strong classification is potentially oppressive because, when applied to domestic space, it restricts interactions and confines children in particular. However, the effects may be unintended. As Alaszewski (1986, p.69) observed in a review of Douglas's work on classification:

> "...we find the classifications used by other cultures strange and therefore feel that they must be wrong [but] we find our own classifications familiar and, therefore, they are right and they reflect objective reality."

If the classification is strong and imposed on individuals or groups who have a different world view, oppression or conflict are inevitable. In this quotation, we could substitute children for 'other cultures' and adult for 'we' and use it to express the conflict between adults and children over domestic space. It is the taken-for-granted nature of adult systems of classification which is at the root of the problem.

Bernstein's argument carries conviction partly because it is consistent with earlier authoritative statements about power and domination, notably Adorno's thesis (Adorno *et al* 1950) on the authoritarian personality, where he stressed the importance of an intolerance of ambiguity, mixing and difference and a concern with rigid rules. However, the imposition of a regime based on strong classification is not the only source of oppression in the home. The model proposed by Minuchin (1974) and developed by Olson *et al* (1979) can be seen as an alternative to Bernstein's schema although their different perspectives overlap and can be combined to construct a more elaborate model of family interactions as they are mediated by domestic space. To summarize Minuchin's argument, there are within families two problem-creating, polar interaction patterns - enmeshed and disengaged. Enmeshment indicates that family members are excessively involved with each other, denying personal space for others. Disengagement, conversely, describes a situation where there is poor communication and individuals feel isolated. Between these poles lie normal states of connectedness and separation, so we can represent the variants of family interactions as a spectrum, with deviant forms lying beyond the range of normal behaviour:

disengaged   (separated......................connected)   enmeshed

There is some similarity between Minuchin's model and our model of spatial behaviour based on Bernstein in that a concern with boundary maintenance (strong classification) or a failure to recognize spatial boundaries which serve to secure privacy (weak classification) could both signal problem behaviour in the extreme. We can then identify boundary styles and communication patterns which, in combination, generate three problem categories, namely:

- Type 1: strong classification/disengagement
- Type 2: strong classification/enmeshment
- Type 3: weak classification/enmeshment

(The fourth combination, weak classification/disengagement, would not be possible because weak classification implies interaction.)

In the first problem case, strong classification and disengagement will be mutually reinforcing in that strong boundaries will discourage communication while poor communication will increase separation and strengthen boundaries. The second describes a situation where the family is positional and a parent attempts to impose a strict regime but is frustrated because little spatial separation of activities is possible. Thus, the strongly classified, enmeshed regime may be particularly associated with families living in overcrowded conditions. The third category is problematic because the disinclination of a parent to recognize or maintain boundaries means that there is a failure to appreciate a child's need for privacy in order to develop a sense of self and to secure some autonomy. This then leaves us with combinations of separateness and connectedness and spatial/temporal classifications tending towards strong and weak which are within the normal range of family interaction patterns and space-use patterns in the home.

The home as a physical space

An analysis of family dynamics should be set in the context of the home as a physical space because the spatial configuration of the home can reinforce or weaken patterns of behaviour. Possible effects of the design of the home are illustrated simply in Figure 9.1. A house in which the spatial arrangement of rooms allows the labelling and isolation of a 'best' room (1) reserved exclusively for adults or for special occasions, would be conducive to a Type 1 regime. Alternatively, a less partitioned space (2) may encourage weak classification and interaction, possibly contributing to problems of enmeshment, as in a Type 3 regime. Where all activities are confined to one room (3), the physical space may reinforce either a Type 2 or a Type 3 regime. The last possibility has been recognized by Sebba and Churchman (1983, cited by Lawrence 1987, pp.149-150) who argued that clear physical boundaries could have a stabilizing or regulating role in the home but that an absence of such boundaries could be a source of tension and conflict. An absence of boundaries in the form of internal partitions, which may be a condition of extreme overcrowding, as in bed and breakfast accommodation for homeless families, for example, could contribute to enmeshment. What we are suggesting, however, is that both the presence or absence of fixed physical boundaries can contribute to anxiety or tension when they reinforce particular problematic modes of family interaction. Thus, it is both family relationships beyond the 'normal' range and configurations of domestic space as they are mediated by such families which we take to define the circumstances in which problem drinking may develop in teenagers.

Accounts of the home which appear in the Mass-Observation archive and the reported experience of family and home which were provided by problem drinkers, and which are quoted later in this chapter, refer to the arrangement of objects in the home, particularly furniture, as well as to the use of rooms. We have described the internal arrangement and use of rooms as aspects of *framing*, by analogy with Bernstein's use of the term to describe the internal organization of subjects in the curriculum - essentially in what form knowledge within a particular subject is transmitted. The distinction between classification and framing does not present a problem in this analysis, however, because framing is simply another aspect of power relations in the family, expressed as control over the use and location of objects in the home - who sits in what chair, what the table is used for, and so on. Some objects in the home are relatively fixed, however, and their design may suggest a particular use and treatment. A fitted kitchen, for example, may encourage a view of tidiness and cleanliness and appropriate use which has an effect on family relationships. Framing, in other words, can be a feature of the geography of the home which conditions behaviour. More usually, however, framing will be associated with choice, with somebody's preferences, and to this extent, it may be a good indicator of authority and exclusionary practices.

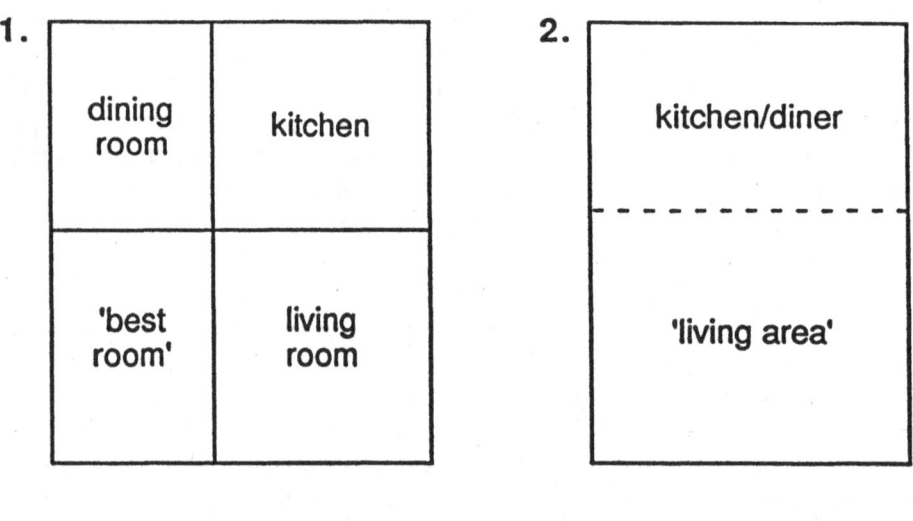

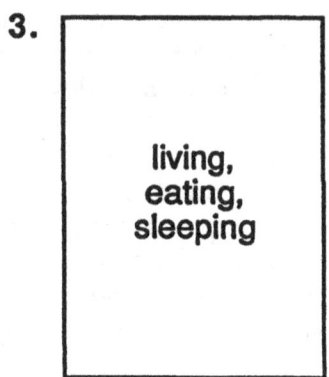

Figure 9.1: Alternative partitions of domestic space

Boundary enforcement in the home environment and adolescent alcohol use/abuse

In observing families we are concerned with where, when and who engages in activities in family space and the methods of control employed. Clearly, in practice, families are likely to exhibit a mix of personalizing and positional characteristics, but the identification of core types could be useful as a means of predicting vulnerability. We would anticipate that teenage alcohol abuse is more likely to be associated with positional than personalizing family environments, given that boundary enforcement is a characteristic method of control in the former and that boundary transgression is manifested in problem behaviour. In order to investigate this connection, we carried out detailed interviews with adult problem drinkers and a more extensive questionnaire survey of 'ordinary' teenagers and parents.

Methodology

Questionnaire data were drawn from two sample populations. First, a voluntary sample of 137 teenagers between 12 and 20 years old and second, a voluntary sample of 109 parents, of which 45 were the parents of one or more of the sample of teenagers, in order to compare their responses. Access to the teenagers was through schools, youth clubs and youth training schemes. Access to the families was through local organizations, such as the National Women's Register.

Two types of data were collected from the teenagers. A questionnaire probed their family composition; the type and scope of accommodation; routine activities and behaviour in relation to the use of space and attitudes to rules and the use of space in the home. The questionnaire was accompanied by an inventory of self-reported drinking patterns and attitudes which we have developed to investigate under-age drinking locally. The inventory focusses on frequency, location and peer/family influences on drinking and experiences of drunkenness. The attitude scale broadly assesses positive/negative associations with teenage drinking. A similar 'boundary styles' questionnaire was administered to parents, without the drinking inventory.

Detailed case studies of self-reported problem drinkers were obtained through structured interviews with 17 adults, identified through the probation service, the Alcohol Advisory Service and the Salvation Army. Data were obtained from the case studies by asking problem drinkers to recall details of their home environment when they were teenagers. These observations were obtained in voluntary and confidential interview sessions conducted by an alcohol counsellor. Although there are some problems associated with this recall technique, within the limited scope of the pilot study the retrospective assessment of 'family boundaries' served to give some indication of the potential development of patterns identified in the teenage sample and elicited substantially more information than the structured questionnaire method. The case study interviews also fed back into the research process as they were conducted in a therapeutic context.

Results

The inventory of drinking patterns and attitudes administered to the teenagers enabled us to plot a distribution of scores along two variables relating to drinking frequency and experiences of drunkenness. The highest decile of scores along these alcohol variables constituted a group of teenagers who reported drinking at least once a week or more and who had experienced drunkenness on more than one occasion. The high scorers (Hi-Ds) on the 'alcohol variables' could be identified as having characteristic family details and an arrangement of space in the home that was less related to the needs of family members. Physical space was a restrictive factor in terms of the number of rooms available for use by individual family members, but Hi-Ds' families were less likely to contain one or more siblings younger than eleven years old. Hi-Ds' families were not larger than the sample as a whole (mean number of children = 2.8).

In order to outline a clearer picture of the subsample of Hi-Ds and to identify any particularly significant variables, the Hi-Ds were contrasted with a subsample from the other end of the distribution of scores on the 'alcohol variables'. This subsample constituted 22 per cent of the full sample and were defined as those teenagers who reported drinking less than once a month and who had never experienced drunkenness. The subsample were labelled Lo-Ds.

Briefly, the drinkers tended to be in the older age group in the sample and lived in households with more adult members. They lived in a variety of types of accommodation, but the terraced dwelling with a separate kitchen, living room and 'best room' typical of older parts of the city, rather than the newer outer estates predominated. Hi-Ds contrasted sharply with Lo-Ds in their lack of access to a bedroom of their own. Their household space was also more likely to be shared with a pet dog. Indoor pursuits such as watching TV or reading were less frequent activities of Hi-Ds than other hobbies which usually took them out of the house. Hi-Ds were less likely to have access to a room or space in which they could engage in activities in privacy, away from other family members. Parental attitudes to allowing domestic space to be shared with teenagers' friends were more liberal, even though privacy was not assured. Lack of physical space did not result in Hi-Ds reporting feelings of being restricted.

The questionnaire data give only limited information about 'psychological boundaries' that operate within families. Questions which may have indicated the existence of rigid household rules and attitudes to discipline did not probe deep enough to suggest any clear styles of parental control and boundary enforcement. However, a comparison of parents' and teenagers' responses to questions relating to perceptions of imposed order in the home and teenagers' access to space in the home revealed some discrepancies between the perceptions of the different generations. Most significantly, parents and teenagers disagreed on their reported feelings of 'being restricted' in almost 50 per cent (22/45) of cases. Where there were disagreements, teenagers were more likely than adults to report that they did not feel restricted. The case studies provided an opportunity to explore these interpersonal boundaries further.

Interviews with problem drinkers

Analysis of the details of 17 structured interviews with self-reported problem drinkers provided a much more graphic illustration of the control of household rules, relationships and use of physical space. The descriptions of the home lives of self-reported problem drinkers enabled us to look at some of the psychological boundaries created by the construction and enforcement of rules and the way in which they interacted with the use of domestic space to govern factors influential in the development of self-identity in the adolescent, such as opportunities for personal expression and privacy.

In categorizing the case studies, household rules were assessed on reported 'strictness' about adherence to:

- pre-set bed times or 'be-in the-house-by' times
- the performance of defined household chores
- attendance at pre-set family meal times

Respondents' descriptions of the arrangements were classified into either 'rigid' or 'relaxed' categories. The two categories were not mutually exclusive, but could be identified separately. For example, the following would be classified as a description of 'rigid' rules:

> *A's mother was a full time housewife who, according to her daughter, made everyone's life a misery with her strictness....At this time, A was still at school and her day would begin at 7.15 am, when she and her two younger sisters would be woken by their mother. Breakfast would be laid out on the kitchen table by 7.30 am prompt. However, in the 15 minutes between 7.15 and 7.30 am, all of the youngsters had to wash and then make their*

> beds. From about the age of 7 years, their mother expected the children to make their own beds. 'Hospital corners' were inspected periodically and if not to the mother's satisfaction the bed had to be remade amid the inevitable tears consequent upon a slap from mother. Should one of her daughters not be at the table by 7.30 am, her breakfast would be scraped into the bin and no second chance would be given.

An example of 'relaxed' rules would indicate the situation where household rules specifically accommodated the interests of the children:

> Because his mother worked weekdays until 6 pm, C would, upon his return from school, begin to prepare the evening meal "out of self-interest, rather than obligation", because if he had waited until his mother's return, he would have been "starving". Apart from helping with the evening meal, C was not asked to help with the household chores. "Mother did everything". C's mother kept the home neat and tidy, but preferred to rearrange furniture etc. once the children had gone to bed. No special rules existed regarding keeping the home clean and cushions could be spread out on the living room floor for comfort, if desired. Parental supervision of homework was not exercised and so long as C did not bring trouble home from school, his parents showed only a passing interest in his studies.

The case studies highlighted the fact that the existence of household rules did not necessarily mean that they were enforced by any sanctions and conversely that discipline was not necessarily used in conjunction with a set of clearly defined rules. The discipline element in the case histories was therefore analysed to identify three features separately:

- by whom it was enforced
- the sanctions of the methods used
- the frequency with which they were used

Indicators of opportunities for self-expression were taken from reported parental encouragement to take up hobbies, interests, etc. and permission to decorate the respondents' bedroom as they wished or to adopt the dress and hairstyles of their own choice. Indicators of opportunities for respondents to attain privacy were taken from direct statements about privacy, such as

> When aged 15, H recalled that privacy was a difficult state to achieve. Her mother did not like family members to lock the bathroom door and would make the point of trying to open the

> door to check access in case of emergencies. Rows were plentiful
> as H tried to frustrate her mother and ensure privacy,

or from reported parental permission to invite friends into the home and entertain them without interruption from other family members.

Of the case studies, seven out of the 17, the largest group, lived in households in which rigid rules existed and were enforced by discipline of various types, with a high proportion of physical reprimands, such as

> F was expected to complete his daily chores. Failure to do so
> would invariably result in "a thick ear" courtesy of his mother.

Of those without rigid rules, the enforcement of discipline appeared to be the cause of family conflict, eg.

> Typically, it was said that the conversational currency was a sort
> of sarcasm with family members sniping at each other with put
> downs of all kinds.

None of the four households which did not have any restrictions due to physical space employed rigid rules and discipline tended to be relaxed. Overall, the case studies revealed a spectrum of types of accommodation, from one-bedroomed tenements to five-bedroomed, owner-occupied, semi-detached houses; and a range of styles of enforcement of psychological boundaries, with the rigid styles providing fewer opportunities for personal expression and privacy.

Before considering individual case studies, let us summarize our observations so far. A high proportion (77 per cent) lived in restricted households, that is, where children over the age of eleven had to share a bedroom, suggesting that density may be important in relation to boundary enforcement. Seven out of the 17 were in families with rigid rules, positional families in Bernstein's terms, and in all these cases there were restrictions of physical space. Conversely, four respondents felt that there had been no restrictions of physical space and two in this group suggested that their domestic regimes had been relaxed. A third group of three did not suggest any particular rigidity in regard to boundary enforcement and appeared to have normal communication patterns within the family. Finally, three experienced weakly classified regimes. Thus, the boundary enforcement hypothesis is not supported strongly although the connection between extreme boundary styles and density is interesting, with ten out of thirteen interviewees from households where there was a lack of space reporting either very weak or very strong boundary enforcement. There was not enough detail in the interview transcripts to characterize all individual cases on the disengagement/enmeshment axis with much conviction although parts of some of the reports are suggestive and in the examples given below the labels are applied tentatively. Conflicts which respondents felt to be associated with boundary style can be better illustrated with extracts from some of the individual accounts, particularly those in the rigid or strongly classified and very relaxed, weakly classified categories. These may be compared with domestic regimes which do not appear to be problematic and where no connection between the onset of alcoholism and the use of space or time in the home is suggested.

Example case studies

1. 'David': strongly classified, disengaged

> David described his home life as a fifteen year old in 1968 when he lived with his parents, a nine year old brother and a ten year old sister in a semi-detached house rented from the Ministry of Defence. The location was rural and there were plenty of recreational opportunities in the area. Boundary enforcement began at the entrance to the house. Only the back door could be used for entry and shoes had to be exchanged for slippers on the doorstep. Only the father had a front door key.
>
> The interior space was highly organized. Dad had his special chair near the TV and radio in the living room and the rest of the family had their own recognized seating places. The other living room was a 'best' room, reserved for visitors but not attractive in any case because it 'was always freezing'. Mother organized the house. She liked everything neat and tidy. Feet were not allowed on chairs, and neither food nor friends could be taken upstairs. David's father was 'a bit unapproachable'. Typically, he would return from work, have his tea and retire to the front room for the night to listen to the radio, watch TV, or read.
>
> David recalled the regular timing of events. Saturday night was always bath night; Monday was always wash day. Bed times for the children were fixed and strictly adhered to. The parents always went to bed at 10.30.

2. 'Ashley': strongly classified, enmeshed

> Ashley is forty-nine years old. When he was fifteen, he lived in a four-bedroomed council house with four older brothers and three

sisters, two of whom were older. Mother was a full time housewife who kept all the rooms in the house neat and tidy. There was one living room used by all the family and space here was at a premium. Father had his chair by the fire. There was a 'best' room but father's permission was needed to use it. Ashley was allowed to take his girlfriend into the best room but 'every ten minutes, a head would pop through the door and father would ask if they were alright'. Meals were eaten in the kitchen with the parents and the six oldest children sitting at the table. Dad was served first.

Dad's word was law. He frequently physically punished the children and physically abused his wife after drinking. When she was about twenty, Ashley's elder sister received a thick ear for talking back to her Dad after she discovered him following her 'to see what she was up to.' The adult sons had to be back by eleven after an evening out and the eldest daughter by ten-thirty. Ashley had to be in the house by nine-thirty in the evening although he was working full-time and had a steady girlfriend. He recalled his eldest brother, then twenty one, being knocked out cold by his father for arriving home late and the worse for drink. He was told, 'If you don't like the rules, you can always go.'

3. 'Joe': weakly classified, connected

When he was fifteen, Joe lived with his parents, a thirteen-year-old brother and two sisters, aged ten and eight, in a three bedroomed council house. His grandfather was also part of the family until he died, when Joe was thirteen, and Joe recalled that he was more like a father, taking an interest in his homework, and so on. Father worked as a lorry driver and mother had a part-time factory job. Although 'we hardly saw Dad', they did do things together, for example, Joe played chess with his father. When father was absent, however, Joe tended to run the house, making decisions about which TV programmes to watch and suggesting bed times for the younger children. He was also involved in preparing meals, largely out of self-interest.

Because there was a shortage of space, several of the children ate their meals away from the kitchen table and the parents did not raise objections to snacks being eaten in the bedrooms. Apart from outdoor shoes having to be left on the doormat, there were no *particular rules about the use of space in the house. He said mother liked to keep the house neat and tidy but would clean up after the children had gone to bed. Neither parent figured prominently in his recollections. Despite the obvious congestion in the house, Joe did not complain about a lack of privacy. However, he did have two paper rounds which enabled him to get out of the house.*

4. 'Norman': weakly classified, separated

Norman lived in a five-bedroomed house with his mother, stepfather, the stepfather's son and daughter, and his mother's father. The house had a large kitchen and a large, open-plan dining/living room. Apart from Sunday lunch, 'a weekly ritual', family members tended to make their own meals and eat when they wanted. Both parents worked long hours. On weekday evenings, they would not return until about 7 pm, when 'they were too tired to mix much'. They occasionally entertained foreign business people, when the children were asked to stay upstairs. Norman recalled that friends were allowed in the house without restriction and sometimes the parents did not know who was actually in the house.

There were few rules. By the time he was fifteen, Norman had flexible bed times. He wasn't allowed to play his records when his father was in the living room. A cleaning woman was employed three days a week and tidiness was not seen as a problem. Norman said that he had an enjoyable, relaxed childhood. So long as he did not bring any trouble home, he was left to his own devices.

Discussion

The first two cases illustrate family and home backgrounds that occurred with greater frequency than the more relaxed regimes experienced by Joe and Norman but, clearly, a causal link between boundary style and problem drinking cannot be suggested. The arbitrary use of parental power has been examined in other studies, for example by Holmes and Robins (1987) who found that "*unfair, harsh and inconsistent discipline by parents predicted alcohol and depressive disorders* [in children] *independently of the effects of parental psychiatric history, and of the respondent's sex and the severity of childhood behavior problems*". Cases like 'David' and 'Ashley', which comprised about half of our sample, appear to support this conclusion but the connection can only be suggested tentatively. The categorization itself is difficult because each account contains elements of order and disorder, control and permissiveness.

Two positive conclusions can be drawn from the study, however. First, space, both in terms of density of occupation and the design of the home can be seen to have an integral role in family interactions and this issue could be examined more systematically in future research. In particular, overcrowding may exacerbate a problem of excessively weak or excessively strong boundary maintenance. Secondly, although the predictive possibilities of this kind of study are limited, a focus on boundaries in the home may have value in therapy in that it may help the client to appreciate an unrealized source of tension during childhood and adolescence.

Clearly, a causal link between boundary styles and problem drinking cannot be proposed as too many combinations of the different styles and other factors predisposing adolescents to problem behaviour exist. However, the case studies suggest a relationship between the amount of physical space available in a household and the use of strict rules and discipline in maintaining parental control. Of the households where there were no restrictions on physical space, rules and discipline tended to be relaxed. In 50 per cent of households that did have restrictions on physical space, respondents reported the existence of rigid rules and discipline. We would argue, therefore, that the spatial dimension of boundary enforcement in the home environment may be significant and any utilization of social and psychological concepts of boundaries must be taken in a 'spatial' context.

In the study we have been concerned to relate these concepts to the behaviour of potential problem drinkers. Generalizations about the interaction of different boundary styles and the intensity of their enforcement in relation to drinking behaviour are not possible, but the case study method used in the pilot study drew our attention to the clinical implications of a discussion of the different types of boundary styles. The researcher conducting the case study interviews was engaged in counselling work with the self-reported problem drinkers and was able to assess the impact of the study interview on the respondent's development. Respondents reported that the 'family boundary aspects' of their personal development had not been explored in counselling sessions previously, but had provided a means of finding further insight into their problem behaviour.

Increased awareness of interactions between domestic space, modes of control and problem drinking is helpful not only to researchers and professionals but also to family members, whether drinking sensibly or otherwise.

SECTION 4

Conclusions and Implications

Chapter 10

Teenage drinking: home and family influences

There is nothing exceptional about most teenage drinking behaviour. What the media tend to report often in alarmist and sensationalist terms is but a feature of the normal transition to adulthood. More than that, it is evident from our studies that alcohol consumption by adolescents has positive aspects, particularly in establishing a pattern of sensible drinking and in contributing *to* family socialization. The perception of teenagers as heavy and irresponsible drinkers reflects the construction of adolescence as a problem period and adolescents as a deviant minority. Clearly, heavy drinking can be a problem in itself and one that contributes to health problems and anti-social behaviour but it is a feature of adolescence culture which has been greatly exaggerated. What teenagers do often fails to match adults' idealized conceptions of what childhood and adolescence should be like. Stereotypes need correction and we have tried to contribute to this by charting the normal range of teenage drinking.

Normative adolescent alcohol use

Although young problem drinkers are a major source of concern, surveys have consistently portrayed teenage drinking as a normal development in the context of the psychosocial environment. Drinking is predominantly a social behaviour and is widely regarded as a key indicator of adult status.

Throughout this book we have developed and emphasized a theme of normative adolescent alcohol use. We suggest that this is the only sensible approach, given that adult alcohol use is widespread, acceptable and even encouraged. Whilst some have proposed that:

> *"young people's drinking is essentially different to the drinking behaviour of adults."* (O'Connor 1984, p.159)

we argue that adolescent drinking is an adult-like teenage behaviour, albeit an immature one for some individuals. The development of alcohol use by adolescents should be regarded as a normal developmental transitional behaviour between childhood abstinence and adult drinking. We cannot expect teenagers to learn how to drink sensibly and appropriately overnight, as they pass the legal drinking age threshold. To some extent English law achieves this by permitting adolescent drinking only under certain conditions, or only when supervised by an adult. In addition, the 'blind-eye' turned to problem-free under-age drinking by many groups in our society, including parents and police, serves to facilitate the learning process.

Nevertheless, a small minority of adolescents misuse alcohol. Our studies have attempted to identify some conditions which may result in teenage problem drinking, specifically, those features of home and family life which encourage transgressions. These transgressions may be expressed as problem drinking or other forms of substance abuse. The family context is crucial here and our analysis of family dynamics differs from previous research in that we have incorporated domestic space as a variable element of the family system. We have been concerned to 'spatialize the social' and 'socialize the spatial' in a locale which has been examined largely in an aspatial way by psychologists and which has been neglected by geographers. Considering the home as a physical space and the family together has been one of the central aspects of this project. We have argued that the constraining and enabling effects of both the design of the home and power relations in the family are elements of the same problem. Individuals, interacting with other members of the family, manipulate space to meet their needs, which may bring them into conflict with others, but at the same time their actions are constrained by the physical partitioning of the house or flat. Thus, the material environment of the home has a presence in family relationships, one which should be incorporated in models of family systems.

As we have seen, there have been numerous surveys of adolescent drinkers. Most have looked at questions of who, when, where, what and why? Most socio-demographic studies consistently report that teenage drinking starts early, is generally widespread, but surprisingly few alcohol abuse problems emerge. In distinguishing between 'normal' teenage drinking and problem drinking we have argued that psychosocial aspects - rather than socio-demographic factors - are likely to be more important.

On the whole, it is inappropriate to portray alcohol use as a deviant behaviour, and it is also inappropriate to encourage teenagers to abstain. However, some researchers and commentators have tried to do just this. For example, an editorial in the *Journal of the Royal Society of Health* (1991, p.2) describes alcohol as a *"food, a drug, a tonic substance, and a social plague"*. In the *Journal of Drug Education*, Stumphauzer (1983, p.40) suggests that adolescent abstainers have a social skill worthy of serious study so that:

> "(1) this skill could be further encouraged in these teenagers. (2) the process of learning abstinence could be understood; and, (3) this social skill, if there is one, could be taught to other young people in terms of drug education or prevention."

These attitudes remind one of the sensationalism in many media reports of teenage drinking, which we pointed out earlier. Alcohol use is not a "social plague", nor should abstinence be regarded or encouraged as a "social skill", at least not in western 'drinking' societies. On the contrary, parents and families should teach their children and teenagers how to drink. It is not adolescent drinking which is the problem, but the failure to teach some young people *how to drink sensibly*.

However, there is also a down-side to the apparent laxity in enforcing the U.K. drinking laws for minors. Some teenagers, because of inadequate socialization, do not develop sensible and appropriate teenage drinking behaviour, and the opportunities therefore to misuse alcohol are many.

Alcohol misuse

How should we approach this problem? Two main schools of thought address this issue. One suggests that the way to prevent problem drinking is to make alcohol more unavailable to the population, either through raising taxes, or in the case of young drinkers, through raising the legal drinking age. Apart from the obvious 'freedom of choice' implications involved in restricting what is historically and currently *for many* a pleasurable and safe activity, it seems rather heavy handed, perhaps perverse, to try and reduce the problem drinking of a few by targeting everybody.

The second school of thought predominates in the U.K. This suggests that the way to tackle problem drinking, including adolescent problem drinking, is to educate and help people rather than control them. Now this is not an easy option. One cannot just simply tell people not to do something because it is wrong or dangerous. Such an approach, typified by the 'Just Say No' campaign, fails to address the complex aetiology involved in the development of alcohol and substance abuse.

It is necessary to understand the complexities of socialization into drinking behaviour, and to this end a programme of continuing research needs to inform alcohol policies. In this book we have brought our own ideas and research to the debate. To our minds, the influence of home environment and family life is central to the socialization of adolescent alcohol use, whether it is optimal socialization and sensible drinking, or dysfunctional socialization and deviant patterns of alcohol use. The family is an important psychosocial influence in the development of social skills: skills which are important in the largely social activity of drinking alcohol. Therefore we have focussed in this book on psychosocial-spatial influences of home and family, rather than on socio-demographic variables which are external to family life.

Parental influences

In 1972 Davies and Stacey's landmark developmental study of teenagers and alcohol in Glasgow examined ways in which young people perceive their parents and indicated that parental behaviour and attitudes were exerting some influence over teenage drinking. They drew attention, in particular, to disapproving or prohibiting attitudes on the part of parents towards adolescent drinking, such attitudes being frequently associated with heavier drinking amongst offspring. Davies and Stacey argued that such parental attitudes increase the likelihood that adolescent members of the family will use alcohol to 'demonstrate' rejection of parental authority, or adult norms and values in general.

Our findings are very much in line with these earlier observations. However, the focus of our research is primarily on the family dynamics within the home environment, which enables us to conceptualize such alcohol use in terms of boundary transgression, rather than negative attitudes and behaviours.

One important recommendation made by Davies and Stacey concerned drinking in the home:

> "It seems advisable...for parents to provide a home environment in which their children learn the controlled use of alcohol, should these young people wish to do so." (p.xvi)

It is of significance to report that in most families in our studies, that seems to have been the case. The deviant drinking behaviour and attitudes of the remaining minority of teenagers were more likely to be associated with 'deviant' family dynamics relating to authoritarian, lax and/or inconsistent modes of discipline, control, support and/or boundary enforcement in the home environment.

In her study of young English and Irish drinkers (1978), O'Connor found it necessary to differentiate the influence of fathers and mothers in order to understand the socialization process within the family circle. She observed that parental *attitudes* towards drinking, rather than parental drinking *behaviour* or general family relationships, were the most important influence on their children's drinking behaviour. While the influence of the mother was evident, the father's influence on children's drinking appeared to be greater. There was a strong relationship between heavy drinking fathers and heavy drinking children.

O'Connor further noted that it was the children's *perception* of parental attitudes, rather than attitudes reported by parents themselves, that was of more importance. Our research emphasizes this point, with our family life questionnaires and interviews relying heavily on teenagers' perceptions of family life and home environment.

Cognition

In chapter 3 we discussed how social cognition might influence drinking behaviour. A teenager's reasons for drinking and expectancies about the effects of alcohol were, we suggested, related to actual drinking behaviour. We can regard such reasons and expectancies as manifestations of a cognitive schema for alcohol use. As we suggested in chapter 7, alcohol-specific family influences (social learning) are important in the development of a schema for drinking. Non-alcohol-specific family influences, such as support and control, are influential in a more general sense in that they are important in the development of moral behaviour, conscience and social competence. It would therefore be useful and appropriate to look at how family socialization influences relate to the development of a schema for drinking alcohol, in terms of reasons and expectancies. Thus it is necessary to move beyond the examination of language-based communications (Wells 1981; see chapter 3) when looking at socialized processing, to also consider social, psychological and spatial influences. It may be that a schema which incorporates drinking to get drunk as a reason for drinking depends both on the more overt language-based communication of this as an appropriate behaviour, and also on the more covert socialization influence of family dynamics.

When asked about their drinking, teenagers may state reasons and expectancies about alcohol use which may be post-hoc attitudes, but as we suggested in chapter 3, it may be that these attitudes influence future drinking in the form of a self-fulfilling prophecy. As such, these markers of alcohol use schemata may serve a useful role as diagnostic tools. Inappropriate reasons for drinking, inappropriate expectations about the effects of alcohol, or indeed just having too many reasons to use alcohol may indicate problem drinking or may predispose to problem drinking. Cognitive modification techniques (eg. Försterling 1985) may be useful in this sense to change the alcohol use schemata of (potential) problem drinkers.

Of course, on an educational and preventative basis, it is the actual development of such inappropriate schemata in the first place which needs to be addressed, and as we stated, we need to understand more about the social, psychological and spatial factors which contribute to the socialization of such alcohol use schemata. Better knowledge of such factors would enable positive socialization behaviours (for sensible adolescent drinking) to be encouraged, and dysfunctional socialization behaviours to be discouraged.

Socially competent drinking

Competent adolescent drinking should be the desired goal of adolescent alcohol education. Although at first glance this might seem a strange thing to say (since a competent drinker might be viewed as someone who drinks a lot - an 'accomplished' drinker), this is not the case. Competence in fact refers to the ability of an individual to behave in an appropriate and acceptable way. The Oxford English Dictionary defines competence as being "properly qualified". In this sense competent drinking is drinking in a properly qualified way. Thus socially competent drinking implies sensible and appropriate (problem-free) drinking behaviour. Competence can also be measured on other levels. Healthily competent individuals do not compromise their health, for example with excessive alcohol use or with risky alcohol associated behaviour. Psychologically competent individuals do not compromise their psychological functioning, for example with excessive alcohol use. So how do we socialize social, health and psychological competence for alcohol use by teenagers?

Family socialization

Family life plays an important socialization role for teenage alcohol use. We have described how family dynamics incorporate non-alcohol-specific and alcohol-specific socialization behaviours. Our results show that moderate support, moderate control, moderate levels of family drinking and a moderating attitude by parents to their offspring's alcohol use all contribute to sensible adolescent drinking behaviour. Low support, low control, heavier parental drinking and parental indifference to their offspring's drinking were linked with heavier drinking. This is in line with family systems theory which suggests that extremes of family behaviour leads to inadequate functioning: in this case in terms of heavier drinking. Importantly, for family theory in general as well as adolescent drinking research, we also clarified the family systems perspective concerning the other extreme of these family behaviours. Previous research studies had failed to find the predicted relationship between perceived family relationships and substance misuse for enmeshed (high support) families. We suggested that this was because previous family systems models and hypotheses failed to consider adequately the range of normality of the target behaviour. If, for example, we take adolescent drinking behaviour, then not only is heavy drinking a deviant behaviour, but so is non-drinking by adolescents in a culture which condones teenage drinking and in which most adolescents do in fact drink. Thus we predicted and found that high support, high control, parental non-drinking and parental disapproval towards their offsprings' actual or potential alcohol use was linked with self-reported non-drinking or low drinking by adolescents.

We can conclude then that good family dynamics have a positive social influence on teenage drinking. This knowledge should inform alcohol education policy and strategies, but not only should teenagers themselves be targetted for alcohol education, but parents and families as well. In line with family systems theory, behaviour is a function of the whole family system, and as such the whole family system needs to be considered when trying to encourage teenagers to drink sensibly.

Boundaries

Traditionally, most approaches to family dynamics have focussed exclusively on psychosocial interactions and relationships. In structural family systems theory for example, boundaries within the family system are defined by psychological relationships. But boundaries also exist beyond the psychosocial plane, as we pointed out in chapter 8. Physical boundaries, such as the geographical layout of the home, confine and restrict, to some extent dictate, the nature of psychosocial boundaries and relationships.

The interaction between psychosocial and spatial boundaries in the home environment throws some light on the anomolous finding of strict levels of control being associated with heavier or problem drinking, which we commented on in chapter 5 (c.f. Barnes et al 1986; Rollins & Thomas 1979). Although we did not replicate this in the large general sample survey which we reported on in chapter 7, the results of the boundary enforcement study (chapter 9) suggest a possible reason for this pattern. A tentative conclusion from the boundary enforcement study of self-reported problem drinkers was that rigid rules and strict parental control were linked to restrictions on physical space in the home. In those households where there were no restrictions on physical space, rules and discipline tended to be relaxed. It might be that 'overcrowding' and associated strict levels of control are linked with (potential) problem drinking. This hypothesis merits further consideration and investigation. We also pointed to the distinction between attempted control and achieved control as a possible factor, which should also be considered in future research.

Peer groups

Peer influences are frequently reported as an important aetiological factor in the development of teenage drinking, sometimes as more influential than family socialization. Whilst not disputing this stance, current theories of deviance (eg. Hirschi's Control Theory) suggest that dysfunctional family environment leads to increased identification with deviant peer groups. Peer group pressure seems to be a less clear-cut phenomenon than previously thought. The important issue here is not peer pressure *per se*, but *why* some teenagers are particularly susceptible to peer influence whilst others are not. We have argued that family processes exert a major influence in the development of susceptibility or resistance to peer influence. Furthermore, recent conceptions of peer pressure may be criticized as being too simplistic. In fact peer-self influences are reciprocal and voluntary. To suggest that teenagers should resist peer pressure to drink implies that these teenagers are somehow coerced into drinking. This is a naive proposition. Young people want to drink alcohol as part of their social behaviour, and the peer group provides an opportunity to do so. This is supported by the finding that most teenagers give appropriate and positive reasons for drinking (Foxcroft & Lowe 1992; see chapter 3).

At the same time the peer group should not be discounted from research into teenage drinking. Peer groups provide an active opportunity for young people to drink in a variety of different ways. If drinking by a teenager and his or her peers is 'deviant' or problematical, then we need to know why. Why do individuals choose to drink in a deviant way with their peers? We can again turn to the socializing influence of parents and family as one important influence.

Teenagers may choose to drink with friends who have similar alcohol use schemata. If individuals have a deviant alcohol use schema due in part to dysfunctional family socialization, then these teenagers are perhaps more susceptible to influence from deviant peer groups (in that they choose to mix with and behave like these peers) than to influence from an inadequately socializing family. Such peer groups may set their own standards of behaviour, and may try to compensate for poor family identity by maximizing their group identity. This might involve taking on more deviant behaviours as a peer group. By "deviancy amplification" (Cohen 1971), labelled as deviant, these groups may in fact become more deviant.

In this context, peer pressure or peer opportunity to drink in a deviant way is symptomatic of family dysfunction. As far as alcohol education is concerned, we need to encourage young people how to drink properly (optimal family socialization) rather than preventing them from starting to drink problematically (resistance to peer pressure).

Moreover, if peer pressure is a form of propaganda against which counter propaganda (in the form of "Just say No" messages and campaigns, for example) is being directed, then many young people may be just as (or even more) likely to "say no" to these messages, which are in any case more indirect and diffuse than the immediate face-to-face impact of peer pressure.

Other substance use

The model of family dynamics we have proposed in this book is not just specific to teenage alcohol use. Other substance use behaviours are also learned behaviours, and as such socialization influences are important. However, the balance of influence between non-substance-specific family behaviours and substance-specific family behaviours may vary depending on the particular substance and the prevailing social and cultural norms for that substance. Alcohol use is regarded in western countries as a socially acceptable and generally positive social behaviour, and alcohol-specific family influences are especially important as we saw in chapter 7.

Kandel and her colleagues, in their stage theory of substance use, suggest that alcohol is the first step, or stage, on the road to further substance misuse (eg. marijuana, solvents, cocaine, heroin, crack). Normal adolescent drinking is widespread, however, and perhaps amongst older teenagers perhaps even more widespread than is adult drinking. One could argue therefore that teenage drinkers are more likely *not* to develop further substance use behaviour since the majority do not go on to use these other substances. What Kandel's data actually suggest is that *deviant* alcohol use in adolescence (eg. use of hard liquor) is predictive of other substance use and abuse.

Smoking, however, is perceived more and more these days as a negative social behaviour, and parental attitudes to their offspring's smoking may contrast with their own smoking behaviour. As such, family process influences may take on more importance for teenage smoking, to the extent that dysfunctional levels of support and control might lead to deviant smoking behaviour, probably shared with a smoking peer group. But there may be a complexity involved here due to the sex of the individual. We pointed out in chapter 7 that young females smoke more than young males, and we tentatively suggested that this might be part of an 'equal opportunity' substance use strategy by females. Thus, in the absence of such a 'strategy', males might be more susceptible than females to family socialization influences for smoking. Supporting this hypothesis, we found in a recent study (Foxcroft & Lowe 1992d) that levels of support and control were linked to smoking behaviour in male, but not female, teenagers. This finding needs to be followed up with more specific research studies, but there are some important implications if this is indeed true.

Other substances, such as solvents, marijuana, MDMA, tranquillizers, cocaine, heroin, probably do not feature strongly in substance-specific family behaviours. Few parents or families will model such behaviours, and parental attitudes are likely to be negative and possibly poorly informed. Therefore family *process* behaviours such as support and control may be implicated more strongly in the family socialization of these substance use behaviours.

Various other risk factors have been associated with adolescent alcohol/substance use (Bloch *et al* 1991). The risk factor approach, especially prevalent in the U.S.A., has implications for prevention and intervention. From our studies of reasons for drinking and alcohol expectancies we have suggested that these approaches could offer useful scope as diagnostic tools for identifying teenagers who may be at risk for developing alcohol-related problems. Unfortunately, there seems to be no general agreement about predictor variables. It is important to emphasize, moreover, that although the presence of risk factors may help to identify those who are most vulnerable, it does not mean that any individual who has these distinguishing features will inevitably develop problems.

Implications

There are a number of implications from our studies in relation to the role of the family in alcohol education, prevention and intervention strategies, and home technologies which influence boundaries and the control of domestic space. The suggestions made below are, however, only tentative, and parents, health educators, planners and related professionals, together with interested teenagers, may well reach different conclusions of their own on the basis of the observations presented.

Home environment

The research concerned with home environment has several implications for intervention strategies. First, it appeared in the counselling sessions that recollections of home and family, the details of individual relationships and spaces in the home, were of therapeutic value for clients. Both good and bad memories which had not previously been articulated contributed to the therapeutic process. We would agree with Godkin (1980) that recollections of place have a role in counselling and, particularly in relation to problem drinking, recollections of inclusion and exclusion in the home environment.

Secondly, there are some possible lessons for the design of dwellings but here we would be rather more cautious. There is some evidence from our study of a connection between the design of the home and patterns of boundary enforcement in families but it does not point in one particular direction. Thus, we could not say that there are certain layouts which improve the quality of family interactions and reduce the chances of exclusion, alienation and problem behaviour. There are behaviours which are potentially damaging, like the parental urge to exclude children from certain spaces in the home, and such behaviour may be facilitated by the design of the house but it is clearly the case that people react differently to the same environment for a number of reasons connected with culture, family structure, neighbourhood influences, and so on. As Miller (1990, p.50) observed:

> "...*one householder's ample space* [could be] *for another 'totally inadequate' (with no evident correlation with numbers of children and similar factors)."*

Apart from the variable relationship between space and the user, one practical problem which renders any proposals for design improvements rather unrealistic is that, for most families, the home is a 'received environment'. The arrangement of rooms is fixed. The only way in which people can appropriate domestic space, that is, make a house or flat designed and supplied by others their own, is to decorate it or make changes to the internal fittings. Thus, some of the more radical critiques of housing, while interesting, do not provide realistic prescriptions for change. John Turner, an advocate of 'self-build' in the 1960s, found greater levels of satisfaction among the inhabitants of self-built shanty towns (barriadas) in Lima, Peru than among families living in municipal apartments (Turner, 1971). He drew lessons from this for housing in the developed world, proposing building technologies and communal forms of resource use which would give people much more control over the design of their homes. However, the state and the institutions which finance housing discourage user involvement. They impose standards to minimize risk and encourage conformity. Practice favours large building firms supplying standardized units and this leaves little scope for architects to innovate. Thus, users are consumers rather than providers of shelter and the opportunites for appropriation are very limited. Predictably, architectural fashions fail to reflect the preferences of many consumers because the world view of the user, the owner or tenant, frequently differs from that of the architect. One Mass-Observation respondent in our study felt uneasy about an open-plan house and would have felt more comfortable with partitions to separate activities in the home. Similarly, Miller (1990, p. 50) noted that:

> "...when parlours are effectively forbidden by the architectural profession, the two-thirds of tenants who mentioned this subject kept a special area in the main room for their best, brought out at Christmas if at all. This was a population (on a working-class estate in London) among which the desire to partition space was strong."

Observations like these can be misleading. Surveys like Miller's indicate preferences but these are generally adult preferences. The differences, and possible conflicts, between the needs of children and the needs of adults are not revealed in most studies of consumption which derive their information from a single adult respondent. If there are changes to the home environment which could contribute to an improvement in relationships between parents and children and reduce the incidence of problem-creating family situations, then recommendations would have to come from more detailed and sensitive surveys which recorded the world views of children and their relationship with the home environment. Similarly, homes might better suit the needs of all their occupants if children were involved in their design but, given the structure of the building industry and its relationship with the architectural profession, this is unlikely to happen.

Inter-disciplinary research

While there may be few implications for practice in this study, we do feel that there is a future for inter-disciplinary research in this area. Geography and psychology have come together before, particularly in environmental psychology and behavioural studies which are currently unfashionable in geography. However, both psychological and geographical research could benefit from closer links with *cultural anthropology* from which many of the theoretical arguments on boundary issues derive and where there is now considerable interest in the home environment. The home is constituted by symbolic meanings which illuminate uses of domestic space and inter-personal relationships. Future research on substance abuse could be usefully set in an holistic framework provided by these three disciplines.

Indeed, we have tried in this book to look at adolescent drinking and family life from the perspective of different academic disciplines. We think that there is a great potential to improve knowledge by the collaboration of researchers and the bringing together of ideas from previously distinct academic disciplines. Although such ideas may have developed fairly independently, and the language and terminology used appear rather different, if we peel back the outer layers we may in fact reveal similarities or, indeed, helpful distinctions.

This does not only apply to models, theories and ideas. Research methods are traditionally quite narrow and conventional within each distinct discipline when compared to the variety of methods used across all social science disciplines. The expertise brought to the study of adolescent drinking and family life from different research methods within different academic disciplines should be beneficial. To this end, a certain amount of deconstruction is needed. We would agree with Bernstein (1971) that researchers need to negotiate and cross the boundaries between distinct academic and research areas.

Methodology

In crossing boundaries there is more opportunity to employ a sensible mix of research methods. In our research we have used quantitative surveys and questionnaires which led to descriptive and subsequently more analytic findings (via multivariate techniques). Another perspective was provided by case studies from semi-structured interviews, counselling sessions and Mass-Observation reports. These qualitative data enhance the richness of observations and complement the quantitative and statistically more powerful surveys and questionnaire data.

Cultural aspects

In the U.S.A. the level of under-age drinking has generally been found to be much less than in Great Britain. Only about 80 per cent of American adolescents aged 16 or over were reported to have consumed an alcoholic beverage (Rachel *et al* 1980, cited by Plant *et al* 1985). In Great Britain the level is nearer 95 per cent. Bearing this in mind, it is interesting to note the cultural variation in parent-child relations between England and the U.S.A. For instance Devereux (1970) found lower support and looser control in English families. Intuitively, this accords with the results of the meta-analysis in chapter 5, in which the majority of studies came from the U.S.A. That is, higher support and firmer control were found to be associated with lower drinking levels.

Social competence, as we pointed out, is heavily influenced by family socialization, and we can draw distinctions between social competence in different cultures. For example, in the U.K. autonomous individuals with good social skills and independence of thought are stereotypically viewed more positively. At the same time British culture tends to tolerate, perhaps respect, individual differences in behaviour, and there is little pressure for everyone to conform to a certain social or cultural stereotype. To quote an English proverb: *"You can't put a square peg into a round hole"*, suggesting that people are generally different from each other, and that it isn't necessary to try and make everybody conform to a given norm, i.e. a round hole. In western cultures individuality is emphasized, whereas, for example, Japanese culture encourages conformity to group norms, and everyone belongs to one group. There is great social pressure in Japan to conform to certain culturally stereotyped roles. To quote a Japanese proverb: *"The nail that protrudes must be hammered into the wood"*.

In this sense optimal socialization behaviours may vary cross-culturally. Remember that we suggested it was the range of functionality of the target behaviour which was important for the structural systems model of family functioning. In Japanese society and culture the range of normality of adolescent alcohol and substance use may vary from that in western societies, and we may find that optimal levels of support and control also vary cross-culturally. Other family behaviours may also be more prominent in other cultures and therefore need to be considered, for example the religiosity of the family which may have direct implications for alcohol use.

Given the established cultural variation in both adolescent drinking behaviour (Rachel *et al* 1980; Bank *et al* 1985) and parent-child relations (Devereux 1970), then it would be folly to directly compare results from different studies in different countries. Research is needed in other countries to discover the pattern and impact of family dynamics on adolescent alcohol use in a particular country. Comparative studies which use similar methods/measurements in different countries would benefit from triangulation with within-culture studies, enhancing the validity of the research. Even within countries there may be regional variations (Marsh *et al* 1986; Fogelman 1978), and it would be wise to take measurements from different regions within different countries.

The ideas and research we have elaborated in this book have undoubtedly been tainted by our own 'Brito-centric' perceptions and by a predominantly western society research knowledge base. It would be illuminating to examine these ideas in different societies and cultures, from both a within-culture and a between-culture (comparative) perspective.

Conclusions about family relationships, attitudes to domestic space and problem behaviour which may apply to white British working-class or middle-class families would not necessarily hold for, say, an Indian family settled in Britain or families in Mediterranean Europe. More importantly, cross-cultural studies would help to clarify issues like attitudes to domestic space or the role of alcohol in teenage sub-cultures and the family.

For example, on an anecdotal level, within Europe different countries have different social and cultural traditions regarding both family relationships and alcohol use. This is sometimes stereotyped as ranging from Anglo-Saxon behaviours in Northern Europe (typically less family centred and more binge or session drinking), to the Mediterranean cultures of Southern Europe (where there is a tradition of high family closeness and loyalty and lighter but more frequent alcohol use).

A large scale comparative study of family socialization and adolescent drinking over, say, a range of different European countries would offer scope for testing the generality of the family links and influences established so far, as well as perhaps providing further useful observations for alcohol education and intervention programmes.

Parenting skills

In the U.K. "parentcraft" classes are run by health service workers (health visitors and midwives) for prospective parents. The aim of these classes is to teach prospective parents how to look after a new-born baby, and how to deal with any problems that may arise. These health service workers also provide a comprehensive (and free) follow-up service after the baby is born.

This "parentcraft" service provides a useful model for a preventative strategy when dealing with potential or actual adolescent problem behaviours. Parenting skills are not only needed when children are very young, they are needed throughout all the growing-up years. Adolescence is, indeed, a period when parenting skills are very important, a period of intense boundary negotiation and transitional behaviours.

There is no reason why health care workers or family workers could not provide parentcraft classes for parents of adolescents or for parents and adolescents. These need not necessarily be run for every family with a teenager, but perhaps for those who feel they need to develop and improve their parenting skills.

Family therapy

Adolescent alcohol and substance misuse does create numerous individual and social problems. How can we help those individuals who misuse alcohol and other substances? One possibility would be to take the whole family system and address the problem there. In this context family dynamics involving psychological, social and spatial boundaries could be examined and re-negotiated. This of course needs to be facilitated by a professional and skilled family therapist. Before doing this however, a full assessment must be made of the problem. It is possible that the family might not be implicated: breaking up with a girlfriend or being bullied at school might be predisposing factors for some problem drinking individuals. However, in such cases families may still have a role to play. Even if family dynamics are not directly related to the problem behaviour, the family provides a useful resource for social support. Coping behaviours could be developed on a family basis rather than on an individual basis.

Research directions

The models and ideas we have presented in this book are at a relatively early stage of development. Future research, using a variety of methods, needs to be undertaken so that these models and ideas can be refined. There are several directions in which research should go. One is to test the theories and confirm the results we have presented so far. Another is to extend our research on adolescent alcohol use to other, distinct, adolescent substance use behaviours, and indeed to other adolescent social behaviours (eg. dating, sports, leisure, diet). It would also be useful to look at family influences together with other influences on adolescent drinking, to build up an overall picture of the complex aetiology.

A useful direction would be to consider our ideas and results in terms of the family health and illness cycle (Doherty & McCubbin 1985: Doherty & Campbell 1988), a model which looks at the impact of the family on health and illness; the impact of health and illness on the family; and families use of health care. Also, as we have already suggested, the family socialization of an alcohol use schema might be a frutiful area for future research.

Finally, as we suggested earlier, other research has shown that heavy drinking in adolescence is generally not predictive of problem drinking in early adulthood (Bagnall 1991). In other words not all heavy teenage drinkers become heavy adult drinkers - it appears to be a transient phenomenon for some. Nevertheless, there are some young people who continue to drink heavily into their adulthood. There are also young people who do not drink heavily as teenagers, but go on to become heavy drinkers as adults. For example, the work of Orford and Velleman (1990, 1991) points to the importance of a poor family life in the development of problem drinking in adulthood.

Longer-term heavy drinking by these individuals, throughout their adult lives, places a great burden on societies, both socially and financially. We suggest that family and home life dynamics might be implicated in the continued heavy drinking of some young people, and also in the development of adult problem drinking in individuals who did not drink problematically as teenagers. A fruitful area for future research therefore, supplementing our own work and that of other researchers in the field, would be a prospective longitudinal study.

Conclusions

Our focus has been on teenage drinking as a normative developmental transition. We have highlighted the influences of family life and of the home environment. This approach has implications for intervention strategies aimed at adolescent alcohol abuse/misuse, and, in terms of prevention, for alcohol education and guidance.

Although we have concentrated on family dynamics, we are well aware that this is only one factor, albeit an important one, in the multi-factorial aetiology of the development of alcohol use. We should not forget this. Nevertheless, our aim in this book has been to demonstrate the importance of family and home life for the positive socialization of adolescent drinking.

On the whole, alcohol use by young people in the U.K. is not a problem for themselves or for others. Family socialization appears to be quite robust, and it is possibly only the extremes of family dynamics and psychosocial-spatial interactions which lead to extremes of adolescent drinking behaviour for some individuals, be it alcohol abuse or abstention.

In reviewing research on the home by environmental psychologists, geographers and anthropologists, we have developed a schema for understanding the family's relationship to domestic space. Models of family systems can be combined with a model of spatial organization in the home. Boundaries are erected and boundary enforcement and transgression are important factors in the psycho-spatial dynamics of the family. We can use the family-space schema to explore childhood and adolescent experiences which link with various types of drinking behaviour.

To close, we hope that our ideas and research have been interesting, that these will inform researchers and practitioners in their study and work with adolescents, drinkers and families, and also in related fields.

Bibliography

Addeo EG, Addeo JR (1975) Why Our Children Drink. Englewood Cliffs, N.J: Prentice Hall
Adger H Jr (1991) Problems of alcohol and other drug use and abuse in adolescents. Journal of Adolescent Health 12, 606-613
Adler I, Kandel D (1982) A cross cultural comparison of sociopsychological factors in alcohol use in adolescents in Israel, France and the United States. Journal of Youth and Adolescence 11, 89-113
Adorno T, Frankel-Brunswick E, Levinson DJ, Sanford RN (1950) The Authoritarian Personality. New York: Harper
Aitken P (1978) Ten to Fourteen-year-olds and Alcohol: A Developmental Study in the Central Region of Scotland. London: H.M.S.O.
Akers RL, Krohn MD, Lanza-Kaduce L, Radosevich M (1979) Social learning and deviant behaviour: a specific test of a general theory. American Sociological Review 44, 636-655
Alaszewski A (1986) Institutional Care and the Mentally Handicapped: the Mental Handicap Hospital. Beckenham, Kent: Croom Helm
Alexander C (1966) The city is not a tree. Design 206, 47-55
Altman I (1975) The Environment and Social Behaviour. Monterey, CA: Brooks Cole
Alvarez FJ, Queipo D, Del Rio MC, Garcia MC (1991) Alcohol consumption in young adults in the rural communities of Spain. Alcohol and Alcoholism 26, 93-101
Amato PR (1990) Dimensions of the family environment as perceived by children: A multi-dimensional scaling analysis. Journal of Marriage and the Family 52, 613-620
Anderson SA, Gavazzi SM (1990) A test of the Olson Circumplex Model: examining its curvilinear assumption and the presence of extreme types. Family Process 29, 309-324
Andersson T, Magnusson D (1988) Drinking habits and alcohol abuse among young men: A prospective longitudinal study. Journal of Studies on Alcohol 49, 245-252
Andersson T, Magnusson D (1990) Biological maturation in adolescence and the development of drinking habits and alcohol abuse among males: A prospective longitudinal study. Journal of Youth and Adolescence 19, 33-41
A.P.A. (1980) American Psychiatric Association Diagnostic and Statistical Manual of Mental Disorders III. Washington D.C.: APA
Aronson E, Carlsmith JM (1963) The effect of the severity of threat on the devaluation of forbidden behaviour. Journal of Abnormal and Social Psychology 66, 584-588
Atkinson P (1985) Language, Structure and Reproduction: an Introduction to the Sociology of Basil Bernstein. Andover, Hants: Methuen
Ausubel D, Sullivan E (1970) Theory and problems of child development (2nd edition). New York: Grune and Stratton

Bachelard G (1981) La Poetique de l'Espace. Paris: Presses Universitaires
Bagnall G (1988) Use of alcohol, tobacco and illicit drugs amongst thirteen-year-olds in three areas of Britain. Drug and Alcohol Dependence 22, 241-251

Bagnall G (1990) Alcohol education for 13 year olds - does it work? Results from a controlled evaluation. British Journal of Addiction 85, 89-96

Bagnall G (1991) Alcohol and drug use in a Scottish cohort: 10 years on. British Journal of Addiction 86, 895-904

Balding J (1987) Alcohol Consumption and Alcohol Related Behaviour in Young People: What Should be the Focus of Health Education? Exeter: H.E.C. Schools Health Education Unit

Bandura A (1977) Social Learning Theory. NJ, USA: Prentice-Hall

Bank B, Biddle B, Anderson D, Hauge R, Keats D, Marlin M, Valantin S (1985) Comparative research on social determinants of adolescent drinking. Social Psychology Quarterly 48, 164-177

Barnes GM (1977) The development of adolescent drinking behaviour: an evaluative review of the impact of the socialization process within the family. Adolescence 12, 571-591

Barnes GM (1981) Drinking among adolescents: A subcultural phenomenon or a model of adult behaviors. Adolescence 16, 211 - 229

Barnes GM (1982) Alcohol and Youth: A Comprehensive Bibliography. Westport, CT: Greenwood Press.

Barnes GM (1984) Adolescent alcohol abuse and other problem behaviours: Their relationship and common parental influences. Journal of Youth and Adolescence 13, 329-348

Barnes GM (1990) Impact of the family on adolescent drinking patterns. In Collins RL, Leonard KE, Searles JS (eds) Alcohol and the Family: Research and Clinical Perspectives (pp. 137-161). Guildford Press: New York

Barnes GM, Farrell M, Cairns A (1986) Parental socialisation factors and adolescent drinking behaviours. Journal of Marriage and the Family 48, 27-36

Barnes GM, Welte J (1986) Adolescent alcohol abuse: Subgroup differences and relationships to other problem behaviours. Journal of Adolescence Research 1, 79-94

Barnes GM, Windle M (1987) Family factors in adolescent alcohol and drug abuse. Pediatrician 14, 13-18

Barry KL, Fleming MF (1990) Family cohesion, expressiveness and conflict in alcoholic families. British Journal of Addiction 85, 81-87

Bates ME, Pandina RJ (1991) Personality stability and adolescent substance use behaviors. Alcohol: Clinical and Experimental Research 15, 471-477

Bateson G, Jackson DD, Haley J, Weakland J (1956) Towards a theory of schizophrenia. Behavioural Science 1, 251-254

Battjes RJ (1985) Prevention of adolescent drug abuse. International Journal of Addictions 20, 1113-1134

Bauman K, Bryan E (1980) Subjective expected utility and children's drinking. Journal of Studies on Alcohol 41, 952-958

Bauman K, Fisher L, Bryan E, Chenoweth R (1985) Relationship between subjective expected utility and behaviour: A longitudinal study of adolescent drinking behaviour. Journal of Studies on Alcohol 46, 32-38

Baumrind D (1972) From each according to her ability. School Review 80, 161-197

Baumrind D (1985) Familial antecedents of adolescent drug use: A developmental perspective. In Jones CC, Battjes RJ (eds) Etiology of Drug Abuse: Implications for Prevention. NIDA Research Monograph 56 (pp. 13-44). Rockville Md: NIDA.

Beardslee WR, Son L, Vaillant GE (1986) Exposure to parental alcoholism during childhood and outcome in adulthood: A prospective longitudinal study. British Journal of Psychiatry 149, 584-591

Beavers W, Voeller M (1983) Family Models: Comparing and controlling the Olson Circumplex Model with the Beavers System Model. Family Process 22, 85-98

Bennett LA, Wolin SJ (1990) Family culture and alcoholism transmission. In Collins RL, Leonard KE, Searles JS (eds) Alcohol and the Family: Research and Clinical Perspectives. New York: Guildford Press

Bernstein B (1971) Class, Codes and Control: volume 1. St. Albans: Paladin

von Bertalanffy L (1968) General Systems Theory: Foundations, Development, Application. New York: Braziller

Blane HT, Chafetz ME (eds) (1979) Youth, Alcohol and Social Policy. New York: Plenum Press

Bloch LP, Crockett LJ, Vicary JR (1991) Antecedents of rural adolescent alcohol use: A risk factor approach. Journal of Drug Education 21, 361-377

Bloom B (1985) A factor analysis of self-report measures of family functioning. Family Process 24, 225-239.

Bloom M (1990) The psychosocial constructs of social competency. In Gullotta TP, Adams GR, Montemayor R (eds) Developing Social Competency in Adolescence (pp. 11-27). Newbury Park, California: Sage

Braucht GN (1980) Psychosocial research on teenage drinking: Past and future. In Scarpitt, Datesman (eds) Drugs and the Youth Culture 4 (pp. 109-143). Newbury Park, California: Sage

Britt DW, Campbell E (1977) A longitudinal analysis of alcohol use, environmental conduciveness and normal structure. Journal of Studies on Alcohol 38, 1640-1647

Broderick C (1990) Family process theory. In Sprey J (ed) Fashioning Family Theory (pp. 171-206). Newbury Park, California: Sage

Bronfenbrenner U (1986) Ecology of a family as a context for human development: Research perspectives. Developmental Psychology 22, 723-742

Brown SA (1985) Expectancies vs. background in the prediction of college drinking patterns. Journal of Consulting and Clinical Psychology 53, 123-130

Brown SA, Goldman MS, Inn A, Anderson LR (1980) Expectancies of reinforcement from alcohol: Their domain and relation to drinking patterns. Journal of Consulting and Clinical Psychology 48, 419-426

Brown SA, Creamer VA, Stetson BA (1987) Adolescent alcohol expectancies in relation to personal and parental drinking patterns. Journal of Abnormal Pyschology 96, 117-121

Brown SA, Stetson BA, Beatty PA (1989) Cognitive and behavioral features of adolescent coping in high risk drinking situations. Addictive Behaviours 14, 43-52

Bucholz KK (1990) A review of correlates of alcohol and alcohol problems in adolescence. In Galanter M (ed), Recent Developments in Alcoholism Vol. 8: Combined alcohol and other drug dependence (pp. 111-123). New York: Plenum Press

Budd R, Eiser J, Morgan M, Gammage P (1985) The young personal characteristics and life style of the young drinker: The results of a survey of British adolescence. Drug and Alcohol Dependence 16, 145-157

Burke R, Weir T (1978) Benefits to adolescents of informal helping relationships with parents and peers. Psychological Reports 42, 1175-1184

Burkett S (1977) Religion, parental influence and adolescent alcohol and marijuana use. Journal of Drug Issues 7, 263-273

Callan VJ, Wilks J (1987) Cross-cultural perspectives on teenage alcohol use. Pediatrician 14, 7-12

Campbell DT (1975) Degrees of freedom and the case study. Comparative Political Studies 8, 178-193

Carman R, Fitzgerald B, Holmgren C (1983) Alienation and drinking motivation among adolescent females. Journal of Personality and Social Psychology 44, 1021-1024

Casswell S, Gilmore L, Silva P, Brasch P (1988) What children know about alcohol and how they know it. British Journal of Addiction 83, 223-227

Casswell S, Stewart J, Connolly G, Silva P (1991) A longitudinal study of New Zealand children's experience with alcohol. British Journal of Addiction 86, 277-285

Children and Young Persons Act, 1933. London: H.M.S.O. 1950

Christiansen BA, Goldman MS, Inn A (1982) Development of alcohol related expectancies in adolescents: Separating pharmacological from social learning influences. Journal of Consulting and Clinical Psychology 50, 336-344

Christiansen BA, Goldman MS (1983) Alcohol related expectancies in demographic variables in prediction of adolescent drinking. Journal of Consulting and Clinical Pyschology 51, 249-257

Christiansen BA, Smith G, Roehling P, Goldman G (1989) Using alcohol expectancies to predict adolescent drinking behaviour after 1 year. Journal of Consulting and Clinical Psychology 57, 93-99

Christopherson BB, Jones RM, Sales AP (1988) Diversity in reported motivations for substance use as a function of egoidentity development. Journal of Adolescent Research 3, 141-152

Cloninger CR, Bohman M, Sigvardsson S (1981) Inheritance of alcohol abuse: cross-fostering analysis of adopted men. Archives of General Psychiatry 38, 861-868

Cohen S (1972) Folk Devils and Moral Panics. London: McGibbon and Kee

Coleman J (1980) The Nature of Adolescence. London: Methuen

Coleman J, Hendry L (1990) The Nature of Adolescence (Second Edition). London: Routledge

Connolly GM, Casswell S, Stewart J, Silva PA (1992) Drinking context and other influences on the drinking of 15-year-old New Zealanders. British Journal of Addiction 87, 1029-1036

Connors GJ, O'Farrell TJ, Cutter HSG, Thompson DL (1987) Dose-related effects of alcohol among male alcoholics, problem drinkers and non-problem drinkers. Journal of Studies on Alcohol 48, 461-466

Coombs RH (ed) (1987/8) Family Context of Adolescent Drug Use. New York: Haworth.

Coombs RH, Paulson MJ (1988) Contrasting family patterns of adolescent drug users and non-users. Journal of Chemical Dependency Treatment 1, 59-72

Cooper M. (1990) Making changes. In Putnam T, Newton C (eds) Household Choices (pp. 37-42). London: Futures Publications

Cotton NS (1978) The familial incidence of alcoholism - a review. Journal of Studies on Alcohol 40, 89-119

Cowan JD (1983) Testing the escape hypothesis: Alcohol helps users to forget their feelings. Journal of Nervous and Mental Diseases 171, 40-48.

Crawford A (1984) Alcohol and expectancy: I. Perceived sex differences in the effects of drinking. Alcohol and Alcoholism 19, 63-69

Critchlow B (1986) The powers of John Barleycorn: Beliefs about the effects of alcohol on social behaviour. American Pyschologist 41, 741-746

Davies JB (1982) The transmission of alcohol problems in the family. In Orford J, Harwin J (eds) Alcohol and the Family (pp. 73-87). London: Croom Helm

Davies JB (1992) The Myth of Addiction. Reading: Harwood Academic

Davies JB, Baker R (1987) The impact of self-presentation and interviewer bias effects on self-reported heroin use. British Journal of Addiction 82, 907-912

Davies JB, Stacey B (1972) Teenagers and Alcohol. A Developmental Study in Glasgow. London: H.M.S.O.

DeJong CAJ, Hartveld FM, van de Wielen GEM, van der Staak CPF (1991) Memories of parental rearing in alcohol and drug addicts: A comparative study. International Journal of the Addictions 26, 1065-1076

Demone HW (1972) The nonuse and abuse of alcohol by the male adolescent. Proceedings of the Second Annual Alcoholism Conference of the National Institute on Alcohol Abuse and Alcoholism
Devereux EC (1970) Socialization in cross-cultural perspective: comparative study of England, Germany and the United States. In R. Hill and H. Konig (eds) Families in East and West (pp. 72-106). Paris and the Hague: Mouton.
Doherty WJ, Campbell TL (1988) Families and Health. California: Sage
Doherty WJ, McCubbin HI (1985) The family and health care (special issue). Family Relations 34(1)
Donovan JE, Jessor R (1978) Adolescent problem drinking. Psychosocial correlates in a national sample study. Journal of Studies on Alcohol 39, 1506-1524
Donovan JE, Jessor R, Jessor L (1983) Problem drinking in adolescence and young adulthood - a follow up study. Journal of Studies on Alcohol 44, 109-137
Dorn N (1983) Alcohol, Youth and the State: Drinking Practices, Control and Health Education. London: Croom Helm
Douglas M (1966) Purity and Danger. London: Routledge
Dovey K (1985) Home and homelessness. In Altman L, Werner C (eds) Home Environments (pp. 33-61). New York: Plenum Press
Downs WR (1987) A panel study of normative structure, adolescent alcohol use and peer alcohol use. Journal of Studies on Alcohol 48, 167-175

Eiser JR, Morgan M, Gammage P, Brooks N, Kirby R (1991) Adolescent health behaviour and similarity-attraction: Friends share smoking habits (really), but much else besides. British Journal of Social Psychology 30, 339-348
Editorial - Journal of The Royal Society of Health (1991) Alcohol in Industry - United Kingdom Alliance Parliamentary Symposium. Journal of The Royal Society of Health 111, 2
Ellickson PL, Hays RD (1991) Antecedents of drinking among young adolescents with different alcohol use histories. Journal of Studies on Alcohol 52, 398-408
Erikson E (1959) Identity and the Life Cycle. New York: International Universities Press
Erikson E (1968) Identity: Youth and Crisis. New York: Norton
Estaugh V, Power C (1991) Family disruption in early life and drinking in young adulthood. Alcohol and Alcoholism 26, 639-644

Feehan M, McGee R, Stanton W, Silva PA (1991) Strict and inconsistent discipline in childhood: Consequences for adolescent mental health. British Journal of Clinical Psychology 30, 325-332
Felsted CM (ed) (1986) Youth and Alcohol Abuse: Readings and Resources. Phoenix: Oryx
Festinger L (1957) A Theory of Cognitive Dissonance. Stanford, California: Stanford University Press
Fishman R, Kuver JM (1984) Family dysfunction: A driving force in adolescent alcohol abuse. In Krasner N, Madden JS, Walker RJ (eds) Alcohol Related Problems. Chichester: Wiley
Flewelling R, Bauman K (1990). Family structure as a predictor of initial substance use and sexual intercourse in early adolescence. Journal of Marriage and the Family 52, 171-181
Fogelman K (1978). Drinking among sixteen-year-olds. Journal of National Childrens Bureau London 29, 19-25
Fontane PE, Layne NR (1979) The family as a context for developing youthful drinking patterns. Journal of Alcohol and Drug Education 24, 19-29
Ford M (1982) Social cognition and social competence in adolescence. Developmental Psychology 18, 323-340

Forney MA, Forney PD, Ripley WK (1989) Predictor variables of adolescent drinking. Advances in Alcohol and Substance Abuse 8, 97-117

Forslund MA, Gustafson TJ (1970) Influence of peers and parents and sex differences in drinking by high school students. Quarterly Journal of Studies on Alcohol 31, 868-875

Försterling F (1985) Attributional retraining: a review. Psychological Bulletin 98, 495-512

Fossey E (1993) Young children and alcohol: A theory of attitude development. Alcohol and Alcoholism (in press)

Fowler P (1981) Maximum likelihood factor structure of the Family Environment Scale. Journal of Clinical Psychology 37, 160-164

Foxcroft DR, Lowe G (1991) Adolescent drinking behaviour and family socialization factors: A meta-analysis. Journal of Adolescence 14, 255-273

Foxcroft DR, Lowe G (1992a) Reasons for drinking: The more the merrier? Paper presented at the British Psychological Society Social Psychology Section Annual Conference, Hatfield, September 1992

Foxcroft DR, Lowe G (1992b) Family socialization factors and alcohol use in older teenagers. Proceedings of the 36th International Congress on Alcohol and Drug Dependence, August 1992, Glasgow. Geneva: ICAA

Foxcroft DR, Lowe G (1992c) The role of the family in adolescent alcohol abuse: socialization and structural influences. Journal of Adolescent Chemical Dependency 2, 75-91

Foxcroft DR, Lowe G (1992d) Family life influences and health lifestyles of teenage drinkers. Paper presented at the B.P.S. Health Psychology Section Annual Conference, September 1992, St, Andrews, Scotland

Foxcroft DR, Lowe G (1992e) Family life and the development of teenage alcohol use and attitudes. Paper presented at the Sixth Annual Yorkshire Regional Addictions Forum, Ripon, July 1992

Foxcroft DR, Lowe G (1993) Self-attributions for alcohol use in older teenagers. Addiction Research 1, 1-10

Freud S (1929) Civilization and Its Discontents. London: Hogarth Press

Friedman AS, Utada A, Morrissey MR (1987) Families of adolescent drug abusers are "rigid": Are these families either "disengaged" or "enmeshed", or both? Family Process 26, 131-147

Furnham A, Gunter B (1989) The Anatomy of Adolescence. London: Routledge

Gecas V, Seff MA (1990) Families and adolescents: A review of the 1980s. Journal of Marriage and the Family 52, 941-958

Ghodse AH, McCartney JM (1992) Systems analysis of a drug dependency service. British Journal of Addiction 87, 1377-1385

Ghodsian M, Power C (1987) Alcohol consumption between the ages of sixteen and twenty-three in Britain - a longitudinal study. British Journal of Addiction 82, 175-180

Glass G, McGraw B, Smith B, Lee M (1981) Meta-analysis in Social Research. Beverley Hills, California: Sage

Gliksman LS, Smythe PC (1982) Adolescent involvement with alcohol: A cross sectional study. Journal of Studies on Alcohol 43, 370-379

Goddard E (1991) Drinking in England and Wales in the Late 1980s. London: H.M.S.O.

Goddard E, Ikin C (1988) Drinking in England and Wales in 1987. London: H.M.S.O.

Godkin M (1980) Identity and place: clinical applications based on notions of rootedness and uprootedness. In Buttimer A, Seamon D (eds) The Human Experience of Space and Place (pp. 73-85). London: Croom Helm

Goffman E (1959) The Presentation of Self in Everyday Life. New York: Doubleday

Goodwin DW (1989) Biological factors in alcohol use and abuse: Implications for recognizing and preventing alcohol problems in adolescence. International Review of Psychiatry 1, 41-49

Goodwin DW, Schulsinger F, Hermansen L, Guze SB, Winokur G (1973) Alohol problems in adoptees raised apart from biological parents. Archives of General Psychiatry 28, 238-243

Graham JW, Marks G, Hansen WB (1991) Social influence processes affecting adolescent substance use. Journal of Applied Psychology 76, 291-298

Green G, Macintyre S, West P, Ecob R (1991) Like parent like child? Associations between drinking and smoking behaviour of parents and their children. British Journal of Addiction 86, 745-758

Greenberg M, Siegel J, Leitch C (1983) The nature and importance of attachment relationships to parents and to peers during adolescence. Journal of Youth and Adolescence 12, 373-383

Greer J (1989) The drinking behaviour of YTS trainees in Humberside. Unpublished MSc Thesis, University of Hull

Gross E (1990) The body of signification. In Fletcher J, Benjamin A (eds) Abjection, Melancholia and Love: the work of Julia Kristeva (pp. 80-103) London: Routledge

Grube JW, Morgan M, Seff M (1989) Drinking beliefs and behaviors among Irish adolescents. International Journal of the Addictions 24, 101-112

Gurling HMD, Clifford CA, Murray RM (1981) Genetic contributions to alcohol dependence and its effect on brain function. In Gedda L, Parisi P, Nance WA (eds) Twin Research Vol. 3 (pp. 77-87). New York: Liss

Gurling HMD, Oppenheim BE, Murray RM (1984) Depression, criminality and psychopathology associated with alcoholism: Evidence from a twin study. Acta Genetica et Gemellogiae 33, 333-339

Gustafson R (1986) Can straight-forward information change alcohol-related expectancies? Perceptual and Motor Skills 63, 937-938

Gustafson R (1987) Lack of correspondence between alcohol-related aggressive expectancies for self and other. Psychological Reports 60, 707-710

Hansen WB, Malotte CK, Collins L, Fielding JE (1987) Dimensions and psychosocial correlates of adolescent alcohol use. Journal of Alcohol and Drug Education 32, 19-31

Harford TC, Grant B (1987) Psychosocial factors in adolescent drinking contexts. Journal of Studies on Alcohol 48, 551-557

Hartcollis PC (1982) Personality characteristics in adolescent problem drinkers - A comparative study. Journal of American Academy of Child Psychiatry 21, 348-353

Hawker A (1978) Adolescents and Alcohol. London: Edsall

Hawkins RO Jr (1982) Adolescent alcohol abuse: A review. Journal of Developmental and Behavioral Pediatrics 3, 83-87

Hays R, Stacy A, Dimatteo M (1987) Problem behaviour theory and adolescent alcohol use. Addictive Behaviours 12, 189-193

Health Education Authority (1989) Teenage Health and Lifestyles vol. 2: Alcohol. London: MORI

Hewstone M (1989) Causal Attribution: from cognitive processes to collective beliefs. Oxford: Blackwell

Hill R (1949) Families Under Stress. Westport, Connecticut: Greenwood Press

Hill R (1971) Modern systems theory and the family: a confrontation. Social Science Information 10, 7-26

Hillier B, Hansen J (1984) The Social Logic of Space. Cambridge: Cambridge University Press

Hirschi T (1969) Causes of Delinquency. Berkeley, California: University of California Press

Hodgson RJ, Rankin HJ, Stockwell TR (1979) Alcohol dependence and the priming effect. Behaviour Research and Therapy 17, 379-387

Holmes SJ, Robins LN (1987) The influence of childhood disciplinary experience on the development of alcoholism and depression. Journal of Child Psychiatry 28, 399-415

Hover S, Gaffney LR (1991) The relationship between social skills and adolescent drinking. Alcohol and Alcoholism 26, 207-214

Hughes SO, Power TG, Francis DJ (1992) Defining patterns of drinking in adolescence: A cluster analytic approach. Journal of Studies on Alcohol 53, 40-47

Hundleby J, Mercer G (1987) Family and friends as social environments and their relationship to young adolescents' use of alcohol, tobacco and marijuana. Journal of Marriage and the Family 49, 157-164

Jahoda G, Crammond J (1972) Children and Alcohol: A developmental study in Glasgow Vol I. London: H.M.S.O.

Jessor R (1986) Adolescent problem drinking: Psychosocial aspects and developmental outcomes. In Silbereisen RK, Eyferth K, Rudinger G (eds) Development as Action in Context. Normal Behaviour and Normal Youth Development (pp.241-264). Berlin: Springer

Jessor R (1987) Problem behaviour theory, psychosocial development and adolescent drinking. British Journal of Addiction 82, 331-342

Jessor R, Chase J, Donovan J (1980) Psychosocial correlates of marijuana use and problem drinking in a national sample of adolescents. American Journal of Public Health 70, 604-613

Jessor R, Jessor S (1975) Adolescent development and the onset of drinking - a longitudinal study. Journal of Studies on Alcohol 36, 27-51

Jessor R, Jessor S (1977) Problem Behaviour and Psychosocial Development: A Longitudinal Study of Youth. London: Academic Press

Jessor S, Jessor R (1974) Maternal ideology and adolescent problem behaviour. Developmental Psychology 10, 246-254

Johnson KA (1984) Peer group influences upon adolescent drinking practices. Mid-American Review of Sociology 9, 79-99

Johnson V, Pandina RJ (1991a) Effects of the family environment on adolescent substance use, delinquency, and coping styles. American Journal of Drug Alcohol Abuse 17, 71-88

Johnson V, Pandina RJ (1991b) Familial and personal drinking histories and measures of competence in youth. Addictive Behaviors 16, 453-465

Johnston LD, O'Malley PM (1986) Why do high school students use drugs and alcohol? Self reported reasons from nine national surveys. Journal of Drug Issues 16, 29-66

Johnston LD, O'Malley PM, Bachman JG (1989) Drug Use, Drinking and Smoking: National Survey Results from High School, College, and Young Adults Populations 1975-1988. Washington, DC: NIDA, Government Printing Office

Kaij L (1960) Alcoholism in Twins. Stockholm: Almquist and Wiksell

Kandel DB (1980) Drug and drinking behaviour among youth. Annual Review of Sociology 6, 235-288

Kandel DB (1982) Epidemiological and psychosocial perspectives on adolescent drug use. Journal of American Academy of Child Psychiatry 21, 328-347

Kandel DB (1985) On processes of peer influences in adolescent drug use: A developmental perspective. Advances in Alcohol and Substance Abuse 4, 139-163

Kandel DB, Andrews K (1987) Processes of adolescent socialisation by parents and peers. International Journal of the Addictions 22, 319-342

Kandel DB, Kessler R, Margulies R (1978) Antecedents of adolescent initiation into stages of drug use: A developmental analysis. Journal of Youth and Adolescence 7, 13-40

Kaplan HB, Martin SS, Robins C (1984) Pathways to adolescent drug use: Self-derogation, peer influence, weakening of social controls, and early substance use. Journal of Health and Social Behavior 25, 270-289

Kellam S, Ensminger M, Simon M (1980) Mental health in first grade and teenage drug, alcohol and cigarette use. Drug and Alcohol Dependence 5, 273-304

Korosec-Serfaty P (1984) The home from attic to cellar. Journal of Environmental Psychology 4, 172-179

Kristeva J (1982) Powers of Horror. New York: Columbia University Press

Labouvie EW (1987) Relation of personality to adolescent alcohol and drug use: A coping perspective. Pediatrician 14, 19-24

Lader D, Matheson J (1991) Smoking Among Secondary School Children in 1990. London: H.M.S.O.

Lawrence R (1987) Housing, Dwellings and Homes. Chichester: Wiley

Lee C (1988) Theories of family adaptability: toward a synthesis of Olson's Circumplex and the Beavers Systems Models. Family Process 27, 73-85

Leonard K, Blane H (1988) Alcohol expectancies and personality characteristics in young men. Addictive Behaviours 13, 353-357

Levine M, Singer SI (1988) Delinquency, substance abuse, and risk taking in middle-class adolescents. Behavioral Sciences and the Law 6, 385-400

Levison PK, Gerstein DR, Maloff DR (1982) Commonalities in Substance Abuse and Habitual Behaviour. Lexington: DC Heath & Co

Lewin K (1951) Field Theory in Social Science. New York: Harper

Licensing Act, 1964 (1964) Law Reports Statutes Vol. 1, Chapter 26

Lowe G, Buikhuisen M (1989) Combined effects of alcohol, caffeine and expectancy on perceptual-motor performance. Paper presented to the Annual Conference of the B.P.S. Psychobiology Section, Warwick, August 1989.

Lowe G (1990) Alcohol: A positive enhancer of pleasurable expectancies? In Warburton DM (ed) Addiction Controversies (pp. 53-65). London: Harwood Academic

Maccoby E, Martin J (1983) Socialization in the context of the family: parent-child interaction, In Mussen PH (ed) Handbook of Child Psychology (pp. 1-101). New York: Wiley

MacKay JR (1961) Clinical observations on adolescent problem drinkers. Quarterly Journal of Studies on Alcohol 22, 124-134

McCord W, McCord J (1960) Origins of Alcoholism. Stanford, California: Stanford University Press

McKechnie R, Cameron D, Cameron I, Drewrey J (1977) Teenage drinking in South-West Scotland. British Journal of Addiction 72, 287-295

McLaughlin RJ, Baer PE, Burnside MA, Pokorny AD (1985) Psychosocial correlates of alcohol use at two age levels during adolescence. Journal of Studies on Alcohol 46, 212-218

McLaughlin L Mann, Chassin L, Sher K (1987) Alcohol expectancies and the risk for alcoholism. Journal of Consulting and Clinical Psychology 55, 411-417

McMurran M (1990) Young offenders and alcohol. In McMurran M (ed) Applying Psychology to Young Offenders (pp. 45-49). Leicester: British Psychological Society

McMurran M (1991) Young offenders and alcohol-related crime: What interventions will address the issues. Journal of Adolescence 14, 245-253

Manson L, Ritson B (1984) Alcohol and Health. London: Medical Council on Alcoholism

Marc O (1972) Psychoanalyse de la Maison. Paris: Seuil

Marcos AC, Bahr SJ (1988) Control theory and adolescent drug use. Youth and Society 19, 395-425

Marcos AC, Bahr SJ, Johnson RE (1986) Test of a bonding/association theory of adolescent drug use. Social Forces 65, 135-161

Margulies RZ, Kessler RC, Kandel DB (1977) A longitudinal study of onset of drinking among high school students. Journal of Studies on Alcohol 38, 897-912

Marsh A, Dobbs J, White A (1986) Adolescent Drinking. London: H.M.S.O.

Martin MJ, Pritchard ME (1991) Factors associated with alcohol use in later adolescence. Journal of Studies on Alcohol 52, 5-9

Mass-Observation Archive (1983) People's homes. The Library, University of Sussex

Mass-Observation Archive (1988) Time - Summer. The Library, University of Sussex

May C (1991a) Resistance to peer pressure: an inadequate basis for alcohol education. Paper presented at the 32nd Scottish Alcohol Problems Research Symposium, October 1991, Pitlochry, Scotland

May C (1991b) Research on alcohol education for young people: A critical review of the literature. Health Education Journal 50, 195-199

May C (1992) A burning issue? Adolescent alcohol use in Britain 1970-1991. Alcohol and Alcoholism 27, 109-115

Mayer JE (1980) Adolescents' alcohol misuse: A family systems perspective. Journal of Alcohol and Drug Education 26, 1-11

Mayer JE, Filstead WJ (1980) Adolescence and alcohol: A theoretical model. In Mayer JE, Filstead WJ (eds) Adolescence and Alcohol (pp. 151-164). Cambridge, Mass: Ballinger Publishing Company

Mead G (1934) Mind, Self, and Society. Chicago: Chicago University Press

Milgram GG (1982) Youthful drinking: Past and present. Journal of Drug Education 12, 289-308

Miller D (1990) Appropriating the state on the council estate. In Putnam T, Newton C (eds) Household Choices (pp. 43-55). London: Futures Publications Ltd

Miller WR, Heather N, Hall W (1991) Calculating standard drink units: International comparisons. British Journal of Addiction 86, 43-47

Minuchin S (1974) Families and Family Therapy. London: Tavistock

Mitic WR, McGuire DP, Neumann B (1987) Adolescent problem drinking and perceived stress. Journal of Alcohol and Drug Education 33, 45-54

Moore LP, Moore JW, Hauck WE (1982) Conditioning children's attitudes toward alcohol, smoking and drugs. Journal of Experimental Education 50, 154-158

Moos RH (1990) Conceptual and empirical approaches to developing family based assessment procedures: resolving the case of the Family Environment Scale. Family Process 29, 199-208

Moos RH, Moos B (1986) Family Environment Scale Test Manual. Palo Alto, Calif: Consulting Psychologists Press

Morgan MC, Wingard DL, Felice ME (1984) Subcultural differences in alcohol use among youth. Journal of Adolescent Health Care 5, 191-195

Moskowitz JM (1989) The primary prevention of alcohol problems: A critical review of the research literature. Journal of Studies on Alcohol 50, 54-88

Needle R, Su S, Doherty W (1990) Divorce, Remarriage, and adolescent substance use: a prospective longitudinal study. Journal of Marriage and the Family 52, 157-169

Newcomb MD, Bentler PM (1988) Impact of adolescent drug use and social support on problems of young adults: A longitudinal study. Journal of Abnormal Psychology 97, 64-75

Newcomb MD, Maddahian E, Bentler PM (1986) Risk factors for drug use among adolescents: Concurrent and longitudinal analyses. American Journal of Public Health 76, 525-531

Noller P, Callan V (1991) The Adolescent in the Family. London: Routledge

Norem-Hebeisen A, Johnson DW, Anderson D et al (1984) Predictors and concomitants of changes in drug use patterns among teenagers. Journal of Social Psychology 124, 43-50

Nye FI (1958) Family Relationships and Delinquent Behaviour. New York: John Wiley

O'Connor J (1978) The Young Drinkers. London: Tavistock

O'Connor J (1984) Models of drinking behaviour and their implications for health education of the young. In Krasner N, Madden JS, Walker RJ (eds) Alcohol Related Problems (pp 159-165). London: Wiley

O'Gorman PA, Stringfield S, Smith I (eds) (1976) Defining Adolescent Alcohol Use: Implications Toward a Definition of Adolescent Alcoholism. Proceedings, National Council on Alcoholism 1976 Conference. Washington, DC, NY: National Council on Alcoholism

Oliver JM, Handel PJ, Eros DM, May MJ (1988) Factor structure of the Family Environment Scale: Factors based on items and subscales. Educational and Psychological Measurement 48, 469-477

Olson DH (1986) Circumplex Model VII: Validation studies and FACES III. Family Process 25, 337-356

Olson DH (1991a) Commentary: Three-dimensional (3-D) Circumplex Model and revised scoring of FACES III. Family Process 30, 74-79

Olson DH, Russell CS, Sprenkle DH (1983) Circumplex model of marital and family systems: VI. Theoretical update. Family Process 22, 69-83

Olson DH, Russell CS, Sprenkle DH (eds) (1989) Circumplex Model: Systematic assessment and treatment of families. New York: Haworth Press

Olson DH, Sprenkle DH, Russell CS (1979) Circumplex models of families and family systems: I. Cohesion and adaptability dimensions, family types, and clinical applications. Family Process 18, 3-28

Orford J (1990) Alcohol and the family: An international review of the literature with implications for research and practice. In Kozlowski LT, Annis HM, Cappel HD et al (eds) Research Advances in Alcohol and Drug Problems 10 (pp. 81-155). New York: Plenum

Orford J, Harwin J (eds) (1982) Alcohol and the Family. London and Canberra: Croom Helm

Orford J, Velleman R (1990) Offspring of parents with drinking problems: drinking and drug-taking as young adults. British Journal of Addiction 85, 779-794

Orford J, Velleman R (1991) The environmental intergenerational transmission of alcohol problems: A comparison of two hypotheses. British Journal of Medical Psychology 64, 189-200

Orwell G (1954) Nineteen Eighty Four. London: Penguin

Parekh B (1974) Class, Colour and Consciousness. London: Allen & Unwin

Parker H (1974) View from the Boys. London: Tavistock

Parsons T, Bales RF (1955) Family Socialization and Interaction Process. Glencoe, Illinois: Free Press

Plant MA, Bagnall G, Foster J (1990) Teenage heavy drinkers: Alcohol-related knowledge, beliefs, experiences, motivation and the social context of drinking. Alcohol and Alcoholism 25, 691-698

Plant M, Peck D, Stuart R (1982) Self-reported drinking habits and alcohol-related consequences among a cohort of Scottish teenagers. British Journal of Addiction 77, 75-90

Plant M, Peck D, Samuel E (1985) Alcohol, Drugs and School Leavers. London: Tavistock
Plant MA, Plant ML (1986) The use and misuse of alcohol amongst young people in the United Kingdom. In Halford T, Armstrong S (eds) The Extent and Nature of Adolescent Alcohol Use. Helsinki: Social Research Institute on Alcohol Studies
Plant MA, Plant ML (1992) Risk-takers: Alcohol, Drugs, Sex and Youth. London: Tavistock/Routledge
Prendergast TJ, Schaefer ES (1974) Correlates of drinking and drunkenness among high school students. Quarterly Journal of Studies in Alcohol 35, 232-242
Protinsky H, Shilts L (1990) Adolescent substance use and family cohesion. Family Therapy 17, 173-175
Pulkkinen L (1983) Youthful smoking and drinking in a longitudinal perspective. Journal of Youth and Adolescence 12, 253-283
Putnam T, Newton C (1990) Household Choices. London: Futures Publications

Rachel JV, Maisto SA, Guess RL, Hubbard R (1980) Use and misuse of alcohol by United States adolescents - recent information from two national surveys. Paper presented at the 26th International Institute on the Prevention and Treatment of Alcoholism, ICAA, Cardiff
Radecki T, Chairman of the National Coalition on Television Violence (1986) Alcoholism and other alcohol-related problems among children and youth. Cited by the National Council on Alcoholism, Inc
Reeves D, Draper T (1984) Abstinence or decreasing consumption among adolescents: Importance of reasons. International Journal of the Addictions 19, 819-825
Regional Trends 1990 (1992) London: H.M.S.O
Reich W, Earls F, Powell J (1988) A comparison of the home and social environments of children of alcoholic and non-alcoholic parents. British Journal of Addiction 83, 831-839
Rhodes JE, Jason LA (1988) Preventing Substance Abuse Among Children and Adolescents. New York: Pergamon Books
Ritson B (1981) Alcohol and Young People. Journal of Adolescence 4, 93-100
Robins LN, Helzer J, Przybeck T (1986) Substance use in the general population. In Barrett J, Rose R (eds), Mental Disorders in the Community: Progress and Challenges. New York: Guilford
Rochberg-Halton E (1984) Object relations, role models and the cultivation of the self. Environment and Behaviour, 16, 335-368
Rohsenow DJ (1983) Drinking habits and expectancies about alcohol's effects for self versus others. Journal of Consulting and Clinical Psychology 51, 752-756
Rollins B, Thomas D (1979) Parental support, power, and control techniques in the socialization of children. In Burr W, Hill R, Nye I, Reiss I (eds) Contemporary Theories about the Family (vol 1) (pp. 317-364). New York: Free Press
Roosa MW, Beals J (1990) Measurement issues in family assessment: the case of the Family Environment Scale. Family Process 29, 191-198
Rosenberg M (1979) Conceiving the Self. New York: Basic Books
Rowe DC, Rodgers JL (1991) Adolescent smoking and drinking: Are they "epidemics"? Journal of Studies on Alcohol 52, 110-117
Royal College of Physicians (1987) A Great and Growing Evil. London: Tavistock
Royal College of Physicians (1991) Alcohol and the Public Health. London: Macmillan
Rutter M, Tizard J, Whitmore K (1970) Education, Health and Behaviour. London: Longman
Rydelius PA (1983) Alcohol-abusing teenage boys. Testing a hypothesis on the relationship between alcohol abuse and social background factors, criminality and personality in teenage boys. Acta Psychiatrica Scandinavica 68, 368-380

Sager L (1978) Insular majorities unabated: Warth v. Seddon and City of Eastlake v. Forest City Enterprises, Inc. Harvard Law Review 91, 1373-1425

Scherer SE, Ettinger RF, Mudrich NJ (1972) Need for social approval and drug use. Journal of Consulting and Clinical Psychology 38, 118-121

Schuckit MA (1983) A prospective study of genetic markers in alcoholism. In Hanin I, Usdin E (eds) Biological Markers in Psychiatry and Neurology. Oxford: Pergamon

Searles JS (1990) The contribution of genetic factors to the development of alcoholism: a critical review. In Collins RL, Leonard KE, Searles JS (eds) Alcohol and the Family: Research and Clinical Perspectives (pp. 3-38). New York: Guildford Press

Sebba R, Churchman A (1983) Territories and territoriality in the home. Environment and Behavior 15, 191-210

Sennett R (1977) Destructive Gemeinschaft. In Birnbaum N (ed) Beyond the Crisis (pp. 171-200). Oxford: Oxford University Press

Seydlitz R (1991) The effects of age and gender on parental control and delinquency. Youth and Society 23, 175-201

Sharp DJ (1989) Young People and Drinking: Results of a Survey Undertaken in Hull. Unpublished report, University of Hull

Sharp DJ (1992) Psychosocial Characteristics of Adolescent Alcohol Expectancies and Drinking. Unpublished PhD Thesis, University of Hull

Sharp DJ, Greer J, Lowe G (1988) The "Normalisation" of Under-age Drinking. Paper presented at the Annual Conference of the British Psychological Society, April 1988

Sharp DJ, Lowe G (1989a) Adolescents and alcohol - a review of recent British research. Journal of Adolescence 12, 295-307

Sharp DJ, Lowe G (1989b) Asking young people why they drink. Paper presented at the British Psychological Society Scottish Branch Conference, Strathclyde, September 1989

Sharp DJ, Lowe G (1990) Teenage alcohol expectancies. Paper presented at the VIIIth International Conference on Alcohol Related Problems, Liverpool, April 1990

Shields R (1989) Social spatialization and the built environment: The West Edmonton Mall. Society and Space 7, 147-164

Shilts L (1991) The relationship of early adolescent substance use to extracurricular activities, peer influence, and personal attitudes. Adolescence 26, 613-617

Sibley D (1988) Survey 13: Purification of space. Environment and Planning D: Society and Space 6, 409-421

Sloper P, Cunningham CC, Knussen C, Turner S (1988) A study of the process of adaptation in a cohort of children with Down's Syndrome and their families. Unpublished Report, Hester Adrian Research Centre, University of Manchester, U.K.

Smart LS, Chibucos TR, Didier LA (1990) Adolescent substance use and perceived family functioning. Journal of Family Issues 11, 208-227

Smart RG (1980) The New Drinkers: Teenage Use and Abuse of Alcohol. Toronto: Addiction Research Foundation

Smart RG, Gray G, Bennett C (1978) Predictors of drinking and signs of heavy drinking among high school students. International Journal of the Addictions 13, 1079-1094

Smith M (1980) The City and Social Theory. Oxford: Basil Blackwell

Smyth M, Browne F (1992) General Household Survey 1990. London: H.M.S.O.

Soja E (1980) The socio-spatial dialectic. Annals, Association of American Geographers 70, 207-225

Southwick L, Steele C, Marlatt A, Lindell M (1981) Alcohol related expectancies: Defined by phase of intoxication and drinking experience. Journal of Consulting and Clinical Psychology 49, 713-721

Special Committee of Royal College of Psychiatrists (1986) Alcohol: Our Favourite Drug. London: Tavistock

Stacey B, Davies J (1970) Drinking behaviour in childhood and adolescence: An evaluative review. British Journal of Addiction 65, 203-212

Standing Conference on Crime Prevention (1987) London: Home Office

Strickland D, Pittman D (1984) Social learning and teenage alcohol use: Interpersonal and observational influences within the sociocultural environment. Journal of Drug Issues 14, 137-150

Stumphauzer JS (1983) Learning not to drink: Adolescents and abstinence. Journal of Drug Education 13, 39-48

Sutherland A (1975) Gypsies: The Hidden Americans. London: Tavistock

Tamerin JS, Weiner S, Mendelson JH (1970) Alcoholics' expectancies and recall of experiences during intoxication. American Journal of Psychiatry 126, 1697-1704

Taylor R, Brower S (1985) Home and near-home territories. In Altman I, Werner C (eds) Home Environments (pp. 183-210). New York: Plenum Press

Teusch R (1980) The drinking habits of teenagers in relation to parental behavior (Ge). Psychol. Erziehung Unterricht 27, 193-201

Thompson KM (1989) Effects of early alcohol use on adolescents' relations with peers and self-esteem: Patterns over time. Adolescence 24, 837-849

Thompson KM, Wilsnack RW (1987) Parental influence on adolescent drinking: Modeling, attitudes, or conflict? Youth and Society 19, 22-43

Turner JFC (1971) Housing by People. London: Marion Boyars

Velleman R, Orford J (1990) Young adult offspring of parents with drinking problems: Recollection of parents' drinking and its immediate effects. British Journal of Clinical Psychology 29, 297-317

Vicary JR, Lerner JV (1986) Parental attributes and adolescent drug use. Journal of Adolescence 9, 115-122

Volk RJ, Edwards DW, Lewis RA, Sprenkle DH (1989) Family systems of adolescent substance abusers. Family Relations 38, 266-272

Waldron RJ, Sabatelli RM, Anderson SA (1990) An examination of the factor structure of the Family Environment Scale. American Journal of Family Therapy 18, 257-272

Webb JA, Baer PE, McLaughlin RJ, McKelvey RS, Caid CD (1991) Risk factors and their relation to initiation of alcohol use among early adolescents. Journal of the American Academy of Child Adolescent Psychiatry 30, 563-568

Wechsler H (1979) Patterns of alcohol consumption among the young: High school, college, and general poulation studies. In Blane HT, Chafetz ME (eds) Youth, Alcohol and Social Policy (pp. 39-58). New York: Plenum Press

Wechsler H, McFadden M (1976) Sex differences in adolescent alcohol and drug use - a disappearing phenomenon. Journal of Studies on Alcohol 37, 1291-1301

Weintraub SA (1990-91) Children and adolescents at risk for substance abuse and psychopathology. International Journal of the Addictions 25, 481-494

Wells GL (1981) Lay analyses of causal forces on behaviour. In Harvey JH (ed) Cognition, Social Behaviour, and the Environment (pp. 309-324). New Jersey: Lawrence Erlbaum

White HR (1987) Longitudinal stability and dimensional structure of problem drinking in adolescence. Journal of Studies on Alcohol 48, 541-550

White HR, Labouvie EW (1989) Towards the assessment of adolescent problem drinking. Journal of Studies on Alcohol 50, 30-37

W.H.O. (1951) Technical Report Series, 42

W.H.O. (1952) Technical Report Series, 48

Wilcox JA (1985) Adolescent alcoholism. Journal of Psychoactive Drugs 17, 77-85

Wilks J, Callan VJ (1984) Similarity of university students' and their parents' attitudes toward alcohol. Journal of Studies on Alcohol 45, 326-333

Wilks J, Callan VJ, Austin DA (1989) Parent, peer and personal determinants of adolescent drinking. British Journal of Addiction 84, 619-630

Williams P (1982) The invisibility of the Kalderash in Paris. Urban Anthropology 11, 315-346

Williams RJ, Wortley RK (1991) Sex differences in the interaction of drinking, positive expectancies and symptoms of dependence in young adults. Drug Alcohol Dependence 29, 63-68

Wilsnack RW, Wilsnack SC (1978) Sex roles and drinking among adolescent girls. Journal of Studies on Alcohol 39, 1855-1874

Wilsnack SC, Wilsnack RW (1979) Sex roles and adolescent drinking. In Blane HT, Chafetz ME (eds) Youth, Alcohol and Social Policy (pp. 183-224). New York: Plenum

Wilson C, Orford J (1978) Children of alcoholics: report of a preliminary study and comments on the literature. Journal of Studies on Alcohol 39, 121-142

Windle M, Barnes GM (1988) Similarities and differences in correlates of alcohol consumption and problem behaviors among male and female adolescents. International Journal of the Addictions 23, 707-728

Wolin SJ, Bennett LA, Noonan DL (1979) Family rituals and the recurrence of alcoholism over generations. American Journal of Psychiatry 136, 589-593

Wolin SJ, Bennett LA, Noonan DL, Teitelbaum MA (1980) Disrupted family rituals: A factor in the intergenerational transmission of alcoholism. Journal of Studies on Alcohol 41, 199-214

Wright R Jr, Watts TD (1988) Alcohol and minority youth. Journal of Drug Issues 18, 1-6

Yin RK (1989) Case study research: Designs and Methods. Newbury Park, California: Sage

Young I (1990) Justice and the Politics of Difference. Princeton: Princeton University Press

Zucker RA (1976) Parental influences on the drinking patterns of their children. In Greenblatt M, Schuckitt MA (eds) Alcoholism problems in women and children (pp. 211-238). New York: Grune and Stratton

Zucker RA (1979) Developmental aspects of drinking through the young adult years. In Blane HT, Chafetz ME (eds) Youth, Alcohol and Social Policy (pp. 91-146). New York: Plenum

Author Index

Addeo EG, 18
Addeo JR, 18
Adger H Jr, 19
Adler I, 82
Aitken P, 26
Akers RL, 79, 80
Alasewski A, 151
Alexander C, 138
Altman I, 134
Alvarez FJ, 34
Amato PR, 115, 116
Anderson SA, 70
Andersson T, 4
Andrews K, 26, 75, 82, 83
A.P.A., 63
Aronson E, 63
Atkinson P, 149, 150
Ausubel D, 56

Bachelard G, 133, 134
Bagnall G, 1, 16, 29, 34, 72, 84, 180
Baker R, 106
Bales RF, 69
Bandura A, 6, 7, 21, 75, 76, 77, 79, 80
Bank B, 26, 178
Barnes GM, 23, 27, 34, 69, 70, 71, 75, 80, 82, 88, 102, 109, 171
Bates ME, 41
Bateson G, 93
Battjes RJ, 23
Bauman K, 36, 37, 72
Baumrind D, 62, 63, 66
Beals J, 116
Beardslee, 52
Beavers W, 70
Bennett LA, 51, 52
Bernstein B, 9, 10, 11, 139, 140, 141, 147, 149, 150, 151, 152, 153, 159, 177
Bloch LP, 24, 27, 174
Bloom B, 65, 66, 70
Bloom M, 56
Braucht GN, 40, 46
Britt DW, 84
Broderick C, 55
Brower S, 136

Brown SA, 16, 35, 37,
Browne F, 23, 108
Bryan E, 36, 37
Bucholz KK, 81
Budd R, 67
Buikhuisen M, 36
Burke R, 56
Burkett S, 27

Callan VJ, 25, 56
Campbell DT, 94
Campbell E, 84
Campbell TL, 180
Carlsmith JM, 63
Carman R, 34
Christiansen BA, 35, 36, 37, 38
Christopherson BB, 28, 34
Churchman A, 153
Cloninger CR, 50, 51
Cohen S, 172
Coleman J, 2
Connors GJ, 38
Coombs RH, 46, 76
Cooper M, 133
Cotton NS, 26
Cowan JD, 37
Crammond J, 11, 78, 108
Crawford A, 42
Critchlow B, 35

Davies JB, 11, 19, 25, 26, 41, 44, 51, 84, 91, 106, 168
DeJong CAJ, 46, 53
Demone HW, 91, 93
Devereux EC, 72, 116, 177, 178
Doherty WJ, 180
Donovan JE, 17, 82, 83
Dorn N, 16
Douglas M, 10, 137, 145, 151
Dovey K, 133
Downs WR, 84,
Draper T, 34

Eiser JR, 19, 35, 84
Ellickson PL, 82, 83

Erikson E, 56, 134, 147

Feehan M, 63
Festinger L, 78
Flewelling R, 72
Fogelman K, 72, 178
Ford M, 72
Forslund MA, 82
Försterling, 170
Fossey E, 108
Fowler P, 116
Foxcroft DR, 23, 29, 66, 68, 76, 85, 94, 105, 110, 172, 173
Freud S, 134, 146
Friedman AS, 60
Furnham A, 2

Gavazzi SM, 70
Gecas V, 2
Ghodse AH, 54
Ghodsian M, 16, 26
Glass G, 67, 80
Goddard E, 105, 106
Godkin M, 174
Goffman E, 9, 135, 139
Goldman MS, 36
Goodwin DW, 16, 23, 24, 50
Graham JW, 43
Grant B, 17
Green G, 26
Greenberg M, 56
Greer J, 105
Gross E, 146
Gunter B, 2
Gurling HMD, 50
Gustafson R, 35,
Gustafson TJ, 82

Hansen J, 136
Hansen WB, 19,
Harford TC, 17
Hartcollis, 40
Hawker A, 16, 57, 78
Hawkins RO Jr, 16
Hays RD, 21, 82, 83
Health Education Authority, 57
Hewstone M, 29, 35
Hill R, 58
Hillier, 136
Hirschi T, 64, 172
Hodgson RJ, 15
Holmes SJ, 63, 162

Ikin C, 105, 106

Jahoda G, 11, 78, 108
Jason LA, 21

Jessor R, 19, 20, 21, 25, 26, 40, 41, 42, 45, 82
Jessor S, 25, 26, 40, 41, 42,
Johnson KA, 42
Johnson V, 82, 83
Johnston LD, 23, 34

Kaij L, 50
Kandel DB, 19, 21, 22, 23, 24, 26, 75, 79, 82, 83, 173
Kaplan HB, 22, 24
Kellam S, 41
Korosec-Serfaty P, 133
Kristeva J, 10, 139, 146, 147

Labouvie EW, 18
Lader D, 23, 108
Lawrence R, 135, 140, 145, 153
Lee C, 70
Lerner JV, 63
Levine M, 23, 27
Levison PK, 19
Lewin K, 75
Lowe G, 23, 26, 28, 29, 34, 36, 38, 66, 68, 76, 85, 94, 105, 110, 172, 173

Maccoby E, 61, 62, 100
MacKay JR, 16, 25, 45
Magnusson D, 4
Manson L, 44
Marc O, 133
Marcos AC, 65
Marsh A, 16, 29, 72, 105, 106, 178
Martin J, 61, 62, 100
Martin MJ 22,
Mass-Observation Archive, 10, 12, 131, 141, 142, 143, 144, 145, 153, 175, 177
Matheson J, 23, 108
May C, 2, 35
McCartney JM, 54
McCord J, 63
McCord W, 63
McCubbin HI, 180
McFadden M, 107
McKechnie R, 26
McLaughlin RJ, 24, 37
McMurran M, 4, 18, 35
Mead G, 146
Milgram GG, 34
Miller D, 175, 176
Miller WR, 2
Minuchin S, 5, 11, 54, 55, 57, 58, 139, 151, 152
Mitic WR, 18
Moore LP, 28
Moos B, 65, 116
Moos RH, 65, 116
Morgan MC, 23
Moskowitz JM, 85

Needle R, 72
Newcomb MD, 21, 23, 27
Newton C, 130, 135
Norem-Hebeisen A, 24
Noller P, 56
Nye FI, 64

O'Connor J, 86, 87, 166, 169
O'Gorman PA, 17
O'Malley PM, 34
Oliver JM, 116
Olson DH, 5, 58, 59, 65, 66, 69, 70, 71, 152
Orford J, 25, 52, 92, 180
Orwell G, 71

Pandina RJ, 41, 82, 83
Parekh B, 148
Parker H, 106
Parsons T, 69
Plant MA, 1, 2, 4, 16, 26, 29, 72, 177
Plant ML, 2
Power C, 16, 26,
Prendergast TJ, 45
Pritchard ME, 22
Protinsky H, 46
Pulkkinen L, 42
Putnam T, 130, 135

Rachel JV, 72, 177, 178
Radecki T, 76
Reeves D, 34
Regional Trends, 105
Reich W, 53
Rhodes JE, 21
Ritson B, 44
Robins LN, 20, 63, 162
Rochberg-Halton E, 134, 146
Rodgers JL, 20
Rohsenow DJ, 35, 36
Rollins B, 61, 66, 69, 171
Roosa MW, 116
Rosenberg M, 56
Rowe DC, 20
Royal College of Physicians, 30, 108, 112, 113
Royal College of Psychiatrists, 14
Rutter M, 63
Rydelius PA, 40

Sager L, 137
Schaefer ES, 45
Scherer SE, 42
Schuckit MA, 23, 24
Searles JS, 50, 51
Sebba R, 153
Seff MA, 2
Sennett R, 149
Seydlitz R, 64

Sharp DJ, 17, 20, 26, 28, 29, 34, 38, 43, 44, 105, 107
Shields R, 130
Shilts L, 33, 46
Sibley D, 135
Singer SI, 23, 27
Sloper P, 116
Smith M, 146
Smyth M, 23, 108
Soja E, 130
Southwick L, 35
Stacey B, 11, 25, 26, 41, 44, 91, 168
Stumphauzer JS, 167
Sullivan E, 56
Sutherland A, 131

Tamerin JS, 37
Taylor R, 136
Teusch R, 25
Thomas D, 61, 66, 69, 171
Thompson KM, 42, 82
Turner JFC, 175

Velleman R, 52, 92, 180
Vicary JR, 63
Voeller M, 70
Volk RJ, 60
von Bertalanffy L, 54

Waldron RJ, 116
Watts TD, 23
Wechsler H, 107
Weintraub SA, 24
Weir T, 56
Wells GL, 35, 169
Welte J, 23, 27
White HR, 16, 18
W.H.O., 15
Wilcox JA, 24
Wilks J, 25, 82, 83
Williams RJ, 36
Williams P, 131
Wilsnack RW, 82, 106, 107
Wilsnack SC 106, 107
Wilson C, 52
Windle M, 34
Wolin SJ, 27, 51, 52
Wortley RK, 36
Wright R Jr, 23

Yin RK, 94
Young I, 146

Zucker RA, 44, 45

Subject Index

A
abjection, 10, 139, 146
abstainers, 19, 40-41, 72, 81, 91, 167
abstemious behaviour, 80
accommodation, 55, 153-159
adjustment problems, 24
adoptive parents, 99, 102
Alcohol,
    abuse, 1, 4-5, 15, 19, 23, 50-51, 63, 155, 166, 181
    after-effects, 14
    acute effects, 17
    dependence, 1, 15
    education, 8, 12, 72, 84-85, 170-174, 179, 181
    expectancies, v, 28, 35, 36, 37, 38, 39, 174
    and substance use, 2, 19, 22, 28, 127, 178
alcoholism transmission, 51, 53
alienation, 22, 24, 34, 41, 134, 175
anti-social, 19, 24, 71, 165
anxiety, 9, 25, 40, 63, 139, 141, 153
appearance, 18
arguments, 9, 45, 176
attentional processes, 77
attitudes, 4, 5, 10, 11, 21-28, 44, 78-88, 92, 93, 103, 107, 110, 128, 132-137, 143, 155-157, 167-174, 178
attribution, 29
authoritarian, 62-63, 101, 151, 168
authoritative, 61-63, 101, 109, 151
authority, ix, 17-18, 57, 61, 101, 109, 130-131, 139, 151, 154, 168
autonomy, 58, 68, 72, 131, 141, 152

B
background, 36
beer, 2, 14, 78, 96, 101, 107, 112
behaviour, extremes of, 48, 109-111, 127
beliefs, 37, 44, 83
belligerence, 17
beverages, 14
biological factors, 22-23
biopsychosocial model, 21
bonding, 57, 66
boredom, 29
boundaries, absence of, 10, 153
boundaries, home, 9, 10, 139, 145, 163, 171
boundaries, imposition of, 147
boundaries, neglect of, 147
boundary control, 9, 12

C
calendar time interactions, 6
case studies, 8, 48, 94, 102-103, 126-127, 155-163, 177
children's drinking, 25-26, 36, 44, 169
Circumplex Model, vi, 5, 58-60, 69-70
classification, strong, 10-11, 139, 141, 147, 150-152
classification, weak, 10-11, 139, 141, 151-153
classified environment, 140, 151
clock time interactions, 6
cocaine, 23, 60, 173-174
cognition, 35, 72, 169
cognitive dissonance, 78, 85
cohesion, 5-6, 12, 46, 52, 57-60, 66-71, 116
cohesiveness, 52
commonalities, 6, 19, 54, 66
communication, 52, 93, 150-152, 159, 169
community, 15, 22, 24, 80, 137
competence, 21, 61-62, 72, 169-170, 177
confidence, social, 29, 34
conflict, 9-11, 42, 49, 53-55, 67-68, 78, 91, 96-97, 116, 129, 130-136, 143-145, 148, 151, 153, 159, 166

conformity, 43, 46, 64-65, 132, 175, 178
connected, 33, 135, 152, 161, 175
consistency, 63, 78, 84, 94, 114, 117, 123-126
consumption, weekly, 30, 113
control, high, 7, 61-62, 71, 93, 108-109, 117, 119, 121, 171
control, loss of, 14
control, low, 7-8, 62, 92-94, 108, 121, 126, 170
control, moderate, 69, 170
control, poor, 45
coping, 18, 21, 22, 180
counsellors, 1, 17
crack, 60, 173
crime, 4
crisis period, 97
cross-cultural, 12, 82, 178
cross-sectional, 81-84, 123
cultural environment, 71, 74, 86
curiosity, 29
curvilinear relationship, 102, 110

D

daily routines, 143
delinquency, 24, 27, 64
demographic factors, 22, 89, 166
dependence, alcohol, 1, 15
depression, 40, 134
deprivation, 24, 45
development, adolescent, 12, 61
deviance, 4, 41, 45, 54, 64, 136, 172
deviant behaviour, 18, 27, 64, 66, 103-104, 167, 171
deviant, socially, 86, 89
diary technique, retrospective, 30, 106
differential reinforcement, 79
'dirt', 10, 145
discipline, 61, 63-65, 68, 127, 139, 144, 157-159, 162-163, 168, 171, 177
disengaged, 5, 11, 46, 57-60, 70, 152, 159
disinhibiting effects, 42
disorder, 9, 24, 63, 135, 139, 145, 163
disruptive, 144
distress, 38, 42, 72
divorced, 72
domestic space, 9-10, 128-145, 149-157, 163, 166, 174-178, 181
dominant, 135, 144, 148-151
drinking behaviour, measuring, 112-113
drinking diary, 30, 111-112

drinking patterns, 18, 80, 84, 113, 129, 155, 156
drinking, level of, 46, 105
drugs, 20-24, 41-42, 46, 60
drunk driving, 17
drunkenness, 16-17, 25, 44-46, 155-156

E

educationalists, 35
educators, parents as, 45
elaborated code, 150
emotional distress, 38, 72
enjoyable, 85, 162, 181
environmental factors, 5, 22, 24, 51-52, 77
environmental psychology, 9, 176
epidemiological, 5, 40
ethnicity, 19-22, 40, 42, 46
excessive drinking, 11, 15-16, 25, 52-53, 64, 71, 74, 91, 129
expectancies, 4-5, 28, 35-39, 42, 107, 169, 174
extremes of behaviour, 48, 109-111, 127

F

familial modelling, 109
families, personalizing, 11, 149
families, positional, 11, 159
family behaviour, measuring, 115
Family,
    boundaries, 156
    cohesion, 46, 52, 60, 70
    contact, 98
    control, 9, 65, 71, 109, 118-119, 124, 129, 149
    culture, 51, 53
    disorganization, 24
    functioning, 52-60, 65-66, 70-71, 115-116, 178
    history, 23-24, 50-53, 111
    identity, 52, 110, 172
    influences, 5-7, 44, 48-50, 88-89, 117, 126, 155, 165, 169, 173, 180
    interactions, 6, 11, 48-49, 149, 152, 163, 175
    links, 25, 110, 179
    process variables, 66, 108, 118-119
    profiles, vi, 8, 104, 123-125
    reasons, 34
    social learning, 8, 48, 73-75, 79, 80-81, 88, 92-94, 102-105, 109, 117-119, 123-127

socialization behaviours, 8, 103, 116, 123, 126-127
support, vi, 7, 61, 67, 71, 75, 105, 108, 117-125
systems, 5-7, 25, 48, 54-60, 69-71, 75, 92, 104, 109, 128, 166, 170-171, 181
types, 58-60, 149
fathers, 24-25, 45, 82-83, 97, 169
field theory, 75
first drink, 1, 11, 26, 44, 53, 78
follow-up, 12, 82, 84, 179
framing, 139-142, 151-154
friendship, 42
fun, 14, 29
functional consistency, 94, 125
functions, social, 42-43
further education, 23, 40

G
general systems theory, 54
genetic, 3, 5, 16, 22, 24, 50, 51
group identity, 52, 172
group interaction, 42
group membership, 29, 38, 42
growing up, 17, 57
guidance, 49, 56, 61, 74, 103, 110, 181
Gypsies, 131, 148

H
habits, 5, 16, 18, 37, 44
hangovers, 16-17
hard liquor, 67, 82-83, 173
heroin, 19, 60, 173-174
high risk, 24, 37, 52
home environment, 9-10, 42-53, 78, 127, 131-136, 148-149, 155, 163, 168-169, 174-176, 181
hostility, 45
house as haven, 9, 132-135
households, restricted, 159
human geography, 9
hyperactive children, 23

I
identity, 28, 43, 56, 110, 150
ideology, 25, 44
imitation, 6, 76-80
impulsiveness, 40
income, 19, 23, 26
inconsistent socialization, 93

independence, 2, 18, 26, 41, 62, 71, 96, 177
indifference, parental, 7, 87, 91, 110, 117-119, 170
inebriation, 14
inhalants, 21
initial drinking, 20-22, 34, 67, 79, 82, 83
insecurity, 18
instability, 52
intoxication, 16-17, 27, 35
isolation, 18, 45, 98, 134, 153

J
juvenile delinquents, 18

L
labelling, 17, 22, 153
lack of direction, 97
lack of family contact, 98
lack of support, 97-98
law, 3-4, 97, 161, 166
leisure, 18, 135, 143, 180
licensing, 4
liminal zones, 140
longitudinal, 12, 37-41, 63, 82-84, 180
low educational attainment, 18
low risk, 30, 37
low self-esteem, 24, 40

M
marijuana, 19, 21-23, 60, 63, 173-174
Mass-Observation, 10-12, 153, 177
maternal control, lax, 25, 45, 46
media, 1, 3, 10, 76, 132-136, 147, 165-167
meta-analysis, vi, 7, 54, 66-75, 80-84, 102, 108, 177
middle adolescence, 43
MMPI, 40
modelling, 5-6, 21, 26, 43, 75-88, 92, 105, 109
models, parents as, 45, 81
moderate drinkers, 30, 81, 86
moderation, 26, 94
modes of control, v, 10, 149-150, 163
money, 18, 100, 144
moodiness, 42, 52
mothers, 25, 45-56, 83, 98, 169
motivational processes, 77
multiple-risk-factor theory, 21

N
negative effects, 35-38

neighbourhood, 9, 49, 132-136, 175
non-deviance, 64
non-drinking, 5, 7, 46, 71, 80, 89-93, 103, 109, 122-126, 171
nonconformity, 41
normative behaviour, 17, 74, 100
normative socialization, 92

O

offenders, young, 4, 18
offspring of problem drinkers, 6, 52-53
operant learning, 79
order, spatial, 11, 130-137, 141, 151
over-protective, 95
overcrowded, 152

P

parental approval, 81-87, 109
parental attachment, 64-65
parental attitudes, 78-93, 110, 128, 156, 168-174
parental behaviour, 5, 77, 168
parental deviance, 45
parental disapproval, 34, 86-87, 110, 117-122, 171
parental disinterest, 45
parental drinking, vi, 26, 52, 77-94, 103, 111, 118-119, 125, 169, 170
parental indifference, 7, 91, 110, 117-119, 170
parental support and control, 45
parents, permissive, 62-63
partitioning, 135, 143-147, 166
paternal drinking, 82-83
pathological drinker, 91
peer group, 25, 46, 56, 98, 102-103, 129, 172-173
peer influence, 84-85, 172, 173
peer-pressure hypothesis, 35
permissiveness, 61, 68, 163
personality, 20, 40-46, 151
personalizing family, 150
physical abuse, 53
positional, 10, 11, 149-155, 159
power relations, 9, 130, 139, 149-153, 166
precocity, 41
prevention, 4, 19, 26, 167, 174, 181
primary school, 78
privacy, 134, 141, 152-162
problem behaviour, 10, 20-21, 40, 53-57, 129, 147-155, 163, 175-179
prohibitive attitude, 80

protection, 53, 55
psychological boundaries, 9, 57, 157-159
psychosocial maturity, 28
public houses, 26
punishment, 24, 45, 61-64, 79, 99-100, 117, 150

Q

qualitative, 8, 111-113, 126-128, 177

R

reasons for drinking, v, vi, 28-35, 76, 107, 169-174
rebelliousness, 22, 24, 91
recommended limits, 33
recreation, 29, 34
rejection, 9, 25, 42-46, 53-57, 62, 68, 91, 109-110, 146, 168
relapse, 23
relaxation, 14, 18, 33-34
religion, 26
restricted code, 150
restricted households, 159
retrospective diary, 30, 106
rewards, 21, 79
risk factor, 23-26, 87, 174
rituals, 52
role-modelling, 26
routine activities, 155
routines, 130, 135, 143-145
rules, 6, 55, 61-68, 86, 100, 117, 129, 139, 141, 151-163, 171

S

self-attributions, 29
self-confident, 61
self-control, 34
self-esteem, 24, 34, 40, 42, 61
self-expression, 158
sensible drinking, 7, 11-12, 16, 50, 57, 71, 74, 80, 86, 89, 94, 103, 108, 109, 112, 125, 165, 168
separated, 58, 61, 85, 95, 102, 152, 162
seven-day diary, 30
sex differences, 8, 29-36, 82-83, 106-108, 114, 119, 120
sex role conflict, 42
sexuality, 38
shyness, 22
smoking, 19-28, 96, 108, 111, 173
sociability, 14, 32-33, 45, 91

social approval, 42
social classes, 26, 148
social confidence, 29, 34
solvents, 19, 123, 173, 174
space, partitioning of, 139
space, shortage of, 161
spaces, naming of, 129
spatial behaviour, 145, 152
spatial boundaries, 141-148, 152, 171, 179
spatial order, 135-137, 141
spatial organization, 128, 181
special occasions, 19, 30-31, 96, 101, 109, 114-115, 153
spirits, 2, 14, 80, 97, 107, 112
stage theory, 21, 173
standard units of alcohol, 2
stress, 2, 9, 14-22, 42, 56-65
strict control, 6, 12, 62-63, 68-72, 93-97, 102, 109, 157
strictness, 6, 68, 157
structural theory, 57
substance use and abuse, 173
system maintenance, 116
systems theory, 54-55, 60, 70

T
taste, 14, 29-34, 76, 78
television, 10, 76, 131-135
temporal regimes, 10, 143
tension, 9, 14, 25, 37-38, 45, 49, 55, 135, 153, 163
therapeutic, 11, 54, 156, 174
therapists, 60
time budget, 144
time out, 17
time, segmentation of, 139
tobacco, 19, 21
togetherness, 57
transgressive behaviour, 9, 147
treatment, 4, 11, 15, 19, 37, 111, 153
truancy, 22

U
uncaring, 45
unconventional, 46
units of alcohol, 2, 30, 38, 106, 112, 115
unreliability, 52
upbringing, 51
urban, 40, 146
utility analysis, 36

violence, 16, 45, 134

W
weak classification, 10, 11, 139-141, 145, 151-153, 160-162

Y
young offenders, 4, 18
young problem drinkers, 18, 40, 165
youth clubs, 155
youth training, 30, 105, 155
youth worker, 98-99
youthful alcohol and substance use, 28
youthful drunkenness, 16-17